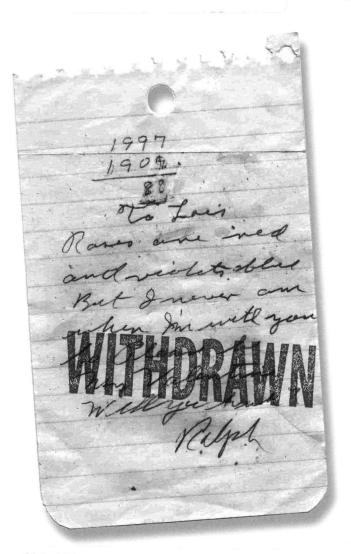

ADVANCE PRAISE FOR *A SONG AT TWILIGHT*

Nancy Paddock's *A Song at Twilight* is a compelling fusion of genres—a memoir, a commentary, a sort of textbook, a biography, and a nonfiction novel—and, most of all, a tragic romance. It is suspenseful even though we know how it must end. Her account of her parents' long struggle with Alzheimer's disease (and the strategies with which she and her sisters deal with it) illuminates the sadness that is through the joy that was, intensified by Lois and Ralph's efforts to retain autonomy. Discovering that she cannot save them from their crumbling reality, Paddock works to rescue the details of their lives and relentlessly seeks to retrieve a pattern from chaos—preserving, examining, and reliving the interwoven stories of lovers, family, and searchers for meaning. Faithful to them, to their struggle, and to herself, the book is straightforward, wise, and intensely moving. It is a love story in all its dimensions.　　　　　　　　　　　　　　— *John Calvin Rezmerski*

A Song at Twilight knocks you over and rips out your heart, then sets you back on your feet again, determined to make the most of every moment you have, especially every moment that's filled with love. In this lyrical, heaven-sent, gritty, earth-bound memoir, Nancy Paddock confronts a monumental question: What can we do to help our parents live a worthwhile, meaningful end of life? Nancy Paddock's mother and father, Lois and Ralph, gave Nancy and her sisters the rarest of gifts: They were wise, caring parents who also carried on a lifelong romance with each other, a love that endured from their courtship before WWII to their death just days apart in the wards of a modern nursing home. The author conveys with searing candor their wisdom and care as parents; their confusion and unrelenting honesty as they age; their sense of loss, grief, and fear as they have to leave the home they love; and their ability to find hope in family, in good words spoken with love. In each journal entry, letter, poem, and anecdote, Ms. Paddock teaches us how to be a mother, father, sister, brother-in-law, teacher, and student. In her words we find grace in pain and truth in despair, as we imagine for ourselves how we might somehow endure and survive, broken and unbroken, at the end of our lives.　　　　　　　　　　　　　　— *Freya Manfred*

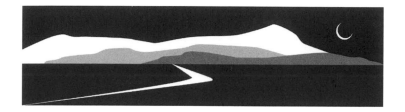

Blueroad Press

2011

A Song at Twilight

Of Alzheimer's and Love | *A Memoir*

NANCY PADDOCK

Blueroad Press

Janesville, Minnesota

A Song at Twilight
Of Love and Alzheimer's: A Memoir
Copyright © 2011 Nancy Paddock

ISBN13: 978-0-9796509-4-9
First Printing

❧

Blueroad Press
34402 15th Street
Janesville, Minnesota 56048

John Gaterud, editor & publisher
Abbey Gaterud, associate editor
www.blueroadpress.com

Book design: John Gaterud
Cover design: Kris Higginbotham
Photograph credits:
Front cover: *Hands* © Supri Suharjoto; Lois & Ralph Pearson, family of Nancy Paddock.
Back cover: *Frozen Window* © Benis Arapovic.
All family photographs, letters, and notes in this book are property of the family
of Nancy Paddock.

❧

Text set in Garamond Premier Pro
Printed in the United States by Sentinel Printing, St. Cloud, Minnesota.

For my family

AUTHOR'S NOTE

ANY MEMOIR IS, IN PART, an imaginative recollection of the past—a selection of elements that tell a coherent story. In the telling, past experiences are clarified and synthesized with current understandings. This memoir is grounded in material set down as it happened. My father's loving World War II letters to my mother, her letters to me, and our family's lively taped interviews tell our early story. And in more recent emails, my two sisters and I support one another and share our concerns. However, my own contemporaneous journal entries provide most of the content of this book. They document family conversations and my struggle to confront and comprehend the events presented here.

Nancy Paddock | *Litchfield, Minnesota*

♋

In Dream

I look out the kitchen window of our old St. Paul home.
Snow is falling, and Mom and Dad are going out together.
As they slowly back out of the garage in a white convertible,
    Dad begins to put its top down.
The roof frame rises, scraping and catching on the garage door.
Then, sprung, it is forced straight up in the air.
Oblivious, as the convertible's fractured roof rocks and breaks free,
    Dad continues backing out.
My parents ride off into the storm, their car filling with snow.

ဢ

The Pearsons, St. Paul, Minnesota—1941

INTRODUCTION

IN AN OLD PHOTOGRAPH, JENNIE AND PAUL PEARSON—my Swedish immigrant grandparents—pose with their six grown sons and daughters and their families in front of a tinseled Christmas tree and a bay window draped by floral chintz and lace. Grandpa stares from the background like a ghost. Stony-faced, Grandma bends forward to fold her arms over her knees. Elmer sits stiffly in his three-piece suit with his hands clasped in his lap. Carl's little daughter, Lois, clings to her father's shirtsleeve, and Marguerite smiles from the flowered, over-stuffed couch. Carol looks as glamorous as a Hollywood star, but her husband, Jack, just glances toward the camera. Against the far wall, Bob stands tall and elegant with his eyes averted.

Front and center on the Oriental carpet, handsome and dreamy-eyed, my father reclines against the shoulder of his vivacious young wife, who is soon to become pregnant with me. It is December 1941. Pearl Harbor has been bombed. And everyone in the family knows the three young men in this room—Jack, Bob, and my father—will have to go to war. By the following October, I will be born, and just months later, Dad will board the train for boot camp. Then my parents' wrenching time apart will begin, their marriage held together by letters, dreams, and longing for the life they hope to share after the war.

Thirty-five years later, my husband, Joe, interviewed his own father, and then numerous citizens of Olivia, Minnesota, as part of a National Endowment for the Arts Poet in the Community pilot project. Struck by the power of these stories, I realized my own family's memories were a treasure that must not be lost. My sisters, Jan and Ginger, and I interviewed family members on both sides, and especially our parents. Feeling a bit like a benign vampire, I recorded their voices, hoarded their photographs. It was as though I had drawn their life's blood into my veins.

My parents, Lois and Ralph Pearson, were extraordinary only in the intensity of their lifelong love that no war, external or internal, could destroy. Having endured hardships and loss in their own youth, they created a remarkable stability for their children. It was easy for us to assume life would go on as it had, immune from the trials and disasters of the world—an illusion that would be shattered in time by Alzheimer's.

Eventually, my sisters and I would be forced by circumstances to violate an almost genetic taboo: to dethrone the king and queen and set up a protectorate. And, as is true for so many families, we would be torn between our parents' needs and the demands of our own lives. Strained by visiting Mom and Dad on a weekend, I'd retreat to my home, ninety miles distant, and dissolve. Half-seriously, I'd claim that, like a *Star Trek* shape-shifter, I needed to spend time liquefied in a pail in order to assume the alien form of English Teacher on Monday morning.

Then, in David Whyte's *The Heart Aroused,* I read: "Whatever you lavish yourself upon grows rich and lavishes itself upon you." This was a revelation: *If,* instead of shrinking away in self-protection, I would turn and embrace my life—as it *was*, with all its exuberance and chaos, its failure, its beauty, exhaustion, and regret—it would feed me. And at last, after several difficult years of avoidance, I retired early to let my parents' broken hearts speak directly to mine. To spill some blood for them. To write my way out of a labyrinth of sorrow.

As a morass of conflicting feelings and hard-won insights became comprehensible, the story grew like a tree in my mind. Its branches spread wide to embrace the lively transcripts of long-ago oral interviews; my father's tender World War II letters; my mother's wise and spontaneous correspondence with me; and the emails and conversations in which my sisters and I supported one another and agonized over our parents' care.

Years ago, at a time when my mother's problems could no longer be denied, I found the broken strands of a pearl necklace in the chaos of her vanity drawer. Just costume jewelry, coated glass, and yet I felt compelled to gather up the loose pearls and take them to be restrung.

Writing this book, it seems to me now, was restringing *real* pearls: our family's humor, devotion, endurance—and the fundamental power of our parents' love. It created order from what had been broken. And it tied together the scattered strands of meaning that would have been otherwise lost.

જી

Lois and Nancy Pearson—1945

PROLOGUE

When I Lived in Paris

Spring 1997

M Y MOTHER'S TRUTH, NOW, IS MUTABLE: the story of the moment. Sometimes it is as though the fabric of her life has been torn apart, then pieced together like a crazy quilt. Today, she who has ever been the keeper of our family stories, telling them over and over so we will remember, says: "When I lived in Paris—"

"Mama," I say as gently as possible, "you were never in Paris."

"But my dad had a pass for the railroad."

"You can't take a train to Paris. You went to New York and Chicago and Seattle as a child."

"I *do* remember—"

"You and Dad went to Copenhagen, Stockholm, Bergen a few years ago. You visited Hong Kong, Seoul, and Singapore with Elizabeth, and Alaska with Helen."

"No, this was early, when I was a girl."

She is silent, deflated. What she *knows* has been denied. Does the memory of Paris wink out, or persist like a ghost, a bright amalgam of other times and places, Impressionist paintings, video travelogues, and stories told by others? A Paris of the imagination: a refuge, an ego-salve, a glamorous cushion against the limitations of old age? Mama shrinks, frightened by the disparity between what she believes and what I say is true.

That night, in dream, Mama tells me her friend May has given her the ornate silverware spread out on the table. May couldn't have done that, I claim; May is dead. Of course, awake, I realize May *isn't* dead. And that I shouldn't set myself up as an arbiter of truth. I do not know Mama's truth.

The dream, like Mama's waking mind, creates its own reality. What is real? We trust our perceptions, but no two people share the same experience. Our fears and desires cause us to see things differently. We trust our memories, but they change with time. We reinterpret past events in light of subsequent experience, and sometimes see them as we wish they had been. Perhaps Mama's mind works as a mind in sleep, transforming details of the world into soul messages that have nothing—and everything—to do with reality.

My first childhood friends were angels with fantastic names. And Mama's delight in my imagination is clear from her entry in my baby book:

> At three and a half years of age, Nancy began asking questions about God and Heaven. One night she said she could see Heaven through the stars and said the angels were playing in beautiful flowers. A few minutes later she came walking into our room holding nothing by the hand, whom she introduced as Hallabrooma, her guardian angel. Hallabrooma is her constant companion. She sits on her crib at night, plays hide-and-seek with her, has birthday parties every other day. Nancy carries on a conversation with her, using two separate voices.
>
> At four years, she added another angel, named Dorothy, who wears glasses, breaks furniture, wrecks houses, and who isn't allowed to go visiting. Oh yes, Dorothy also is very careless; she doesn't keep her wings clean. Then suddenly Dorothy is put in jail and a new guardian angel is sent by God to take her place. When we asked what her name was, Nancy said, "God hasn't told me yet." Then she listened and said, "Her name is Symphanasia." Now the three of them run and play all day. Hallabrooma hides behind the dresser and gets her wings caught. Both of them get showers in the bathtub and evidently squeal with delight. It is very interesting and shows a vivid imagination. Nothing is too impossible for Hallabrooma and Symphanasia to do. I hope they stay with us forever.
>
> At five, the guardian angels were sent on extended vacations. I imagine it's because she has so many children to play with now that we have our own home and yard. She said, "You know that Hallabrooma, Mommy? That was a lot of malarkey."

It took neighborhood children to tell me my angels were "malarkey." Even when Mama's friends pitied her for having borne a child with "something really wrong, that wasn't just an unusual imagination," she let me keep my angels. She played along, believed in them with me.

"When I lived in Paris—"

What will Mama tell me if I let her speak? What fantasy will she construct? What memory from her youth will she transpose, recombine to form a truth about the soul? Will some message lie hidden in the jumbled details? Even if her story has no meaning, why do I, who once played with angels, need to correct her? Is it my terror of losing her that I oppose?

It may be better to let Mama go into the wonderland of her mind. A story could lift her for a while out of her aging body, its gnarled feet and ineffectual hands. Out of purposelessness, boredom, and confinement. If I let her, could she at least have Paris?

℃

YOUNG LOVE

The Life We Had

1933–1956

Looks of love and delight. Lois Christensen and Ralph Pearson
marry in the Pearson family home—1940

That Terrible Bet

M Y PARENTS DELIGHTED IN EACH OTHER. And they loved to tell the story of how they got together. That their deep and stable union could begin as it did makes their daughters' existence seem at once accidental and fated. Out at the Hippodrome, an indoor ice skating rink on the Minnesota State Fairgrounds, Dad had just finished hockey practice when he saw Mama for the first time. He began his story with a sly smile:

> "Well, let me tell you how it *was*— After hockey practice, I saw a girl skating around in time with the music, and she looked pretty nice. She wore a blue-and-white checkerboard sweater. Looked like a *real* nice girl. So I put my skates back on and asked her to skate with me. *No soap!* Absolutely wouldn't skate with anybody wearing hockey skates. Well, I—gave up."
>
> "Why should I?" Mama laughed. "I had all those other guys fighting for me. It's true."
>
> "Later on in the year, after we'd played down at the St. Paul Auditorium," Dad said, "I saw the same girl skating around there. I thought, well, this long-blade stuff must have something, so I bought a pair of long-blade skates. But the next time I saw her, I *still* couldn't get to skate with her. The girls carried cards, and guys would sign up for the different bands. She had all her numbers filled all the time. So then I started going out to the Hippodrome, where all the long-blade skaters went. Even though Lois wouldn't skate with me, other girls did. And I got a little better. I was practically born on skates, so I could handle long blades, too. Finally, I asked her for a date to go to the *Ice Follies* way into the spring. And she agreed to go."
>
> "He didn't know I was still in high school."

"No, I didn't. She looked more mature. Then I started taking her out once in a while, as often as I could—"

"You'd better tell the truth, Ralph Pearson!" Mama laughed. "Tell about that terrible bet! He was bragging how he could get me. See, I was a popular skater."

"Well," Dad said, "there'd been a masquerade party at the Hippodrome Club, and I hadn't gone skating that night. I'd played hockey or something. Anyway, I was down at a saloon on Payne Avenue afterwards with Jack Hagglund, and his brother Rudy came in. Had been at the party—"

"I had gone as a pirate," Mama said. "And I had little short pants on and a pirate hat and a pirate vest. I'd made oilcloth pirate boots to fit over my skates. And I don't know if that had anything to do with Ralph—"

"Well," Dad continued, "Rudy started telling me, 'Boy, that girl that you kinda have taken a shine to out at the Hipp, boy, you shoulda seen her to-night. Oh, did she look nice.' I'd been rebuffed by Mama, so I acted real casual about it— 'Oh, I could have her for a girlfriend if I wanted to.'

"Rudy said, 'I'll bet you couldn't.' And I said, 'I'll bet I could.' Then he said, 'Tell you what: your car needs a ring job. I'll bet you ten dollars against that ring job—'"

"I thought it was *twenty*," Mama squealed. "*Ten dollars!*"

"Well, twenty then. 'Twenty dollars against a ring job on your car that you can't get her to go with you by summertime.' Oh! Did I get to work *then!*"

Mama giggled. "He'd call me up and say, 'This is Ralph.' And I'd say, 'Ralph who?'"

"In any other circumstances I would have said, 'Good-bye!' Bang!"

"But, see—" Mama leaned forward and whispered, "it was a matter of macho."

"Then I started getting dates with her," Dad said, his voice softening. "And found out, more and more, she was the kind of girl I wanted. I couldn't believe how innocent she was. Naïve. I thought she was putting on an act, 'cause she was definitely not the kind of girl I'd been used to. I was older, 24. She was 17. And so we were going out pretty often. Then came a Hippodrome powwow down on St. Croix and Al Searle wanted to take you."

"He *did*," Mama crooned. "We spent the whole day at the Hippodrome picnic. We went swimming, and we just had the most beautiful time—"

Dad rolled his eyes. "Anyway—you came home from *that*, and I gave you an ultimatum. It was me-and-nobody-else or everybody-else-and-not-me." He winked at her, then swung an arm around her shoulder and pulled her close. "I don't know why she ever chose me—"

"Well, the thing is, that I liked the way he was, too."

"So I won out both ways," Dad proclaimed. "I got myself the most won-derful woman in the world for a girlfriend—and I got my car overhauled."

"Boy! If I'd had *any inkling*!" Mama laughed. "Those guys!"

That bet led to a seven-year courtship during which the two lovers fought nearly every night. Mama would shout, "I never want to see you again, Ralph Pearson!" She'd slam the door and leave him standing on the steps. But, by the time Dad called her the next day, she was eager to continue working out their differences. And, over the years, they created a remarkable harmony.

☙

ON THE DAY OF MAMA'S FIRST BRIDAL SHOWER, Dad's name appeared in the paper as No. 12 in the draft. It was 1940 and, in the shadow of the Nazi blitz over England and the signing of the Axis Pact, they feared they would never live in the apartment they were furnishing. But they gambled with fate and went ahead with their November wedding. Due to the large number of volunteers, Dad's number didn't come up right away, but by the following September, duty and desperation led him to enlist. As luck, or fate, would have it, an emergency appendectomy and a temporary deferment bought them time to have a child. Thirty-six years later, Mama described the day of my birth in a letter sent to me from San Diego:

> *Happy birthday, darling—and hello, Joe*
> *36 years ago the world was at war and we were having our firstborn—Grandma was worried that Ralph would go and get killed and I would have a child to support—I was worried that he would go and get killed, too, but that was why I wanted a child—anyway, it turned out very well indeed and you arrived one day earlier than expected.*
> *Did I tell you that I was standing in the kitchen in Auntie's house on Sherburne Avenue, packing something for the picnic supper we were going to have with the Bohns at Como Park—when, lo and behold, such a new and different small pain came and went quickly. Pretty soon it came back again, then again, and all of a sudden I knew you were trying to escape. No one would let me go to the picnic and I was insisting that I could have birth pains out in the park as well as home.*

Anyway, between my mama's insistence that we call the doctor and our own inexperience in these matters, we arrived early enough to have to go thru all the small tortures they dream up for the PGs in the maternity ward. I swore I'd never let them get to me again! So after awhile, to the sad strains of "Nearer My God to Thee," all hell broke loose when the water burst and sent Daddo out into the hall with one leap to get help. I'm sure I don't know what he thought had happened— must have been the music!

When I was in the delivery room, without our doctor, the house doctor tried to hold you back, but I was cooperating with you to get you born. They all finally gave up and there you were! Grandma Christensen was delighted you were a girl—Grandma Pearson said she thought Ralph would have a son—but from that day on, you became the darling of both sides of the family. Carol and I laugh at the many times on Sundays at 501—how we all sat in a circle watching your every move—like you were a TV or something! Firstborn feelings stay with you forever.

Dad added a few words in that letter's margin:

Mom's comments on your coming into this world brought back some memories. The hymn she mentioned came from a little church near the hospital that was having a vesper service. Mom's right. I was scared. I remember the woman doctor came running down the hall, her high heels clicking. Too late, you were already there. They gave me five dollars off the bill for that! Big deal!

c⁄ɔ

The Life We Had

WHEN DAD RETURNED FROM WORLD WAR II, he and Mama bought our first house, a little two-bedroom bungalow on St. Paul's East Side. That York Avenue neighborhood, only half built-up back then, with great places to play in the grasslands and woods gracing it on two sides, is easy to idealize. There I had what novelist Thomas Mallon describes as "the kind of happy childhood that is so damaging to a writer—where our fathers were all World War II veterans and our mothers were always at home." In that place and time, it was safe to play Starlight, Moonlight in the summer dark. The only menace came from our own imaginations, and the only outrages we knew were the small cruelties and skirmishes of youth.

After his war years in England and France, Dad had a clearer-than-ever appreciation for home and neighborhood:

> "It was a community," Dad said proudly. "Neighbors were real neighbors back in those days. If you got in any kind of trouble, your neighbors would help you."
>
> "Well, that was true on the East Side," Mama conceded, "because it was like a little town. But that wasn't true where I grew up."
>
> "Out on York Avenue—the first house we had—that was really a close-knit four or five families there. I remember when we moved in I had a small trailer that I'd loaded with a lot of stuff. I was trying to push it back by the garage, but there was a little bump on the edge of the driveway that I couldn't get it over. All of a sudden, it *moved*." Dad's voice was full of feeling. "There was Al helping me. And I hadn't even met him yet. That's the way they were."

"How old was Janet when Russ took that darling picture of her?" Mama asked.

"He was a milkman who came home during the day," Dad remembered. "And he went out there and took a picture of Janet sitting with the rainwater running over her in the gutter." He shook his head. "She must have been about three and had this gleeful smile on her face."

Mama chuckled. "Well, I think that out there on York was a nice place to live and grow up. There were kids, and they had a place to play. It was a safe time."

"There were 24 kids between our house and the corner, the way I remember it. I never was sorry we lived there." Dad grinned. "I enjoyed it."

Jan told another story about our good little community on York Avenue:

I was two or three, I guess, so I don't remember, but it's been told to me so many times that I feel like I do. Mom had put me down for a nap, and she was in the kitchen when she got a phone call from Mr. Hoff, the grocery guy.

"Lois, do you know where your daughter Janet is?" he asked.

"Yes. She's in taking a nap."

"No, she isn't. She's right here with me."

Evidently, I'd gotten out of my crib and toddled up there. He looked out of the door of his grocery store and saw me sitting in the middle of Seventh Street!

Mom had no idea how that could have happened or how long I could have been gone or anything. It was lucky Mr. Hoff knew who I was but, well, neighborhood.

❧

ON THE DAY GINGER WAS BORN, Dad sighed, "Born on *D-Day*." Though the grave tone of his voice struck me, I didn't ask him what that meant. Nor did I know we'd soon need a bigger house. A year later, we found one with three bedrooms and a bath upstairs, a real dining room, and a front porch. Location—still on the East Side of St. Paul—meant everything to Dad. Only six blocks from his family home, our new Nebraska Avenue house was also walking distance from Dad's church; Lake Phalen, where we swam; and his old alma mater, Johnson High

School. Dad was finally back home. In our taped interviews, Mama described our move:

> This is how we bought 688. Red Rolig called up Ralph at work and said, "Eddie Anderson is going to move and sell his house."
>
> And Daddy said, "Tell Eddie we'll buy it."
>
> It was not exactly sight-unseen. We had been there once before at night. But Daddy said it was exactly where we wanted to live. Walking distance to everything. And it had an upstairs so you could put the kids to bed and just close the door.
>
> I remember when we arrived at the new house, Ginger slid down the stairs, bumpity-bumpity-bumpity-bump. *On purpose.* But Jan hadn't wanted to leave the old neighborhood. She didn't want to leave her friends, so we told her that she'd be able to see the Christmas lights on Wheelock Parkway from her bedroom window.
>
> Oh, that was so funny when Jan came running downstairs. She had gone up there the minute we arrived to look for the lights and she came down and said, "I don't see any Christmas lights!" Of course, it was summer.
>
> The day we moved, Daddy had been helping the movers, and he came in and told me, "I'm too tired to hook up the stove."
>
> So we all went down to Nelson's Drive-in, and Janet looked out over all the cars and said very seriously, "My, but there are a lot of people moving today."
>
> Oh, I have told that story to so many people, and everybody thinks it is so darling. It's a sure giveaway of how often we took the kids out. "My, but there are a lot of people moving today." She analyzed everything, always, from the very beginning, even when she was five.

✌

WHEN HER MOTHER RETIRED FROM A JOB as cook for a Beverly Hills millionaire, Mama wanted to take care of her. Grandma moved in with us, and I lost the "room of my own" that had made moving almost acceptable. Forced to share a double bed in a space crowded by Ginger's crib, I took it out on Jan, egging her on, pestering her in sneaky little ways, till she'd yell and get the blame. "Go to sleep!" Mama would call up the stairs, but we wouldn't.

Finally, Dad had had it. He'd heard about the bundling boards Pilgrims once used to keep young couples chaste while they courted warm under bedcovers on cold winter evenings. Dad's bundling board had rubber caps on each end so it could be wedged between the foot and headboards to keep us separate. History abounds with fences that do not make good neighbors. And we were no exception. Our parents would put us to bed, cover us, and force the board in between us. Naturally I did my best to defeat it, sticking fingers underneath to poke Jan. And, of course, she'd wail. Sometimes we'd get such a struggle going, jabbing at each other, that the whole thing would just BOING! loose, and then Dad would stump upstairs, threaten us, and force it back into place.

Eventually Grandma, who was an independent sort and, at seventy-two, perfectly able to take care of herself, decided she needed a place of her own. She set up a cozy apartment a mile away, and I reclaimed my room. Though its walls remained Grandma's favorite dismal brown, with green pine boughs climbing the wallpaper, it was my cell and refuge throughout the storms of adolescence.

∽

MY SULLEN TEENAGE REBELLION shocked Mom and Dad, but they had adopted a far more relaxed approach to parenthood by the time Ginger—ten years younger than I—reached high school:

> "Lois," Dad asked, "do you remember the time Ginger was going to go to some kind of a party with Brian and he came over to get her and he had an outfit on?"
>
> "Oh, ho ho! He had on a long white body suit that was real tight."
>
> "And he had a fig leaf over his—middle," Dad groaned and shook his head. "And Ginger was dressed about the same way and we thought, oh, what are they going to do? They had a snake!"
>
> "Yes! Adam and Eve," Mama giggled. "And Ginger had an apple! Afterwards, Brian said, 'I wish I had taken a bite out of that apple.'"
>
> "I don't know where that party was. Was it at church?"
>
> "It was at school! And it was a Sadie Hawkins dance. A picture of Ginger and Brian in those costumes was even put in the yearbook." Mama shook her head. "I don't know how the minister's wife found out, but when she said, 'I was a little bit shocked at their being Adam and Eve,' I said, 'I thought it was wonderful.'"

Dad's eyes rolled back, and he sighed, "We always thought what our kids were doing was wonderful."

"If parents don't stick up for their kids, even if they're wrong—" Mama shrugged. "I used to tell all of the kids, 'You're the joy of my life.' And pretty soon something would happen and I'd say, 'You'll be the death of me yet.'"

⁊

SOME OF MY STRONGEST MEMORIES of the life we had open on the kitchen of our Nebraska Avenue home and almost reclaim that lost, precious, and undoubtedly idealized space. Late summer suppertime, 1956. The house is hot, the air heavy with cooking and the sweat of the day. Low sun gilds the yellow kitchen where Mama in her faded black bathing suit hovers over sizzling frying pans and steaming pots. Blue hand-stenciled words from the *Lord's Prayer* stretch across the arch of the breakfast nook: GIVE US THIS DAY OUR DAILY BREAD. In those years before air conditioning, the little brown fan hums and oscillates feebly on the floor. Daddy, home as always at 5:03 PM, has shed his suit, his white shirt and tie, and lies on the living room carpet in undershirt, cotton wash pants, and headphones, lost in *Claire de Lune*.

I'm thirteen, Jan is eight, Ginger is four. Our swimming suits are still damp from our afternoon at the beach. When Mama calls us for supper, our thighs stick to the bench as we scramble into the breakfast nook, tired, waterlogged, sun-bronzed. Sidling past the stove to his chair, Dad pats Mama's ample bottom. "Raalphie!" she yelps and flashes him a grin. Her bare feet grind sand on the linoleum as she fills our plates too full of hamburgers, corn on the cob, mashed potato patties fried in butter, red wheels of tomato from the yard.

Maybe it's one of the times we didn't fight. Maybe we beg: "Wiggle your muscle, Daddy." And when he raises his arms, clasps his fingers behind his head and makes the big muscle of his pitching arm bounce as it flexes and relaxes, we giggle. Maybe it's one of the times we play our word game. It just sort of happens, but usually Dad starts it. Someone mentions a word, maybe the plot of a story. And that sets off the puns on all possible meanings of "plot." We do it deadpan, without ever saying the word again:

"Oh, you could never *plant* anything in that."

"Well, you could *bury* somebody in it."

"Or end up in prison for all your cloak-and-dagger *strategies*."

Once we've cleaned our plates, Mama places Pierre, the fat yellow French chef cookie jar, in the middle of the table and lifts off its upper body to reveal a heap of fresh baked-from-scratch oatmeal raisin cookies.

"Oooh, cooo-kies," Daddy croons, and Jan and Ginger, their braids sun-bleached almost white, reach out. Then wail in protest as I grab one first.

After Ginger has plunked a one-finger tune on the old upright in the dining room and Jan and I have fought over and finally finished the dishes, after the sun has dropped below the arching elms along the quiet street, Mama says, "Let's go down for a dip." Dad switches on the exhaust fan in the attic trapdoor that sucks the day's heat out of the house and draws in cool evening air through the open windows. Then, barefoot, he drives us to Lake Phalen.

The beach is nearly deserted in the twilight. A last sunset blush dances on the water as we wade in. We drift in the pink lapping waves, cooling our heated bodies, washing off the turmoil of the day, laughing, talking softly until first stars appear. And then, dripping and wrapped in towels, refreshed, we climb back into the old gray Plymouth and head home to bed—with no idea of the dry years to come.

✑

Nancy, Janet, and newborn Virginia Pearson—July 1952

LOIS

The Dying of the Light

1991–1998

Looks of love and delight. Lois and Ralph celebrate their
50th anniversary at Janet's house—1990

JOURNAL | *Universe*

June 1991

MAMA HAD A TERRIBLE TIME trying to pack for the Great Fiftieth Anniversary Scandinavia Trip we gave them. Confused, unable to decide what to take, she said she felt old. At seventy-four, she had lived longer than her mother and was the age at which her dear Aunt Ida died.

The "trip of a lifetime" turned out to be taxing. Their suitcase fell apart in the airport. Long-lost Copenhagen relatives were never found. And with few pictures and no great stories, they returned jet-lagged and exhausted. Depressed, Dad stayed in bed with a cold. And Mama's sleeping was turned around. Though less dithery than before the trip, she was disoriented for days, saying, "I don't feel like I live in this place or that any of this stuff is mine."

She made distracted comments about "how far up everything goes" and "where the universe ends in space and begins in time"—the sort of things astronauts said when they returned to Earth. If only we'd given them that trip five years ago.

Today, Dad tells Joe, "I wish Lois would read instead of watch TV. It would be good for her mind. She's getting forgetful."

And he tells me, "I do a lot of things for your mother, and I'm glad I can. But I worry about what she'd do if I wasn't here."

✧

JOURNAL | *Spy*

December 3, 1992

OVER MANY YEARS OF ARTS, humanities, and environmental work, I often felt like a sort of evangelist carrying a message from the soul. When, last fall—turning fifty, a bit burned out, and needing more financial security—I took this part-time high school English teaching job, I felt like the poet who came in from the cold. Poets are a bit like spies anyway, the watchers in the shadows, the secret agents of the other world.

Part-time teaching, I believed, would take part-time energy and still leave time to write. Right! That's why this journal hasn't opened since September. But weird as it seems, teaching is a framework my life can form around, like a crystal grows from its molecular structure. And, as much as they exhaust me, I do care about the kids.

Even so, Christmas vacation hangs out there like a sweet sunny clearing in the jungle.

ᘓ

Journal | *Cookies*

December 23, 1992

WHEN JOE AND I ARRIVE, Mama meets us at the door of their White Bear Lake condo holding out a handful of almonds.

"Are these pecans? I'm making butterballs." Then, in the cluttered kitchen, she starts fishing for pecans in a can of mixed nuts.

"You can't use salted nuts in butterballs, Mama."

"I'm going to wipe them off."

We stack our presents under the artificial Christmas tree in their living room. Its big ornaments dangle precariously from high branches, too many in front, nothing in back. A shriveled garland of last year's cranberries has slid off onto magazines, cassette tapes, and junk mail scattered on the soiled carpet. The light-filled rooms of ivory, apple green, and gold proudly decorated when they moved in just seven years ago have become somewhat shabby recently—but this mess is shocking. Dust and grime everywhere. And in the kitchen, the sinks are filthy, and pans and canisters crowd every work surface.

Once we find pecans, Mama stirs the cookie dough together, but it's runny. Too late she discovers she'd hidden the flour under a cookie sheet and fished out powdered sugar instead. Dismayed, she starts over, though it's 10 PM. Without complaint, Joe leaves the TV movie he's watching and takes Mama to the store for more pecans.

As they close the door, Dad looks scared. "We always tried to have an equal relationship," he says. "Now I have to take care of her. I don't mind doing that, but I'm eighty-three. What if something happens to me?"

Fit and sharp, Dad plays golf, does daily crosswords, reads mysteries and the newspaper—with his one good eye. Takes care of everything.

"There are still good times to be had with Mama," I tell him, "and we just have to let go of the desire that it be different."

But *he* can't do that. She has always brought life and love to all of us. And he needs her to connect him to the world.

☙

JOURNAL | *Bridge*

December 25, 1992: Christmas

MAMA HAS ALWAYS MADE HER legendary apple pies by heart, but the crust she rolls out this morning bakes hard as cardboard. She couldn't follow the recipe even after I found it in the chaos of her cookbook. Distracted as she sets the table, she complains, "I didn't sleep. I kept thinking I was supposed to be doing *something*, but I didn't know what it was."

When Jan was five, she came down to breakfast with a sleepy-eyed announcement that cracked us up and became an instant family saying. I try it on Mama. "What you think in bed isn't always true."

Mama doesn't laugh. She adds a new line: "But the trouble is, you don't know what's true and what isn't."

"Mama, you really don't have to do anything, because Jan planned a menu from *Bon Appétit*."

"But, *I* planned a menu, too," she sighs.

Shortly after we arrived last night, Mama assured me she'd taken the roast out to thaw. But this morning it's still in the freezer. We thaw it in a neighbor's microwave and coat it with ground red, green, and white peppercorns and Dijon. But once finally roasting, the meat sizzles alarmingly. Smoke billows from an oven set on broil.

"I'm never going to cook anything for anybody again," Mama mutters. "I'm not good for anything. I'm going to the bridge."

I take her in my arms. "We all love you for who you *are*, not what you can do. Do you believe that?"

"Yes," she whispers, unconvinced. And Dad shoots me a significant look.

Later he tells me about the last time Mama offered to go to the bridge.

"I was trying to shock her out of feeling bad, and I said, 'You'd get down there and forget what you were there for. Do you want me to write you a note?'"

"Then," he says, "she laughed."

❧

Journal | *Charmed*

June 1993

INSTEAD OF A BAPTISM, Ginger and Ned planned a nontraditional naming ceremony for baby Ian in the park across the street from their house. Friends and relatives were asked to write blessings, invent small rituals. Joe and I were to be godparents. Because Ginger had asked them to come early to take care of Ian, we dropped off Mom and Dad and went to help Jan cook.

When we returned, they were walking the pavement in front of Ginger's house. Mama was slumped, disconsolate. And Dad, both arms around her, seemed as much to be keeping her from falling as comforting her.

With Ian in a stroller, Mama had gone for a walk. But instead of circling the long block as always before, she crossed the street and headed west. And got lost. Ned and others rushed out to look for them, frightened by a scenario fit for a TV melodrama: baby kidnapped on the day of his blessing.

"When Ned returned alone, he was desperate," Ginger said. "I jumped in the car and drove right to Mama and little Ian. Mama was smiling, but clearly distressed, as she asked a woman for directions to 'the park.' Minneapolis is *full* of parks. As I helped Mama into the car, I know she saw the fear and anger on my face. She was sick at heart. 'You're never going to let me take him again,' she said, and I told myself: *Don't say anything.* But I was too horrified by what could have happened, and I said: 'Mom, I *can't* let you take him out anymore.'"

It required everything we had to convince Mama people would feel worse if she went home. I had to hold on to her as well-wishers welcomed Ian to the world.

"I will always regret not comforting Mom with some gentle evasion," Ginger told me later. "I was angry at her for abandoning us. I wanted her to be the vital contributing Nana for Ian that she'd been for my Alia."

⌘

MAMA MEETS ME AT HER BEDROOM DOOR, naked. "Stay away!" she shrieks. White hair wild, eyes staring, she is the archetypal hag, a madwoman from the back wards—until she melts, sobbing in my arms.

The very young and the old are the usual victims of scabies, and both of my parents have it: red, scaly, itchy—and cured by a three-day treatment.

Dad is fine, but Mama is distraught. She itches, she bitches, she says she should sit by the road with a sign that reads UNCLEAN. Though the bugs are microscopic, she sees bugs everywhere—not only ants but coffee grounds, crumbs, small print on paper.

"The washer and dryer ran all day for a week," Dad reports. "Mama washed and rewashed towels, and sheets, and clothing. She took shower after shower and scoured her hair with bar soap."

Then, clearly horrified, he whispers, "I never thought she would be this way. She was always so full of life."

Shampooed, conditioned, curled, and combed out, Mama's hair looks and feels better. Dad covers her with lotion, but she remains fixated upon her spots from scabies and age. She continues to believe she is contagious and looks too terrible to go anywhere. It is my job to talk Mama into attending Ginger's birthday party, but I fail.

☙

THE NEXT DAY, MAMA AND I WALK for a while at Lake Phalen, where we so loved to swim, and then sit by the northern shore. As has become her custom, she wears a white long-sleeved blouse, white pants, white socks, white shoes. In any weather, she veils her spotted body in polyester.

Mama is delighted to be near water, but she won't even wade. "It would be too much of a tease if I couldn't go in."

"No foreplay if you can't go all the way?" I ask, and she chuckles.

After visiting the East Side lakes, we eat big juicy hamburgers at Annie's Parlor and split an old-fashioned chocolate malt too thick to drink with a straw. Then we go to Lake Harriet, where we walk among roses just past full bloom, their bright petals slightly singed. Mama is ecstatic, exclaiming, "Beautiful, just beautiful." Shaded benches appear wherever we want to rest. The whole day is charmed—and declared wonderful.

"Were you worried about bugs today?"

She was not.

Back home, Mom and Dad seem apprehensive as I prepare to leave. But Dad has seen how going out helps.

ᥴᕟ

ON SATURDAY, MOM AND DAD ARE GONE ALL DAY, and when I call at night they still glow from their visit to the historic St. Croix River town of Stillwater. During the next week, Dad takes Mama out several times. Both are happy. And we begin to hope.

"This bug crisis reminds me of what Dad told me two years ago," Ginger says. "Mom wanted to attend a White Bear High School production of *South Pacific*, but Dad didn't want to see a high school show. 'Oh, you never want to do anything,' Mom grumbled and left the room.

"That night, Dad dreamed he and Mom were young again and she was just as pretty as before. Because all he ever wanted to do was stay home, she left him. He woke from that nightmare devastated and put his hand on Mom to make sure she was really there. The next morning, he told her he loved her and asked if she'd like to go to that high school play.

"It fits with what Mom told me years ago," Ginger adds. "There was a time when she was upset with Dad for just wanting to play sports or stay home. But they worked it out. Mom said she knew Dad *needed* to play sports."

A life-long athlete, Dad required physical activity to counteract his insurance-company desk job. He played and coached softball, collecting trophies and medals around the East Side until he was fifty years old. He even pitched some no-hitters.

But in 1960, a bat broke off, shattering his cheek and blinding his left eye. Softball was over for him. He bowled in winter, but in summer he just hung around the house, depressed. Mama encouraged him to find other activities, but he was beaten. Finally, on her own, she went across the alley to ask a neighbor who was an ardent golfer whether a one-eyed man could play the sport.

"Well, I don't know why not," he said. "The ball doesn't move till you hit it."

Once our neighbor lent him a set of clubs and took him golfing a few times, Dad found a new passion though he'd never been interested in that gentleman's game. And over the years he won trophies for two holes-in-one.

Needs, and the ability to meet them, change with the years. Dad's response now—to a deteriorating golf game, aging, and thoughts of dying—is to escape into thrillers and crossword puzzles. But Mama needs to get out and see people. Their condo has become a sensory-deprivation tank where he reads and she watches TV or fiddles with things.

Even though driving is harder for Dad and there is danger there, it's not talk but activity that pulls Mama out of her living hell.

✌

THOUGH HER SPOTS ARE ALMOST HEALED, the bugs are not forgotten. On my next visit, Mama points out a dark speck in a bag of mixed greens. "I know a bug when I see one."

"No, you don't!" I reply and to her horror eat the sliver of purple cabbage.

"I know a bug when I see one" becomes one of our jokes.

✌

JOURNAL | *Stone*

December 1993

TODAY AN OLD JOURNAL FELL OPEN TO THIS: Mom, Dad, and I were talking about their friends, the Torgeson twins, and how they looked so much alike, when Mama said, "Now it's easy to tell them apart because one has lost part of a leg—I don't know which one."

A punchline fit for Gracie Allen. But these days talking to Mama is more like pulling the string of a Chatty Cathy doll. Out rolls one of a limited number of programmed remarks:

I want to go see Honeybun.

I want to have people over.

I want to give you kids some of these things.

It broke my heart when Alia went to school and couldn't play with me anymore—and how she doesn't remember that.

When are you coming here again?

Are you liking your job now?

We're so lucky to have this place.

I don't want to do those church things anymore.

I tell Daddy he worked for forty years and then retired; I retired from cooking.

I wish I could have a puppy.

When is Janet going to go away so I can take care of her cats?

I love the fact that my three girls are so close.

We've got wonderful kids.

And after every one of Dad's corny jokes: *Nobody knows how I suffer.*

She is like a peach reduced to the essential stone of her nature: love, interest, generosity, humor, self-doubt, worry.

∽

JOURNAL | *What Remains*

June 29, 1994

FIVE-YEAR-OLD ALIA, protected from all woe like the young Buddha, is slowly discovering the time bomb that is her love for her grandma. "Will you die?" she asks, and is answered, "Yes."

A world of sorrow resonates in that exchange.

For Mama, these years are a time of relinquishment. An ankle injury means giving up her beloved long-blade skating. Getting lost on the way to Ginger's, and having to call for rescue, ends driving entirely—and destroys her independence. Cataract surgery sends her into weeks of disorientation and dizziness. Then a bad knee keeps her from joining Dad on the golf course. She admits she'd lied when she told us that didn't matter.

Perhaps we all float on a precarious raft of denial.

Looking back, I can see that even in the early 1980s Mama experienced high levels of anxiety and despair, but it was not until 1990 that several events forced us to focus on her problems. When Alia started nursery school, Mama lost the weekly playdays that had filled her life. Though she repeatedly said she understood the change was necessary, she couldn't adjust to the loss.

The Christensen family reunion we planned for Mom and Dad's fiftieth anniversary that same year brought Mama's brother, Ed, and his family from Nebraska, and her dearly loved cousin, Helen, whom we called Honeybun, from California. Ninety and in fragile health, Honeybun almost died and later said she could never again visit Minnesota. Mama bitterly grieved this decision.

At that time, some of us took a driving tour of the many St. Paul neighborhoods where Mom and Ed had lived as children. At each site, they told stories about the financial hardships that had plagued their family.

And 1990 was the year money anxieties began to keep Mama awake at night. It was also the year of the first Gulf War, which for her evoked painful memories of World War II when Dad was in Europe and she and I were alone.

"Seeing those young couples on TV kissing each other good-bye and those young mamas crying on their babies brought it all back," she told me. "I cried on you plenty."

And when, that same year, Ginger had a miscarriage, Mama was desolate.

It was as though the ghosts of the war years and the hard times of the Depression had rematerialized. All of the old stressors were present again to haunt her: money anxieties, the insecurities of change and loss, fear and sorrow for loved ones, war—

Recognizing Mama's unmistakable signs of memory loss doesn't mean we truly understand what these changes mean for her, for Dad, for all of us. What must it be to feel your hands shake, to work for fifteen minutes to thread a needle or fasten a pin to your coat? To return the church shut-in list unfinished, to botch recipes you knew by heart, to grope for the spelling of simple words, to abandon the mystery of the typewriter, to be taken everywhere like a child? To wake in the night worrying about things real and unreal?

In hushed discussions, we vacillate between shock at what Mama has lost and hope of finding solutions to this or that specific problem, between fear of the future and anger at being thus abandoned. But it's not as though *we* are in control. So much of civilization is dedicated to maintaining that illusion—throwing up frail systems against chaos, fencing off the abyss. Nevertheless, we will all eventually fail—a strange usage of a word that means a lack of skill or effort.

Ginger takes Mama for a gerontological exam, and afterward we discuss with Dad the experimental treatments the doctor suggests. We all agree the limited and temporary improvements that drugs offer aren't worth their considerable side effects. We turn up the lights with brighter smiles, warmer hugs in a strange savoring of precious time left. It is the reverse of the way a mother wants to watch her baby grow into a unique human being. We want to hold on to what *remains* of Mama. Conflicts of the past dissolve in a new way to be with her that I call "timeless time": living in the present moment with no agenda, just doing what presents itself. Trying to let things be what they are.

"I don't know why some people want to live to be really old," Mama says. "The older you get, the more that goes wrong. People should die at their peak. My brother is right: it's hell to grow old."

℘

JOURNAL | *Mystery*

July 5, 1994

IN THE DARK, RAINY STREET-SCENE PAINTING hanging over the TV, Dad sees an idealized picture of the little French towns he served in during World War II. But Mama sees a sorrowful reflection of her mind. She stares at it, obsessed.

In one of our attempts to fix every problem, we ask Mama to pick out a new painting, and she chooses a forest path that winds through sun-dappled trees to a mysterious end.

Now she smiles, looks at it long, and wonders what lies just beyond those trees. And Dad takes his French scene down to the basement, paints the dark clouds bright, and hangs it above his workbench.

જી

JOURNAL | *Perils*

July 22, 1994

IN MY DREAM, WE ARE HAVING a family party, but our house is the home of family friends where, in real life, Mama received the ankle injury that ended her skating. And where their good friend Harry who, far gone into memory loss, said to his wife of fifty years, "I've been noticing you working around here. What's your name?"

Mama and Honeybun have gone off to church—walking more than a mile in winter through a dangerous neighborhood. It is getting dark, but the rest of us are enjoying the party and not paying attention. An artistic man, with the look of a Gypsy fortune teller, peers out into the darkness and confronts us with the uncomfortable truth that Mama and Honeybun are still out there alone. Only then do we become concerned. Only then do we go out to look for them.

I wake to fuller understanding of the perils of Mama's journey now. The dream is saying, be present with her. Be aware of what she needs. Know it is your own journey, too.

෧ඁ

Jewels

December 1994

FOR YEARS, MAMA HAS MADE GLITTERING wall hangings out of junk. Gluing tiny ceramic birds, fragments of earrings, and rhinestone necklaces to black velvet, she constructs Christmas trees. The ultimate in kitsch, like pink flamingos. Calling her the Great Destroyer of Jewels has never slowed her down. Her work table in the basement is piled with fishing tackle boxes full of sequins, beads, and gaudy costume jewelry from garage sales and the Goodwill store.

But now bric-a-brac and baubles for her crafts are jumbled together with Christmas ornaments and her own good jewelry—all her shiny treasures spread out on the dining room table.

"I've got to do *something*," she says.

After all these years, I ask her to make me a jeweled Christmas tree. Something she still can do.

She is past sorting her trove, so I try. But it seems like some fairy-tale task that can only be accomplished with magical help. Rescuing a gold earring serving as the cover for a lotion bottle, I search out its mate, hoping it has yet to meet the metal snips. It is urgent work, as if the effort might keep Mama's mind from unraveling. Soon it will all be a pile again.

And then a glint of light from beneath the couch reveals Mama's engagement ring— discarded or abandoned while several clunky junk rings adorn her fingers. "Mama, this is your diamond. Why don't you put it on again?"

"It's loose. My fingers have gotten so thin. But maybe *this* one will hold it on." She slides on a ring that sports a garish chunk of red glass.

At my next visit, Mama holds out an imperfect, glue-splotched square of black felt, to which she has affixed most of a rhinestone choker. It forms a misshapen circle that doesn't quite enclose two green glass buttons stuck to the leaves of a cheap pin. She knows she has failed, but gives it to me anyway. I hold this broken mandala in my hands, this uroboros whose teeth just miss its tail. This jewel.

⁌

Journal | *Moments*

December 20, 1994

I N THE GARAGE THIS MORNING, warming up the car, exhaust fumes rising, I think: *I could just close the door*— Then get a grip: *Not today. Think about it tomorrow, Scarlett.* But, if I *had* closed that door—and somehow survived—they'd take me away for a nice long rest. Good for nothing but writing, I might even qualify for disability—my madness being, at least in part, job-related.

Teaching full time is hell. The day begins with two ninth-grade classes on two different floors in the middle school, followed by dashing off to the high school for two journalism classes, a study hall, and a final tech communications. Three different preps in four different rooms. Years of *Poetry in the Schools* residencies ruined me for this job. All that creativity and freedom, with a regular teacher in the room to keep the lid on. You can't teach poetry in a straightjacket. But here, when I don't hide my delight at their antics or don't humiliate some brash kid trying to find his power, I'm fair game. For disapproval and more shenanigans. Most of the kids are well-mannered, even sweet, but some few say and do things they'd never try in a class where they'd end up doing pushups in the aisle. And then it's my fault for not controlling them.

Work occupies my life like an armed force. Dreams assail, their warnings ignored. Quick notes for poems press in vain for completion. And somehow, not every lesson is perfectly organized, not every assignment corrected on time. And little energy remains to give what Mom and Dad most need from me—a loving presence. But school does have its moments. In first hour, Tommy, brilliant (and what I prefer to think of as *eccentric*), announces from the back row, "I was an accident. I was born after my mother had her tubes tied."

"Miracle child," I offer.

But Zack, front and center, rolls his eyes and mutters, "Must be the work of the devil."

This job is my fate, both terrible and wonderful. Instead of saying, "It's all right," and enduring whatever happens, I must grab hold and squeeze some sustenance from it.

And hang on for winter break.

☙

JOURNAL | *Octopus*

So NOW IT'S A FACIAL TIC! Tell me how to face the heartless scrutiny of teenagers with *this*. Reminds me of my second-grade teacher who would stand in front of the class with her face going crazy. She never said a word about it to us, and we dared not laugh. But it was freakish. Ridiculously distracting. What a way, all these years later, to find some empathy for her.

Meanwhile, the word that describes the current trajectory of my life is *entropy*, defined as "a lack of order or predictability; a gradual decline into disorder."

Like my parents' lives. And their condo. They run short of money every month, and Jan has to make it up. We all bring groceries and often refuse payment. Or sneak food into their fridge.

The phone, the TV, both fans, coffeemaker, timer—so many things wearing out and bearing signs of Dad's way of fixing them: wire wrappings, duct tape. We should replace everything with state-of-the-art technology, but Dad has even forgotten how to record a movie on the VCR. He needs no new failures.

Totally taken over by school and trapped by the need to do an impossible job well, I feel like an octopus outlet disconnected from its energy source. Drained by all the power-sucking responsibilities plugged into me. Still trying to love the kids.

But even as the word "love" appears on this page, the phone startles me with one of their prank calls! Ah! They're thinking of me!

෨

This Too Will Pass

October 1995

ONE MORNING, MAMA CALLS JAN to tell her Dad is sick. At least she knows to do that. When Ginger enters their condo, the place is in chaos, and the refrigerator is bare. She takes both parents to the doctor and learns Dad has pneumonia.

After the appointment, Ginger sets them up in Jan's guest bedroom. At first, Mom and Dad are relieved to find themselves cared for. Thankful for the Family Medical Leave Act that supports time off work, I take my turn staying with them. But after a few days, Mama is desperate to go home.

We resist her pleas as long as we can. Dad had been taking care of *her* and is not completely recovered. And we wonder if Mama knows how to call 911 and give their address in an emergency. Ginger flatly refuses to take them back to White Bear, but Jan finally gives in.

Over all objections, we use this crisis as an opportunity to arrange Meals on Wheels—"till Dad gets better." Tortured by personal expectations based upon what she has always been able to do, Mama now feels even more a failure. She cannot understand that by resisting help she is making it harder for Dad. For all of us.

Gradually, at home, they get used to Meals on Wheels, and like it. They eat much better, *are* much better. And on weekends, one of us brings supper and groceries. We fill their refrigerator with fresh fruit and vegetables, frozen entrées, but all too often they eat wiener sandwiches and cottage cheese or baked beans and chips.

❧

DAININ KATAGIRI, the former Roshi of the Minneapolis Zen Center where Joe and I occasionally sat in meditation, had an inspiring presence that could lift me out of my everyday mind. His smile was transcendent, his Zen teaching full of compassion for human suffering. In *Returning to Silence*, he wrote of staying fully alive when life, for all of us, is continually passing away.

> Human life, which includes sorrow, is nothing to say, nothing to grasp, nothing to throw away. It is very painful. You can't stand up there, but you can't escape either.... We cannot despair, we cannot be arrogant, we cannot say anything, but right in the middle of dangerous situations we have to live, we have to let our life force bloom with our best effort. At that time the flower of our life force becomes beautiful.

"Let our life force bloom with our best effort," he said—not force it. Defensive postures or clever words just get in the way. Especially in adversity, we must learn to let go of fear (throwing away) and desire (grasping), and surrender to the present moment. If we can truly be there, life can open like a flower.

"I don't understand how I got this way," Mama moans, as she and Dad slip all the holds we have set to keep them.

Nothing to grasp.

"This too will pass" becomes my parents' motto, and my mind leaps ahead to a neater, easier time.

Nothing to throw away.

On the phone, Dad hangs on long after he has said everything. My parents' lives have narrowed down to their "wonderful kids." Without us, they have no appetite, no energy. And yet, nothing we do can save them.

Just be present with them.

Whether psychologically or physically, being present is the one thing most difficult, especially when home and work are ninety miles away in Litchfield. And yet they say:

If you're bored while Joe's gone, you can always come here.

When will we see you?

You're always welcome here.

We'll miss you when you go.

Would you like to move in? (A joke that is not a joke.)

Years ago, Mama would sometimes erupt in an operatic scream, just to let off steam—especially when Dad had put on classical music. She has always claimed she cannot carry a tune, but she can. And these days, after a few hours of our presence, Mama often slips from vague passivity into humming.

Today, while doing the dishes, she drifts through a wordless, disjointed medley in which "and let the rest of the world go by" segues into snatches of *I Wonder What's Become of Sally?* and then *I Come to the Garden Alone*, her mother's favorite hymn. After "I'll cherish the Old Rugged Cross till my trophies at last I lay down" slides into *Please Release Me*, she calls out:

"It's been so long since I've used it. Could you come and show me how to use this?"

She points to the dishwasher.

❧

Journal | *Gift*

December 10, 1995

AUNT CAROL AND UNCLE BOB give Mom and Dad a gift certificate that will take them to California. And that sets off a burst of emotion. For me, it's guilt for not wanting to take them out there. Jan calls to tell me she's gotten a letter saying Honeybun is worried about Mom staying with her. Carol had phoned to warn her about Mama's condition, and she doesn't know if she can "take care of her."

On the phone, Honeybun asks me whether Mama can "do anything." I explain she just lets Dad be her memory and make decisions. She forgets to eat or doesn't think she's hungry. She has a hard time deciding what to wear, and wears the same clothes too long. But she's still fun to talk to and still tells stories from the past. She doesn't do anything dangerous. Honeybun is reassured. But how strange to have Mama's ninety-five-year-old cousin worrying about her. And Dad's brother and sister making all these careful arrangements for them.

It will be a much-guided trip. In San Diego, they'll be picked up at the airport and taken to Carol's. Mama is afraid she'll have to get together with the Rancho Belles—she was one of them—and these stylish clubwomen will see how she's changed. But that won't happen. And Carol will drive them to visit Honeybun.

Luckily, all of this will take place after Christmas.

✢

JOURNAL | *Switch*

October 27, 1996

WE BUSY DAUGHTERS BUSTLE IN and stock the kitchen with food, but Mom and Dad can't really feed themselves. They eat junk and let fruits and vegetables mold and liquefy in the fridge. That's scary. Today I found a hunk of cheese stuck in an open jar of mustard. Yellow matched with yellow.

We help Dad pay bills and taxes, and try to fix every problem, but usually don't stay long. And what Mom and Dad want is our presence. Of course, on every visit we tell them what they *should* be doing.

"That's the way it goes," Mama says today. "When you kids were little I told you what to do. And now that we're old, you tell us what to do."

"Maybe it's like what Jan said when she was still in grade school," I remind her. *"Just you wait till I'm big and you're little."*

Mama thinks that's hilarious. She *is* little now. So is Dad. I shortened five pairs of his pants to twenty-nine inches, the same length as mine. But height isn't the problem. Dad got lost taking Mom to the doctor the other day, and we wonder if he should be driving. What will we do about that?

❧

JOURNAL | *Christmas*

December 26, 1996

THE PLAN WAS FOR MOM AND DAD to stay overnight at Jan's on Christmas Eve. We were even going to take them to church. But they both got the flu last week. Ginger wanted them present on Christmas Eve despite that, but Jan thought it would be inconsiderate to expose other guests to the flu.

Instead, Joe and I bring the traditional Christmas Eve meal out to them.

Mama is naked when we arrive, so I help her get dressed. A little later she says, "I feel smart. I got dressed before you came."

Both of them have forgotten they're sick. "Why can't we go?" Mama asks. Dad says he just has no energy.

To set their places at the table, I have to clear off plastic containers of moldy Meals on Wheels desserts, wrapped bread slices with pats of margarine, a plate of cookies from somebody, and a jumble of Christmas cards—though Mom and Dad haven't sent any for three years. I trash the accursed sweepstakes materials that have become Dad's main business these days.

Ginger had asked me to pick up the gifts that she brought out for Mom to wrap for the kids. I find one box with a doll dress in it but the pants loose in the junk on the table. The rest of the gifts are scattered around the guest room.

"Did we pay for them?" Mama asks anxiously. "It's no fun otherwise."

I cry hard on the way back to Jan's. We are leaving them alone on Christmas Eve, but might as well have stayed out there with them. This year at Jan's, "Merry Christmas" greetings seem ironic.

❧

JOURNAL | *Talk*

May 20, 1997

JOE AGREED TO TALK TO DAD about "contingency plans." Because I can't and neither can my sisters. When the two of them were alone in the car, Joe began by reminding Dad what his younger brother has been saying about *his* plans for care, should he need it. As Joe recollects, their conversation unfolded as follows:

"When Bob was talking about what he is going to do if he can't get around," Joe said, "it made us feel guilty about not discussing contingencies with you. Your daughters have been cautious about interfering, but it's something we need to talk about."

"Where we are now is just the perfect place," Dad said quickly.

"Yes, it *is* a wonderful place, but we're worried about you being overwhelmed by taking care of Lois. What are your plans if Lois can't manage or something happens to her?"

"She *does* cook. It's not too bad yet."

"Well, suburban living means driving, for groceries, doctors, everything. And that could become a problem—"

"Yes, but it's okay as long as I can drive," Dad argued.

"Are there senior services in White Bear?"

"Yes, there are—"

"Have you thought about where you'd go if something happened?"

"Not really," Dad mused. "Well, you think about it, but not really."

"What about Litchfield? You could find a place near us that's fairly cheap, but nice."

"But we wouldn't know anybody there."

"Your daughters have been thinking, wouldn't you like a place like Honeybun's? A senior assisted-living apartment?"

Dad let himself drift into what was clearly his expectation: "I don't think my daughters would want me to live with *them*." Then, in the uncomfortable silence that followed, he quickly added, "I guess I wouldn't want to do that, either. My grandmother lived with us, and I was her pet, but it wasn't so great for the rest of them. It caused problems."

"You can expect your daughters will want to talk about this."

❧

AFTER HIS CONVERSATION WITH JOE, Dad tells me, once again, "We want to be independent as long as we can."

"We want you to live where you feel comfortable and safe and happy," I assure him, knowing independence is an illusion we all create for them with every visit.

"That's what we're doing now," he insists.

❧

WE LET THE ARGUMENT GO, but begin to search for an assisted-living apartment. When we find one that seems suitable, we take them to see it. They hate it and refuse to move. That visit, however, softens their resistance to our adding much-needed support services.

Meanwhile, through Eldercare Locater, Senior Linkage Line, Senior Housing Directory, and Housing Special Services, we intensify our search for other options.

❧

Folie à Deux

June 1997

D AD HAS ALWAYS KNOWN NOT ONLY THE ROUTE but also the exact lane to follow at each point along the way. He has always carried the map in his head, but now he gets lost on old familiar trips—going to and coming from his brother Bob's in South Minneapolis, and even going home from Jan's house.

"I traveled all over Northern Europe during the war, and I get lost in South Minneapolis," he says.

Mama seems to gain a little confidence from this. "I wasn't paying any attention, so I couldn't help. I told him when you get old, you've got to be extra careful. I try to be."

He of the maps and clear directions cannot find his way. The next time we go to Bob's, he lets me drive, blaming the sun shining in his one good eye.

Focusing on Mama's problems, we have not been paying enough attention to Dad. He has forgotten the location of Mama's hairdresser and how to play the VCR. He forgets that I am teaching, that he has a cordless phone, that a few months ago he had pneumonia. He writes two checks for the cleaner, but neglects to pay the rent. On Mother's Day, he asks if there is a Father's Day. Last Christmas, he thought *he* had ordered the treats sent by Honeybun.

We lose most of what faith remains in his judgment when, after all we have been through with Mama, he talks about getting her to drive again.

Meanwhile, Dad's car registration and driver's license have come due, but he has put off renewing them. On some level does he know he should not drive? Reluctant to intervene, I leave the notices with his bills. If they expire, it will be because he lets them, and if he lets them, he will not be driving.

Around Mama, gravity fails. Facts break loose and collide with each other. History, continuity, even cause and effect dissolve. It is as if the very ground gives way. Has Dad's bond with Mama's muddled presence somehow untied his mind? Although she usually keeps quiet to hide her confusion (she has said as much), what must this be for him? They have always been *one*.

Joe's sister, Shirley, told me of an old man who asked his wife where his Linda was.

"I'm Linda," she said.

"No, you're not!" he exclaimed. "I want my old Linda back."

This morning, Dad echoes that loss: "I went in to check on Mama, and there she was sitting on the bed. Of course, it wasn't really *her*."

Later, as we watch Mama slowly shuffle into the hairdresser's, he sighs, "And *that* is my wife—I never thought she'd be this way—" Then hastens to add, "She's still good company."

And now, in despair at her failing functions, Mama tells Dad, "I should go jump off a bridge."

"What?"

"I think I'm ready to go to heaven."

"Oh, stay here with me, if you don't mind," he croons, taking her in his arms. "I like having you to cuddle with in bed. And when we meet in the hall to pat you and hug you."

My parents continue to talk about their romance and the war years. They tell the same stories again and again. But the love of Dad's life has abandoned him. Some blank and dispirited imposter has taken her place. Is his growing befuddlement caused by grief and loneliness? Is he joining Mama in what the French call *folie à deux*—a madness shared by two?

Folie à deux is psychosis. I use the phrase as metaphor only, but the question remains: Is seeing himself and their life reflected in the funhouse mirrors of Mama's dementia causing my father to let go and follow her into the darkness?

෴

Short-term Memory Loss

June 10, 1997

ALL WINTER MY SISTERS AND I have been going to Mom and Dad's on alternating weekends to do whatever needs to be done. Ginger handles medical issues. Jan and I have power-of-attorney. And we have gotten more outside help. In addition to Meals on Wheels and a cleaning service, Meg, a home-care provider, comes every Tuesday to escort Mom to the hairdresser, or both Mom and Dad to the dentist or doctor. Lay ministers deliver taped church services and leave notes saying they have been "communed." On occasion, friends stop by. Still, we find chaos whenever we arrive. Somehow Mama seems less real to me when she cannot remember. Words and thoughts pass into the air like smoke—even this honest talk:

"I told the cleaning lady I'd call her if I wanted her to come," Mama confesses.

"But we scheduled her to come every two weeks."

"Oh, I did the wrong thing—but when she comes I feel guilty. I go down and sit in the basement."

Though cleaning has never been a major concern for Mom, she is dismayed she can no longer do it herself.

"But, Mama, nobody wants to clean if they don't *have* to. You worked hard all your life. This is your time to be free. I'll talk to Ginger about it."

"Are you going to tell the cleaning lady to not pay any attention to what I say?" Mama asks.

"Well, not exactly—but sort of."

We both laugh and relax a bit.

"I realize I am like my mother about accepting help," she says, "and I remember how mad it made me when my mother wouldn't let *me* help. I'll try to change."

"Mama, in order to be happy, people have to be in harmony with their stage in life. Everyone is born needing help and then gradually—"

"We're able to do things."

"Yes, and then we eventually need help again. And it's sad and it's a loss, but it's the way things are, and if we try to be like we were in a different stage it doesn't work. I'd be a fool to act like I'm twenty-five. At fifteen, I couldn't act twenty-five, either. When you're eighty-one, you can't expect to do what you did at fifty."

That is easy for *me* to say. And "You have to let go and let it be what it is or you can't be happy" sounds too glib, especially when I cannot do that.

"I want to stay in White Bear until I die."

"We want you to stay here and get help here. Getting you help is easy; what makes it hard is how you react, your feelings about it."

So it is all out in the open, and for now she understands.

After supper, we sit on their balcony. Out in the yard, a line of sunlit poplars and elms creates a golden oasis that almost obscures the nearby houses. With the little spruce we always decorate for Christmas and the flowering crab-apple tree we planted for Mother's Day, this suburban environment is the materialization of our parents' dream. Even though it has become a soft prison for Mama, they both bask in it.

"The White Bear Senior Community Center has lots of programs you could take part in," I urge. "You should get out more."

"The worst thing that could happen to us is if I couldn't drive," Dad says. "I think I still have all my marbles—"

He waits for me to confirm this, but I have to say it outright: "You do have memory problems."

He does not seem ready to admit it.

"It's short-term memory loss, Daddo. You just have to make lists, write things down."

Mama says *she* has memory problems, and I agree—sitting here, the definer of reality, passing judgment on my parents' minds! And they dependent on that judgment.

"It seems like we've grown old in about a month," Dad sighs.

"All I want is to have Honeybun come here, but I know she won't do that now," Mama says. "I always thought I could go to see her, but I don't know how to do that anymore."

The gulf between impulse and action is filled with longing.

For the very old, unrealized dreams will not come true. The dashed hopes, false starts, defeats, losses, abandonments, the failures of nerve, momentum, or heart cannot be remedied by some fresh ambition.

What is it to live beyond the lives of friends and loved ones? Alone among strangers, to flounder in a morass of incomprehensible technical, cultural, and political change? Without work, purpose, or power, to be continually corrected and humored? To lose pride and the freedom to choose? To find life a burden to self and others? And, if lucky enough to avoid chronic pain and increasing medical intervention, to yet know life is nearly over? What happens to a person who is no longer able to trust strength, judgment, and memory—qualities that in all previous life had been taken for granted?

Here on the balcony, her face a dark silhouette against the setting sun, my mother says, "I miss who I used to be."

❧

HOPING TO ENTERTAIN MAMA and to remind her of her life, I dig out all the letters she had ever sent me and put them in a ring binder. She is amazed.

"You saved them *all?*"

"Of course. They're great."

When I read one she asks, "Did I *really* write that? Was I that smart? Could I type?"

In addition to insightful letters, Mama always wrote thoughtful and compassionate notes of thanks or condolence. But today, stuffed in among cards, bills, and sweepstakes junk mail, I find scrawled, labored drafts of a note to her godchild, whose husband has died:

Dear Connie, ~~Ralph Ralf~~ We wish We wish ~~we could find the right~~ words
we could find the   right words
of comf   We just can't find There just ~~does~~ doesn't
I've tried to find a few words of comfort All I can think to say to you is

but all there is   to tell you how sorry we are ~~that~~ this happened.
We will Ralph and I will pray for ~~some comford~~
Dear Connie
After
~~well, I've been~~ trying to find ~~the words~~ something ~~to right~~ comford you all
~~There isn't~~

We wish we could find the right words to comfort you in these sad days, Connie.
Ralph and I want you to know that you are in our ~~thoughts and~~ prayers, along
with all your family ~~and friends~~ and we pray that you will find strength to help
you through. God bless.

෴

Mama's Writing

ONCE, WHEN I WAS A TEENAGER ARGUING WITH MAMA, she went to the basement, dug out her high school diary, and called me down to hear some of it. She thought it might help me understand she too had once been young and had problems with her mother. Sulking, I refused to go. Immediately, she burned her diary in the incinerator. I never asked how she could do that.

Mama had hoped to be a writer, but when after high school she took a class, the teacher's judgment of her efforts as clichéd destroyed all confidence. One of Dad's letters to her during World War II made encouraging reference to her "novel," but she never mentioned it to any of us. However, for my thirteenth birthday, she gave me a five-year diary with its own lock and key, thus inviting a lifelong dialogue with myself.

"Nothing has a stronger influence on children than the unlived lives of their parents," wrote psychologist Carl Jung. No doubt, Mama's frustrated dream contributed as much to my writing as the stack of journals kept since the gift of that first little diary.

Dad boxed up and sent home all the letters Mama wrote to him during the war, but she destroyed them. In one of his letters to her at the time, he wrote:

I guess you're right about not saving the old letters, it would just make us feel bad to read them over after we have maybe forgotten all about this trying period. There are a few of mine I would like to have to remind me of things to tell you about.

Mama characterized her own letters as "so mundane I thought no one would want to read them." She later apologized to me. "You would have wanted to read them. They were about you."

Mama did not destroy Dad's letters. She kept them in a sealed box in the basement under a sort of taboo. I didn't open that box until both parents were dead. His letters praised hers and responded to stories she told and questions she asked. They described what he could about his life in the Army and his longing for home and family. I ache for her strands of the fabric that held their marriage together during those anxious and lonely times.

Over the years, for special occasions, Mama wrote clever rhyming poems. She would read them aloud, expecting derision, but never saved any of them. Once she said, "Sometime I'll show you my *real* poems." But she never did.

But, always, her words flowed. After our parents retired to California in 1976, Mama's letters were full of love and humor, passion, and compassion. Using an old manual portable typewriter, she banged them out on onionskin with two carbons so she could send one to each daughter. And scribbled afterthoughts and personal notes in the margins.

Distance did not stop our family from gathering for Christmas. It was almost mandatory. In 1978, Jan, Joe, and I traveled to San Diego expecting a lonely time because Ginger and her first husband, David, were Peace Corps volunteers in Chile. Their surprise arrival delighted us. Believing they had been given jobs that should have been filled by Chileans, they had left the Corps in disillusionment.

Back at home, I wrote a positive poem (difficult for me at the time) about the family as made up of:

> *pieces whose bruising edges have been smoothed*
> *by time,*
> *a puzzle that finally fits.*

The poem was cynical about San Diego:

> *a manicured suburb of exotic plants*
> *where it is safe*

to pretend there is no death—
no darkness and no light.

Mama's response included her own real poem:

Dear Nano—

I could feel you waiting for my response to your family poem, either by mail or by phone, but I hadn't settled it yet—I was trying to figure out why I cried, why I was so sad, why I couldn't discuss it with Daddo, either. I still do not know. It isn't that I don't understand your poem completely, because I'm sure I do, and I am thankful that we all have learned that alone, "we are not complete" (that's a wonderful line) and that it is enough just to be together even if for a short time, no matter how we spend the time.

Sometimes I try to recapture my joy of having you all here for Christmas— how I even shopped with a smile on my face for all the world to see—how great it was that we were together at Christmas, with even Ginger and David coming back so unexpectedly from Chile, when we all thought we would miss them so much. I still do not know why I cried about your poem, though. Perhaps my poem will tell. It is from my point of view, naturally, so I think you have to be an old mother to understand it.

When you were in those years of rebellion and we were hurting each other, I often remembered harsh words I had had with my mother and how irritated I used to get with her—so I sort of figured I had it coming—and now when I look back on all of it, I have learned that she forgave me and still loved me no matter what I had said—know why I know that? Because I loved you, forgave you. Hope you have done the same. It is tough to be the first-born, too bad we couldn't have been wiser, but then, guess we were doing the best we could—you have to think that way, you know. Otherwise we'd be haunted by guilt forever!

Well, let us hear what you feel about my prosy-poem—sometimes it is easier to write what is in your heart than to say it. I find it so—

THE BEST CHRISTMAS

They came to California, thousands of miles from Minnesota, Chile
To gather together in a house no longer their home
And fill it with the sweetest joy old parents can know—
A time when once more the family is complete, whole.

Emotions deepened by separation, tears came first, then laughter
The excitement of telling everything at once—
And plans hurriedly made
Until, finally, very late, the house quieted
And each settled to sleep, to think, to count blessings.

As she lay encircled by his arm
The old mother whispered contentedly in the night
Once again their shared and familiar phrase—
"Dad, our babies are all safe in their nests."

With my love, Momo

*P.S. I think I got the tears out of my system since I wrote the above! My love
and best to Joe—*

Horrified that my attempt to express love had sharpened the old "bruising
edges," I rewrote my poem, taking out all cynical references. If it comforted her,
it was not the whole truth. It just outlined the barriers that remained. And I
missed at that time what was perhaps the real reason for her tears: by moving to
California, she, herself, had widened the distance between us.

❧

Love Made Flesh

July 1997

MY LONG-TIME FRIEND KATHLEEN watches her daughter and her mother as they lie together, arms entwined. Physical contact between bodies that must soon be separated. Her mother—skin drawn taut, desiccated, reduced to bony frame—is precious and passing away.

For Kathleen, all old conflicts dissolve in the present need for physical care— the exhausting, repetitive process of lifting a spoon to lips, of helping the frail body into a wheelchair or onto the toilet. Her anger from all the years shrinks, and grief washes it clean, even as her mother slips away, becoming small, help- less, unreachable.

"Washing the body after death is a Judaic ritual," Kathleen says. "I don't know if I can do that, but I didn't think I could ever diaper her. And I do."

Patience, gentleness, and care are love made flesh.

What is patience? First, what is *im*patience? Wanting to control someone or something. Reaching toward some future time or place and throwing away what rests within the open hands. Saying no.

But patience, that rare gift, is letting life be what it *is*, surrendering to the present moment, saying yes. The moment that cannot be escaped can be savored. Even its whole bitterness.

"If you want to learn life, you must learn death," says Zen master Dainin Katagiri.

Life is life. Fragile and ephemeral as a flower. Beautiful *because* it is passing away. We so rarely let life be life. We have to shape it, extrude it through some kind of system to make it mean something. We have to be going somewhere, accomplishing something. We devise regimens to create harmony and balance, to give meaning, purpose, and structure, to make us feel we are in control—not pathetic victims of natural forces, wisps blown by the winds of chance, pawns of fate. Mere mortals passing away.

But life will be life, in all its incongruous juxtapositions. *This Is My Father's World* rings out from the Lutheran church's electronic carillon in concert with the neighbor's howling dog. And everything we love is held hostage by time.

In her confusion, my mother waters tattered silk flowers. She sets out cheap molded glass alongside her crystal. To restore order, I wash the china on the buffet, polish the silver, arrange yellow gladioli in the cut-glass vase. The late afternoon sun lights the display in a glorious blaze. And all around it the clutter and dust, the stained carpet and scarred walls lay bare my mother's dementia.

Letting life be life may be the hardest thing to do. Being present here and now. "Right in the middle of the road—where there is completely nothing to do, to say, to grasp, to throw away—you have to do constantly," says Katagiri. "There is nowhere to go, just right now, right here. This is an open space for you."

There is only now. This touch, this look, this word is all. In the presence of a failing loved one, we may alternate between grasping at the hope of cure and almost wishing for the death that will set us free. Hardest of all, perhaps, is to be present with dissolution. Loss breaks the heart, but opens the soul. And when the soul opens to the present moment, love is made flesh.

℀

Bloodsuckers

November 1997

T HE READER'S DIGEST AND PUBLISHER'S CLEARING HOUSE hype has sucked in my parents. Dusty audiotapes teeter on the shelves: *Sentimental Journey: 80 Original Hits of the '40s, Great Romantic Memories of the War Years*. Unopened *Great Train Ride* videos accumulate on the TV. Unread books and magazines pile up in corners. And always, the bill, the reorder blank, and the sweepstakes entry form fit neatly on one piece of paper. Their financial cushion having gone flat, Dad orders junk to lay his final bet on the American Dream.

We do not know if our parents should stay in their White Bear Lake condo, even with help, but sitting on their balcony is heaven to them. Or is this only something they tell themselves? To me, their life looks like hell. Mama falls asleep in front of the television. She fiddles with things, hangs little ornaments in weird places. She fishes through drawers for old letters she cannot read, old photos of people she has forgotten, and mixes them in with the current mail or the recycling. She cries when we arrive, "Oh, I was so down!" And she cries when we leave, pleading, "When will you come again?"

Dad's conversations are spirals, telling not only stories he has told before but stories he has *just finished* telling. Even so, he reads mysteries and the newspaper, completes his daily crossword, and regularly enters the sweepstakes.

Ah, the sweepstakes dream: the jokes about winning, the extravagant and generous plans for the money, the careful filling out of forms, and the unending mailing of entries and orders for magazines, calculators, books, videos, and any number of other useless trinkets.

"It's a scam," I declare.

"Well, I'm just about done with the sweepstakes—"

But is he? The sweepstakes are something he can still do. They give him some contact with the outside world and keep alive a wild dream of the wealth that will solve his problems. He and Mama are easy prey.

Last month, Dad read a sweepstakes letter aloud to show he understands what an evil piece of work it is. He pointed out every qualifier, every trick. All the while Mama heckled him.

"Did you *do* it?"

She showed me a sweepstakes form. "Is there still time to send it in? Read this and tell me if I won a million dollars."

Her words set me off on a personal campaign to purge their home of bloodsuckers. Each visit means trashing half a grocery bag of catalogues, contests, subscription offers, and requests for donations, then venting all manner of wrath on these "businesses" that take advantage of the gullible: book clubs, video clubs, health letters, the case of canned grapefruit arriving every ninety days, and several scam sweepstakes.

One letter is not enough to drive a stake through their hearts. Only the intervention of the Minnesota Attorney General will finally hang some garlic over the mailbox. In the meantime, I write repeatedly, and it feels so good! On November 8, 1997, I sent this to Publishers Clearing House:

> *I need your help! Last month I asked your company to remove my parents from your mailing list. I also asked that no further offers to buy magazines or books or videos or any other materials be sent to them. And that any club memberships or series to which they may have subscribed be canceled at once.*
>
> *But instead my mother got a letter from you saying she was "scheduled to receive Lifetime Payment Entitlements in the amount of $5,000 per week" should she "have and return the winning SuperPrize Number...." You included a direct deposit slip! And the reminder that she should order because that's the only way you can award so much money.*
>
> *My mother also got a letter from "Dorothy Addeo, Contest Manager" suggesting she should help Dorothy out! Dorothy, it seems, was in trouble with her boss for not letting my mother win. And she could "personally guarantee that you'll win a prize in our sweepstakes!" All my mother had to do was return the Guaranteed Winner Document. And make an order.*

You should be ashamed. I am appalled at the number of companies such as yours who offer all manner of false hopes to people on fixed incomes. How can you ask them to spend their limited money for overpriced books and videos on the negligible chance of winning your prize!

My parents have granted me power-of-attorney because they can no longer manage their own affairs. They cannot deal with the sweepstakes mail. They will not order more merchandise from your firm. Consider this letter notice of cancellation. They will not pay for any shipments that may be sent after this date. Thank you for your immediate attention to this matter.

For the United States Purchasing Exchange, I pull out all the stops:

Congratulations! Your sweepstakes materials are the most outrageous, misleading, manipulative con job I have ever seen. Orange envelope indeed! And small print informing only the most careful reader that you are not connected or affiliated with the U.S. Government—despite the torch of liberty, the laurel wreath, the internal audit, the security exchange, the time-sensitive package, the official issue and seal, the Courier Authorized Express (which apparently means bulk rate).

Using a sweepstakes and promises of prizes—along with time allotment cards, check-like releases, suggestions of highly prized customer status, declarations of issuance, Lotso Value Quick Match Tickets, Lincoln Town Car Giveaway Questionnaires and U.S.P.E.'s Giveaway Times—is perhaps the ultimate in underhanded marketing. It is especially egregious to prey upon people in their eighties who might hope that buying your merchandise will allow them to "finally live [their] dreams." The "STOP! If you're responding WITHOUT a catalog order, stop and reconsider for your own benefit" is especially disgusting. You should be ashamed....

☙

MOM AND DAD ARE SLIPPING AWAY, a problem that cannot be solved. I cannot defeat old age or forgetfulness or a universe in which life requires death. But I *can* battle the sweepstakes bloodsuckers. It is one way to "rage against the dying of the light."

☙

The Hanging Angel

December 1997

E VERY CHRISTMAS SEASON, an angel hung from the ceiling of my parents' living room. But this year, it is gone. "Mama said it looked like we'd hanged somebody," Dad says.

Though she had never mentioned it when we were children, Mama once told Jan that it always tortured her to see Halloween ghosts and skeletons hanging from trees. She did not explain. Some wounds never heal. Some secrets weigh upon the heart and lie in wait like live depth charges.

When we were recording our family history, my mother and her brother, Ed, told stories they had never shared. As I was transcribing Mama's account of her father's death, it disappeared from my computer screen as though a ghost had touched it. Such was the power of her secret. Typing the words again felt like violating a taboo. After all the years of silence, was her telling of this story healing or traumatic?

In 1990, when they read our family book, Mama and Ed finally shared their memories of their father. Mama saw him as a gentle man with charming idiosyncrasies:

> My dad, Edward C. Christensen, was the third son and a very good-natured, very nice man in every way. Everybody had kind words to say about my dad. I don't think he was too strong emotionally, because he did have two nervous breakdowns in his life— Before he was ill, he had been a wonderful father. He did the best he could. Oh, he had a *few* extravagances: baseball tickets and gambling tickets that were illegal. And he never gave any of his

Lois's parents, Edward C. Christensen and Anna Dahlgren Christensen

winnings to my mother. He would say, "Here, Sis" (that's what he called me), "here's five dollars. Now, don't tell your mother."

Of course, Mama was like that, too. When she'd do something for me, she'd say, "Now don't tell Daddy."

Ed, four years older than Mama, expanded upon the frustrating financial aspects of their family life.

> Mother was a very poor manager of money. There were so many instances of her charging items on department store bills and not telling Dad. He'd find out the hard way, a phone call or a knock on the door asking for payments. All Mother's lady friends were independent, and she didn't want to have to account for anything she did.
>
> Things started coming to a head in October of 1933, when Daddy's father died. Oscar, Dad's oldest brother, thought Dad had received some money, and he came roaring up from Chicago right away. It was the first time in many years that he'd been back to St. Paul. His purpose was to take over Grandpa's house. And at that time we were renting the upstairs.

Mama saw Oscar as a villain straight out of a melodrama. Twenty or more years earlier, when he was an attorney dealing in real estate and mortgage loans, he had been "disbarred for cheating widows and orphans," she said. To keep Oscar out of jail and repay his victims, her grandpa had liquidated John Christensen & Son, Contractors and Builders. Robbed of his future in the construction business, Emil, the aforementioned *son*, moved permanently to a tiny town in North Dakota. And Mama's father, essentially disinherited, held on to his blue-collar job. Nevertheless, in the difficult time surrounding their father's death, Oscar shamelessly pressed his youngest brother for money. Fifty years later, Mama's bitterness was unabated:

> Oscar heckled my dad. And Daddy used to worry a great deal about that. I remember my mother saying, "Don't pay any attention to Oscar!"
>
> But Oscar was big and handsome, a four-flusher, talking the big stuff. He had a big car and put on all this jazz. He was a lawyer. Everything was swish— he stayed at the Edgewater Beach Hotel. But he was a rat. A fake and a fraud. The final blow struck when Daddy was laid off from the railroad. They were

cutting workers, and those with the least seniority went first. The next person could bump down the line. But Daddy refused to bump when it came his turn, because the man below him had a big family. And I can remember him coming home and saying, "Ann, I'm not going to do it. It has to stop, and it's going to stop here. I'll just wait this out."

Between that and what Oscar was doing, it was just too much for him. He went to work the next day, and when he came home he started to cry. Mama told me later how terrified she was because she *knew*— It had happened before. By that time I'd graduated and was working at Wards. I was going with Ralph, and I was always sorry that he never knew Daddy when he was—himself.

Old wounds bled anew when Mama read Ed's haunted account of the time that changed everything for their family:

Dad kept brooding about the family and finances. And none of us realized how much this was contributing towards a breakdown. We tried to assure him we were getting along. But it did no good. Dad was put in [St. Paul's] Mounds Park Hospital for a year or more. We sold Grandpa's house, but I don't know who got the money. Mother borrowed money on everything and from everyone who could lend it to her.

Finally, we had to take Dad to a mental hospital. We'd visit him when we could find someone to drive us down there. He'd know me, and all of us, but didn't know why he was there or what had happened. When we had to leave one time, I saw them take him back to a padded cell. I cried all the way home.

In October of 1935, the doctors thought Dad was improved and it might help his condition to be at home with the family for a few weeks. In those days, they didn't know how to treat nervous breakdowns.

One morning before I went to work, Dad was in bed and he called me in there. He started to talk and then all of a sudden he grabbed me, hugging me, kissing me, and asked me to take care of my mother. I tried to tell him that he was getting along better and that we were, too. That things were going to get better in the future.

After lunch, I was called at work and told to come home right away. When I arrived, there were police cars, ambulances. He had hung himself in the basement in a small bathroom closet. They had already cut him down and asked me if I wanted to see him. I was so stunned, I said no. I didn't care to see him that way. Mother called Lois at work, and I met the streetcar to tell her what had happened. We were both going around in a daze. I had to chase some of the nosy neighbors out of the house. They had just walked in to find out what was going on.

I found out later that my mother had gone downtown to pay Dad's life-insurance policy. It was the last day of the grace period, which made it 29 days overdue. She had arranged with her sister Ida to come over to watch Dad. He had never been alone before. Auntie was to be there by 11 AM, but she missed a transfer point on the streetcar. Don't know why Mother had to leave before Auntie arrived. Never did find out. We didn't think to talk about it.

Auntie said she had come in the house hollering his name. She looked over the whole place, but never did look in that closet. She thought that when she was late maybe Mother had taken him with her.

Well, when Mother returned she found him in the basement. He had tied a perfect hangman's noose on a very strong rope at just the right height, so when he jumped off the potty seat, his feet hung off the floor.

The officer told me that when he came in, Mother was still holding up Dad's body, trying to work him out of the noose. She was a very strong woman—

Her father's suicide tormented Mama. As she told the story years later, her grief was fresh.

Auntie told me she thanked God for the rest of her life that she hadn't opened that closet. She was sure she'd have had a heart attack or a stroke. She said when Mama found my dad, she just gave one anguished scream.

I never looked at Daddy in the funeral home. And I remember all the relatives came, and you know how people do. Bring food. They're supposed to comfort the family. I don't know what the hell that's for. It made me bitter. I couldn't stand it. I was upstairs listening to all those people laughing. The whole family—hadn't seen each other—enjoyed being together. I hated it. I remember Mother came upstairs and said, "Go downstairs and talk."

And I said, "I'm not going anywhere near any of it."

After a while, Ralph came over, and we sat and talked in the back hall.

Almost immediately, Mom and Ed and I moved to an apartment on Laurel. But there are only a few things that stand out. The shock of it. And then I didn't understand. I blamed God for a long time, and I felt guilty, too. Dad had been depressed all the time. He couldn't get interested in anything. Not reading, not anything. He was supposed to go for walks, but he said people were staring

Lois, called "Little Sis," about age three

at him. My mother had gone through different doctors and different advice about how to treat him. First it was sympathy and understanding. Later they said to try scolding him to see if that would shock him out of it. He would sit around the house and sigh loudly, almost like a moan. One time I was doing my homework, and when he sighed I said, "I wish you would stop doing that."

He said, "You're getting to be just like your mother."

That's what I regret. I never forgave myself for that.

When I was sixteen or so, my parents called me into the kitchen to disclose, in very abbreviated form, the secret of my grandfather's suicide.

"You must never tell anyone," Mama said.

It was years before I realized it was not *my* secret, and wondered why, if it *was* a secret, she had needed to tell me.

When his daughters asked why he rarely talked about his father, Ed looked at his wife and said, "I guess now they're old enough to know."

Unable to forgive himself for not somehow preventing his father's death, Ed feared that he, his father's namesake, might be drawn into that same suicidal vortex. And now, after all her years of unresolved grief and guilt, my mother sees her father in the hanging Christmas angel.

☙

IN *SELF-DESTRUCTION IN THE PROMISED LAND: A Psychocultural Biology of American Suicide*, psychiatrist Howard I. Kushner presents his theory of "incomplete mourning." He believes a person's early loss of a parent, before or during puberty, must be completely mourned to allow a "catharsis of grief" that can cleanse the soul of rage and guilt. If this does not happen, the feelings are often directed at the self, leading to depression and dangerous behavior, even suicide. Without such a catharsis, writes Kushner, some people are nevertheless able to transform their grief into significant achievement and thus to exorcize the demon. Mama had hoped to be a writer, but once discouraged, she became a tireless worker in her church and community, valued for her kindness and generosity.

When asked what a person should do if a nervous breakdown seems imminent, psychiatrist Karl A. Menninger replied, "Lock up your house, go across the railroad tracks, find someone in need, and do something for them." On her own, Mama came up with the same solution, and it became her most frequent advice to me: "Oh, stop worrying about yourself and go out and do something for somebody!" Her own self-directed guilt was not so easily appeased. When hurt or frustrated, she would often mutter, supposedly in jest, "Nobody loves me, everybody hates me, I'm going to eat some worms," or "I'm going to the high bridge."

Neither she nor her brother looked into the face of their dead father. It is unlikely they ever found catharsis from guilt and shame. Silence may have allowed their grief to fester, perhaps contributing to the dementia that, in old age, ravaged their minds. Would their fate have been different if they had clung together in the cold wind of their loss? In the fourth act of *Macbeth*, Malcolm warns Macduff, whose wife and children were murdered, of the danger of burying emotion:

> *Give sorrow words: The grief that does not speak*
> *Whispers the o'er-fraught heart and bids it break.*

☙

The Baloney Club Brunch

December 6–13, 1997

MAMA ACTS AS IF WE ARE RESCUING HER when Joe and I arrive. "Oh, I've been hoping you'd come!" She is scattered and helpless, and there is much to do before the party next weekend.

We place the red-and-green stained-glass wreath in the living room window where the sun can catch it, set out red Swedish candleholders, and hang sequin-encrusted felt Yule stockings from the mantel. Mama's eyes begin to shine as we light the little ceramic tree she made so many years ago. And once we've pulled the artificial Christmas tree up from the basement and decked it with strings of lights, she opens a box of ornaments and smiles. As she lifts out a tiny glittering wreath, does she recognize her work?

Soon old family treasures, gifts from her daughters, and an array of her own crafty efforts adorn the tree. As a finishing touch, I drape the glimmering branches with worn foil garlands Mama helped us string when we were children. Sticking a final plastic candy cane on the patio door, Mama says, "It's so pretty, I should have company."

"You *are* having company."

And I tell her again about the brunch we are hosting the following weekend. December 13 is Saint Lucia Day, when granddaughter Alia, dressed in white and wearing a wreath of candles on her head, will serve coffee and delicate kringler to their long-time church friends who call themselves the Baloney Club.

Thrilled, Mama repeats, "The thirteenth, the thirteenth," and asks Dad if he knows about it.

Ian and Alia serve Saint Lucia's Day coffee and kringler
—December 1997

ↅ

MOM AND DAD ALWAYS WENT to the early morning Saint Lucia Day breakfast at a Swedish American church in our old St. Paul neighborhood. Afterward, they brought home little red-and-white felt hearts, inscribed *God Jul*. Before the reform of the Gregorian calendar in the sixteenth century, Saint Lucy's Day fell close to the winter solstice. Undoubtedly, our Swedish ancestors found the day of the sun's turning toward spring numinous after a dark northern winter. They lit Saint Lucy's fires and trusted incense from the smoke to ward off the terrors of darkness. According to legend, with a crown of candles lighting her way, the original Lucia carried food to fourth-century Christians hiding in Roman catacombs.

Alia, the first grandchild in our family—born eleven years earlier on the current winter solstice—had brought light and renewal to all of us, but especially to Mama, who said, "I didn't care if I died, but now I want to be with that baby."

ↅ

WHEN JOE LEAVES TO GO BACK TO THE CITY, I ask Mama if she remembers what is happening on the thirteenth.

"I know it's something good!" she says, and then, "I know you're doing this because we're moving."

"What do you mean?" Dad objects from behind his thriller. "We haven't found a place yet. We have to find a place that's acceptable to us."

How can a man who lets his daughters pay his bills and do his shopping, who calls repeatedly to say he is no longer competent to handle his affairs, who has a cleaner, a home-health aide, and Meals on Wheels, who does not know how old he is or what year it is, and who repeats the same stories twice in one conversation and too often forgets what he did or said—how can this man think he can live independently? But then, how can he *not?*

Though we sisters have been forced to take over our parents' lives, we feel we have violated a holy of holies. With trepidation, we discuss whether to move them or continue to help them stay in this place they've loved since 1985.

"We should each think about what we'd do if we were in it alone," Jan counsels.

I would move them to Litchfield as soon as possible; Ginger would move them to South Minneapolis. But Jan fears such an uprooting would kill them. So does Sue, their upstairs neighbor, who loves them dearly and apparently believes our care is insufficient.

"One of you should check on them on the weekends," she tells me in the hallway today.

"We *have* been," I say, but cannot explain further because Mama is standing next to me.

But checking on them, even staying with them on weekends, is *not* enough. Every visit reveals chaos and potential disaster: an aluminum pan in the microwave, an unidentifiable substance moldering in the fridge, a burned votive candle in a paper cup. Dad can no longer distinguish his blood pressure medicine from vitamins. And, most unsettling, is the gas stove that could obliterate the building.

Meanwhile, we sisters keep working out the details of creating an "acceptable" place for our parents. Once we have sorted the mess, gotten rid of the junk, and set up the care they need—financial help, activities, congenial people, better food—life can flow abundantly into that new space. Position the furniture just right so Dad will have a comfortable place to read, use bright colors to cheer Mama. Instead of quietly watching autumn leaves spiral down one by one, we are scurrying anxiously about trying to paste them back on the branches.

It is the same with my own life. If I can just get, do, learn, or write some unknown magical entity, the bubble will remain intact. And protect me from the relentlessness of life, the uncertainty of living in real time: the Now, which is all there is.

❦

DECKED OUT FOR CHRISTMAS, my parents' place is almost as festive as it used to be. But, before our guests arrive, Mama needs help to shower, fix her hair and makeup, put on her red blouse and black velour pantsuit, pull nylons over her twisted swollen feet, tie the laces of her sensible white shoes.

"Are those *mine*?" she asks.

After much misdirection about the names of her old friends, and who is coming and when, she asks, "And *why* are we doing this?"

"You always used to get together with the Baloneys. And last week, as we decorated the tree, you said we should have a party. When I told you about *this* party, you said, 'Oh, goody-goody!'"

"I suppose I can get used to it," she sighs.

Ginger arrives early carrying Jan's egg casserole, croissants, muffins, and fruit salad. She sets the table with the good dishes and sterling, arranges red roses and green candles in crystal, and, for each place setting, fills the little red ceramic Santa boots Mama made with nuts and candy.

Then Mama's old friend Lucy enters with a toy Santa that, when its belly is squeezed, shouts, "Ho-Ho-Ho! Merry Christmas!" Mama loves it and, for a while, responds to each "Ho-Ho-Ho!" with a surprised yelp of laughter. As more friends arrive, her eyes overflow, and some of them cry with her. Happy talk fills the room, and everything happens as it should.

Once all are seated at the table, we hear the sweet sounds of *Santa Lucia* sung in Swedish, and Alia stands before us in a long white dress, her blond hair crowned by a wreath studded with glowing electric candles. The group applauds as she approaches with her tray of Jan's delicate kringler. And little Ian follows, ceremonially holding up the tape recorder with both his hands. Mama's smile is a bit dazed, but Dad's eyes gleam. The others, East-Siders familiar with the tradition, coo and purr as Lucia serves them.

Soon Jan rushes Alia off to an art class, and after lunch and some talk, the friends leave with quick hugs and choked good-byes. They know an ending when they see one.

While Ginger and I clean up, Mama tells Dad, "This is the first time I've doubted myself. I couldn't have done this without their help."

She thinks *she* gave the party—and after years of bemoaning failing abilities, *this* is the first time she has doubted herself.

"Mama," I call out, "This brunch was a gift, a two-years-late birthday present. You were the guest of honor. You weren't *supposed* to do anything."

"Did I act all right? Did I talk at the table?" she asks.

Back in his chair with a thriller, Dad is content. Without much to say to his old friends, he'd turned down his hearing aids on their loud chatter.

"I'm glad we had daughters," he says, "because sons would go with their wives' families. We have the best kids in the world."

Dad accepts our work without thinking twice, but Mama understands.

"Oh, let me give you something. You've worked so hard! You'll be exhausted."

Then she discovers a present bag in the bedroom and ponders the card until I read it to her.

"It's from Trudy. Go ahead and open it."

She pulls out a Christmas hand towel, chocolate mints, a *Lutheran Digest*, and a devotional book, but hardly looks at the gifts. For her, the real issue is the thank-you notes. *You get back what you give out* has always been her motto and her counsel—a sort of economics of the heart.

"Did I *thank* Trudy? I don't know where they are or what their telephone numbers are—"

"You thanked her when she was here."

"She was *here?*"

⁓

A Move Might Kill Me

WITHOUT MEANING TO, Mama initiates the moving process. In September, returning from Joe's sixtieth-birthday surprise party at our house, she became convinced they had been at Jan's house. And that Jan—not Joe and I—lives ninety miles from White Bear Lake.

"Mama said over and over, 'Oh, this is so far for you. Dad, it's time for us to move,'" Jan told me. "And when we finally got to their place, she again talked about moving and got all teary. Something needs to happen fast."

Moving is one thing Mama does not forget, but Dad resists discussing it. The day Joe and I take them to visit the Tower, an assisted-living high-rise only ten minutes from my sisters' homes in South Minneapolis, Dad stalls. An hour late and still not dressed, he is unwilling to go, but unwilling to say so. We'd "discussed" the move till 2:00 the night before. He did not want to leave his garage. He would be lost without his workshop.

"Just the other day, I wanted to cut something, and I just went down and cut it," he said. "It was so nice. Of four boys in my family, I'm the only one who was interested in that sort of thing. I've always had a workshop."

All through our tour, Mom and Dad allow us to shepherd them and point out the features of the Tower: a dining room on the top floor, a library, an exercise room, a coin-operated laundry, security doors, balconies with picture-postcard views of the city, and any number of social clubs to join.

"A move might kill me," Dad grumbles once we are back home.

And now that he has fallen asleep in his chair, Mama remarks, "I know this will be our last Christmas in this place. I don't want to move, but I know we have to. Nothing stays the same, and you just have to be flexible. And—adjust to it. I'll talk to Daddy and get him to understand."

☙

MOVING IS NOT SOMETHING my parents do lightly. Once we had settled in our own home after Dad got home from the war, we moved only once. But when Mom and Dad retired, and all three daughters were on our own, they traveled to California every winter. After a few years, they were torn between settling in San Diego, near Honeybun and Dad's sister, Carol, and her family, or staying close to their kids and community. In 1976, their decision to move sent them into panic. Mama told me:

> Moving to San Diego—that was a big adventure. We weren't very adventuresome. Oh, Daddy and I didn't sleep at all. In fact, I shook all night after we decided to buy the house, and the next day we were both exhausted. We took a drive, and we sat by the sands of Del Mar, and we looked at the mountains, and we looked at the sea, and we said, "Nobody cares what two insignificant people like us do." And then we both fell sound asleep there sitting in the car.

The rolling of the unbounded sea lulled them to sleep. The strength and endurance of the mountains gave them courage to break free. And a new world opened. Retirement in San Diego rewarded them for their years as parents, workers, and servants of the community. They became, as they liked to say, "just plain Lois and Ralph." But *this* move to Minneapolis in their old age is their daughters' decision.

"I dreamed everything we own was carried out into the street," Mama said. "And I stood there crying." Then she backed away from her nightmare: "It won't *really* be that bad."

We get but one chance to help our parents in decline. Fear and trembling in the face of such responsibility sucks at my life the way the moon pulls tides away from shore. Stranded on this desolate and incomprehensible coast, I say, *I know what you mean, know how it feels, that must be hard*—but cannot know how hard. Or with what diminished capacity they face their losses. Their irreplaceable losses.

☙

THE SOCIAL SERVICES STAFF THINKS Dad's memory loss could be related to depression. And that Dad, as Mama's primary caregiver, needs support. Isolation in White Bear, with Mama not herself, *has* strained him. In forgetfulness, he zones out in his chair, basks in our offerings. "I've noticed that if I don't do it, someone will take care of it for me," he said today.

Jan and Ginger found an assisted-living facility in South Minneapolis that, at first, looked perfect to them. Smaller and more intimate than the Tower, it provides more care and three meals a day. It's subsidized and has an opening in February. But today they have doubts.

"It's so small," Jan says. "And it isn't as nice as the Tower. It's like putting them on welfare. We're worried about Daddo just closing down."

As she speaks, I recall the previous weekend when Mama said, again, "We're thinking it's time to move."

"*I'm* not thinking about moving," Dad shot back from behind his paper. And he meant exactly that: He's not *thinking* about it.

"But Daddo, it's got to happen."

"If it has to happen, it has to happen, but I'll think about it then. I like it here." And then, wistfully, he showed what he had been thinking about: "I don't suppose I'll ever drive my car again. Neither of my sons-in-law has any interest in my tools. I'd like to give them to *some*body —"

☙

No Choice in the Matter

December 25, 1997–January 2, 1998

AFTER A JOLLY CHRISTMAS EVE WITH JOE'S FAMILY, we drive late to Jan's. *The Nutcracker* on the radio and lights strung along the way preserve our cheer. When we arrive, Mom, Jan, Ginger, and the kids are leaving to go to a late-night service at Mount Olivet, the largest Lutheran church in America, and maybe the world.

"If I can't go to my own church, I don't want to go," Dad grumbles, refusing to leave his chair.

❧

ON CHRISTMAS NIGHT, the long stairway to Ginger's front door is aglow with luminarias. Electric candles shine from every window. Dad follows behind as we guide and support Mama on her arduous climb. Once inside and greeted with hugs all around, Mom and Dad sit down and stare into the radiance of the Christmas tree until called to the table. After a lovely meal and toasts all around, we pass out gifts.

"Oh, we don't have anything for the kids!" Mama exclaims.

"It's okay, Mama," Ginger says. "Jan and I bought presents for you to give the kids."

"Oh, Daddy, give her some money for them. Right now."

Mama greets the gifts we bought for them to give each other with the same anguished response.

Joe and I have decided to spend the night at Jan's after we take Mom and Dad home. The work and stress of Christmas and just being with my parents has burned out both of us. We need a break. And it is not *our* week to help them.

At home again in White Bear, Mama unpacks their suitcase and holds up her new nightgown.

"What's this?"

"Our gift to you."

Her face contracts in panic: "But what did we give you?"

The cut-glass bowls she had pressed upon the three of us had been somehow forgotten in the basement during our holiday scramble. Retrieving them, I gush, "Oh, Mama, these are just beautiful! I love them, and Jan and Ginger will, too. Thank you, thank you."

Mama is content, until we prepare to leave.

"Don't you want to sleep at our house?"

"I'm sorry, Mama. We can't. Joe's compulsive about getting home to work on his book."

At least there is some truth in that. Yet Katagiri's dictum haunts me: *Nothing to throw away, nothing to grasp. Just be present with them.*

It is the hardest thing in the world, and it is my practice. But such Zen seems impossible now. Even my poor attempts to let go feel like *grasping*. Grasping at letting go.

☙

THREE DAYS AFTER CHRISTMAS, when I finally call my parents, Ginger answers. She and the kids have brought out dinner. And she is looking for drivers' licenses so Jan can sign up Mom and Dad for county health aid and subsidized living.

Jan wonders if we should take Mom and Dad to see the new place before they move in, but we fear it could be too depressing. That cramped, empty apartment and the less-than-appealing common spaces might cause them to close down.

"I don't know how you can move them into a place they haven't seen," Joe says. "Unless they have no choice in the matter."

Choice? They cannot stay where they are. And this is the only appropriate place we have found.

The list of reasons for the move is long. Some we can tell Dad and some we can't. We cannot tell him his judgment is bad. Or that everything has to be done for them now by five different people, and even coordinating it all is difficult. Or that we are all overburdened by our own work. Or that I am getting burned out and do not want to spend my meager free time cleaning their place when it is unnecessary.

Of course, it would be different if it *were* necessary.

I tell him: *Move closer so we can see you more often. Mama needs an easier shower, and more help. You'll get three meals a day, and you won't have to cook them. You'll get your laundry and cleaning done, and have twenty-four-hour staff in case of emergency. We won't have to worry about you. This place is becoming a prison for Mama. She'll have more social life and things to do. It will take that burden off of you. And you do have memory problems—*

⁓

A WEEK AFTER CHRISTMAS, while I am lifting from a branch one of the red Popsicle stick sleds she and Dad made for all of us years ago, Mama says, "Taking down the tree makes me sad, because you never know what it will be next year."

And then she brings up moving, though she has been told nothing of the small two-room unit we have reserved for them.

Dad's head jerks up from his crossword. "What's the rush?" he snaps. "In a couple of years—"

"It will have to be sooner than that."

"Well, I'll adjust," he sighs. "It won't be for long."

Whether threat, manipulation, or prediction, that comment shakes me into blurting, "I hate this! You make me feel like a bad person *when I'm only trying to do what's best for you.*"

Hearing my own voice echo the very words my parents used on me during my teenage years, I retreat to the bedroom, but leave the door open.

"Shame on you!" Mama scolds him. "You should apologize to Nancy."

Suddenly it feels like maybe 1958 and one of many conflicts with Dad that I had ended by storming upstairs and slamming my bedroom door. Once inside my barricade on one such night, I realized my book was still in the kitchen and started back down to get it. Until Mama said my name. Then I settled down out of sight on the steps to listen. My parents were calmly discussing how to deal with *me*. Mama gently told Dad he had been too rigid, and he listened to her suggestions. Without anger or defensiveness, he explained his feelings.

Growing up, we sisters never once heard our parents fight. We did not know how lucky we were. And now, all these years later, Mama comes into the bedroom and apologizes *for* him.

"He's just scared, Mama."

She winces and turns away. In a few moments, meekly, Dad stands at the door. "I don't even remember what I said."

"You acted as if you wouldn't like that place, no matter what. But you and Mama *need* to move," I say. "It'll be so much better if you can make the best of it."

"Oh, that's what I should have done in the Army," he sneers.

He has begun comparing the move to going to war, that other time he was taken from home.

"That's what you *did* do in the Army. You did the best job you could, you learned how to work with the French, and you treated people well."

"I know," he mutters, "you get what you put into it."

Joe rescues me, and we get ready to go to the store. Afraid Dad will attempt to carry the bare tree down to the basement while we are gone, we do it ourselves. When we return with groceries, Dad remembers to pay me but has trouble with the check. Several times he asks the date and the amount. And then my name. Only Joe realizes Dad is not kidding and spells P-A-D-D-O-C-K for him.

As we leave for home, Dad hugs me several times, and Mama cries and thanks us again and again. I am a wreck.

"It's too bad you got the job of telling us," she says.

Her intuition is undiminished. But Dad seems to be several people: one who believes he is still a strong and capable man. One who periodically wakes up to reality in fear and despair. One who drifts passively, not dealing with anything. One who, without ever announcing a decision, has quit driving and let his license lapse. And one who still thinks he needs a garage.

"We'll do what our kids tell us to do," Mama says. "You have your life, your work, not just taking care of us."

At times, she seems almost eager to move, perhaps hoping it will solve her problems. She keeps asking, "What can we take?"

How can these confused, dependent people be my parents? In my heart, their images remain strong, kind, beautiful: Mama singing "Father will come to thee soon" as she rocks my infant self to sleep during the war, and Dad on the day he returned, a handsome hero in uniform kneeling down to greet me.

ᏆᎦ

When Daddy Came Home

England—22 June 1944

Dearest Lois,

If you find it hard to realize that little Nancy is all ours you've got a little inkling of how I feel when I try to make myself believe that I've really got a loving wife and darling daughter waiting for me to come back to them after the war. Sometimes it seems that I've never been anywhere but in the army. Anything else is just a dream. I don't suppose I'll really believe it until I have the two of you in my arms again. I can picture in my mind every step of the journey home and, going that way, the hardships of a troop transport won't bother me at all. What a great day it will be when we pass the Statue of Liberty and steam up into New York harbor. And I don't think I'll be responsible for my actions when I finally step off a train at the Union depot in old St. Paul. Hoping with all my power that all this comes true very soon, I remain your loving husband, Ralph.

AS A TEENAGER, I WOULD SNEER whenever Dad said, "I've been to New York, Paris, and London, and no place can compare with the East Side of St. Paul." He meant Mama, my sisters and me, his family and friends—all of the life that war had taken from him. Years later, he told his story of coming home:

It was three months after the war ended. Way into September. I'd put in for a pass to the Riviera. One three-day pass to Paris was the only one I'd had the whole time I was in Europe, so I had a lot coming. Well, the pass came on the same day that I had enough numbers to start on my way home. They were doing it by individuals and this nice young captain said, "What do you choose, Ralph?"

Lois's caption on the back: "You don't look very unhappy to leave me—and I don't look like I care, either—but we know better, don't we darling." —September 1943

I said, "The heck with the Riviera, I've been away from home too long. Let me go."

And he said, "Jeez, I sent two of our jeeps back with fellas just a couple days ago and they're not back yet."

We had *three* jeeps. And my face must have fallen—so he said, "That's all right, Ralph, you can take the last one."

After that we went to the cigarette camps. Camp Chesterfield, maybe there was a Camel, a Lucky Strike, but there was another one, too—Philip Morris, and I was in that one. It was October by that time, and we'd been put through all kinds of physicals and were waiting for a ship. Then one day, I looked at the blackboard and my name was under a ship called, of all things, the *Santa Paula*. A little 11,000-pound cork, Jeez! And across the North Atlantic in the wintertime.

When I finally arrived in New York City, I called Mama. "Hello, Lois...." But neither one of us could talk. I had stood in line for a long time to get the phone, and then all we could do was cry. That was awful. I just said, "I'll be home soon."

In St. Paul, I left the Union Depot and walked up to Fourth Street. The Mississippi streetcar came down, and I stood out in the back with my big bag. I didn't want to sit inside because—well, there were tears in my eyes. I didn't want to talk. Can't talk now— As I was coming through the East Side, I saw the neighborhoods I had grown up in, and I felt I was getting it all back.

That day in November 1945 my parents' lives would begin again. And they would, as one of Dad's letters had promised, "show a united front to the world."

"We were on the front porch at 501," Mama told me, "waiting for the streetcar, and it stopped and Daddy got off and came across the street—looking so handsome in his uniform, and in wonderful shape—and he kneeled down, held out his arms, and you went to him. We cried for joy."

Though Mama told it that way, I remember running out onto the porch, tripping, and being saved from falling by strong arms. After Mama's constant talk of "when Daddy gets home," Daddy was finally home.

A few weeks later, after the first snowfall, he took me outside to play. And he did not want any daughter of his to be a sissy.

> I was shoveling the sidewalk, and I turned around, and Nancy had a little shovel and was putting the snow back on the sidewalk. I took a whole shovelful and threw it on her. After I finished, we went out in the back yard. I laid down in the snow and made an angel, and she laid down in the snow and made an angel. Oh, we came in and we were happy and wet.

Of course, his idea about how a three-year-old girl ought to be treated differed from Mama's:

> When Ralph came home in November, a while later he took Nancy out in the back yard and showed her how to make an angel in the snow. I looked out the window, and there was my baby lying out there in the snow. My goodness!

Sitting on Daddy's lap, entranced by the colored lights reflected in his glasses, is my only memory of Christmas 1945. Somehow he *was* the Christmas tree—the lights, the wonder of the season, embodied and real—just as the angel he had made in the snow was real. It would be years before I would truly see his human eyes. Or understand how much he valued home.

ↀ

The day Daddy came home.
Nancy with Ralph—November 1945

OLDER LOVE

In the Tower

February 15, 1998 – November 11, 1998

JOURNAL | *Change*

February 15, 1998

A PLACE HAS OPENED ON THE TWENTY-SECOND FLOOR of the senior high-rise Joe and I toured with Mom and Dad. With a startling view of the Minneapolis skyline, big windows, and a kitchenette, it is one of only a pair of two-bedroom apartments in the entire complex. An exceptional opportunity. We let the smaller place go, and begin measuring and drawing floor plans to set things up perfectly. Almost all of their furniture will fit.

The Tower has a foot clinic, a dentist, a beauty shop, a puzzle room. My parents' floor has a plant room with greenhouse windows where, at Christmas, a huge lighted tree will extend up into the dining room. The place has pianos, church services, tenant groups, coffee and birthday parties, a Toastmasters club, entertainment programs, and buses that take residents to shopping centers. Pets are welcome. A nearby nursing home provides activities. We can set up a schedule that will take care of everything.

When Joe and I take Mom and Dad to tour the place again, we stand in the white, empty apartment looking out over the tops of bare trees. Selling its advantages like a real estate agent makes it almost possible to ignore the lost look in Dad's eyes and the quivering of Mama's lips.

During screening to qualify for assistance, Dad is charming, cracking jokes, but unable to say what year it is. Mama cannot count backward from ten.

"I still know my A-B-2," she offers, aware of her mistake but unable to correct it.

They get an "A," meaning "A-level" care. For an additional $180 a month, they will receive three hours of housekeeping a day with the option of personal care and escort service to and from the various activities. Their income is right on the line. If it decreases, that care will be free. The Tower offers a great and compassionate arrangement. A perfect solution.

To set up the lease, Mama has to sign her name three times. But she must be told each letter: L-O-I-S. Confused on the second one, she can't make a capital "L," but for the third she writes out her name with no trouble.

In the car, she turns her face away and stares out the window in silence.

"Mama, we're doing this because you said it was time to move," I lie.

"It's different doing it and talking about it," she murmurs, eyes filling up.

Dad is quiet until we get home. And then he says again, "All my life I've had a workshop." This and his car are the most difficult to give up. Breath comes hard as he paces aimlessly around the room. "You own your house so you won't have to move when you get old."

"As long as we don't need services," Joe answers.

"You can bring help in."

We *had*, of course, brought help in, and they had resisted it at every step. Jan, who bought the condo with Mom and Dad, was willing to keep it as long as it worked for them. Dad may find it easier to believe she wants to sell the place.

ↄ

ONE DAY AFTER THEY SIGNED THE LEASE, neither Mama nor Dad remembers their visit to the Tower. Instead, they repeat an anxious litany of questions:

When are we moving? In two weeks.

Where is this place? In Minneapolis.

It has one bedroom? It has two.

But no basement? Your workshop will be at Jan's.

Can we walk there? No, it's two miles.

Well, we can walk two miles. Not in that neighborhood.

Can we see the water? How far are we from the water? We'll come and take you to the lake.

But we can walk there— You can walk in the dining room or go to the exercise room. Groups go walking outside, or we'll come and get you.

And when is this happening?

And what can we take with us?

Will we have our own entrance?

There isn't a garage, is there?

ↄ

Garage Sale at the End of the World

March 1998

THESE DAYS, THE BLACK-SCARFED HARPIES in *Zorba the Greek*, crouching in the death chamber of Madame Hortense, would have a garage sale. But, in that film—as voices in the audience whisper, "Vultures!"—they rise and whirl to snatch Madame's riches.

They, at least, wait till she is dead. We just move our parents out of their home, decide what they should keep, and dispose of the rest. If we try to involve them, they cry, so we do not ask what clothes they want or what dishes. We decide where, when, what, and how. Life has provided the *why*.

Dad agrees to sell his car. To spare him trouble and pain, Joe and I check the market and buy it for a fair price. It is all necessary and done with love, care, and trepidation, but my sisters and I have now taken charge of our parents' lives. Of course, we are doing what they can no longer do. Of course, we deposit the money into their account. We try to do everything right, but their bones are being picked.

The idea of justice that Jan held at age four happens to be the way of the universe: "Just wait till I'm big and you're little."

❧

I AM STRUCK BY THE KINDNESS of Jan's and Ginger's friends during the move into the Tower. Like members of the family, they do what few would do for pay. They carry in so many loads of furniture and heavy boxes that the lineup of elderly women who sit by the elevator waiting—for something, anything—murmur snide queries about where we're going to put it all. Not only a desk, a bookcase, a couch,

On their last day in White Bear Lake, Ralph and Lois
look toward an unknowable future—March 1998

two side chairs, several end tables, a dining room set, a buffet, an exercise bike, and any number of huge boxes, but two beds, two dressers, and a massive obsolete stereo cabinet with separate speakers Dad had made and cannot part with.

David, Ginger's former husband, still close to our family, hangs Mama's plate rail and stained-glass ceiling lamp in the dining area. We set up a reading chair for Dad and, in a separate nook for Mama, the new TV, a gift from Aunt Carol and Uncle Bob. We fill vases with flowers, string white lights above the windows, and ready their "penthouse" for the housewarming.

The following Sunday afternoon, we take our parents to the Tower. With friends, wine, and lovely food, we make a party of it. Uncle Bob envies their fabulous urban view. Aunt Carol sends long-distance blessings. And then on the phone Mama tells Honeybun, "Pretty soon, we're going to move."

To ease the transition, Joe and I stay with my parents that first night. Snug in the TV corner, we all listen to the Beatles sing, *I get by with a little help from my friends.*

"That should be 'a *lot* of help,'" Dad remarks.

But when Mama whimpers, "You kids are so good to us. I don't know what we'd do without you," he mutters: "We wouldn't have *moved.*"

And late that night, he believes they will soon go home again.

On Monday morning, Joe leaves to research his book, and I stay on. Meals are delivered, but Mama refuses to get dressed. We do not leave the apartment. When the social worker arrives, Dad is charming, but Mama, in her unevenly buttoned nightgown, is disoriented. Both qualify immediately for services that promise to make this new place work for them.

❧

In the Tower

March 1998

O N CARD XVI OF THE TAROT, lightning blasts the crown from the Tower and two royal figures fall headlong through flames. When one consults this ancient way of divination, five cards are laid down as a cross, and four as a scepter. Depending on its position and orientation, each card has several meanings. Drawing the Tower portends "suffering of an individual through the forces of destiny being worked out in the world" or "natural disasters which strike all, just or unjust alike." The Tower reversed signifies "the calling down of disaster which might have been avoided. Unnecessary suffering. Self-undoing."

Struck by the uncanny correspondence between this medieval fortune-telling card and the architecture of my parents' new home, I consider whether their distress in the Tower is due to their own inability to adjust to changing circumstances, their daughters' poor judgment, an imperfect care system, or simply fate.

Dad refused to face the need to move until it was actually happening. Then he became cavalier. "This bothers Mama more than it does me. I'm used to moving. During the war, I never knew where I'd be, and I adjusted. One night it might be an open field, the next a castle with a feather bed that was too soft." Now, his depressive comments alarm us.

"Well, anyway, it won't be for long." And: "The windows don't open so you can't jump."

The windows *do* open.

So far Mom and Dad are unable to learn the systems of the place. All our work has fallen into forgetfulness, which in some ways is just as well. Help makes Mama hate herself. Whether or not we made the right choice, it seems at once to be the "least lousy alternative" and a perfect hell.

"When I was young," Dad said today, "if we had a situation like this we took care of it as a family, all under one roof."

With his mother's care, his Swedish grandmother lived and died in their extended family home when he was a child. And after the war, by signing over the house to their brother Carl, who would stay on, he and his siblings provided a home for their mother until she died at seventy-four. Theirs was a solution from a different world. My sisters and I are tormented by this generation gap in expectation. Ginger recounts a haunting comment she overheard when Mom and Dad were visiting her house: "Every time I come here I never want to go home. Ralph, why did we ever leave here? Why can't we stay here?"

Mama thought she was visiting her own old house. And Ginger realized she had never told her why she had not taken them in.

"You and Dad need a lot of help now, and I just can't do it."

"I suppose that's true," Mama said, her jaw tightening. Then she turned and wiped it all away with, "It's so lovely this evening."

When Mom and Dad are with us, we are all together with beautiful food and drinks. Everyone pampers them. It is like heaven, but it could not be that way every day. Ginger's marriage is fragile. Her husband runs an alternative-healing practice in their house; clients wait in the living room. She has no real space for Mom and Dad. Home schooling requires not only teaching her own and other children but driving them to classes in other locations. Ginger desperately wants to take care of our parents, but cannot find a way. She has even considered looking for a house with a separate apartment for them, but Jan rightly told her that would not provide a life for Mom and Dad.

Jan lives alone, but her demanding administrative job in a large law firm often keeps her at work until 8 PM or later. If our parents lived with her, when Jan came home tired, they would want to talk, and she would want to hide upstairs. Mom and Dad need all-day caregivers. In the absence of planned activities, they would be more bored and lonely than at the Tower. And despite help from Ginger and me, Jan would be overburdened on a daily basis by increasing levels of caretaking she is not trained, or emotionally able, to provide.

Our little house in Litchfield has no guestroom. Its one small bathroom is not handicapped accessible. My English teaching job—our primary income and our retirement plan—fills my waking hours. Joe is deep into writing *Keeper of the Wild*, his biography of environmentalist Ernest Oberholtzer. And, in any case, he could not give my mother the intimate physical care she requires. Even if our parents lived elsewhere in town, my sisters would have to drive out every other weekend to visit them—which would mean far fewer visits with grandchildren. But this town has no acceptable options. Senior residences have long waiting lists and offer insufficient care. There is a nursing home—but Mom and Dad are not ready for *that*.

In the face of our parents' growing dissatisfaction, our reasons for placing them where we have feel like mere justifications. Had it been financially and logistically possible for one of us to live with them in White Bear Lake, would we have solved their problems? Or merely delayed their move to a care facility? And what would such care, all day and every day, have done to us? We did what everyone told us was right, but it feels wrong. In anguish, we chose the Tower. It may seem heartless, but it is breaking our hearts. We *are* taking care of them in the best way we can.

"We shouldn't agonize over this," Joe tells me. But now, high in the air, Mom and Dad look out their windows at a sky pierced by edifices of steel and ice-blue glass. Strangers come in to do things for them.

☙

WE MOVED WHEN I WAS ELEVEN. With three kids in a two-bedroom bungalow, we needed a bigger house, but our York Avenue neighborhood was my soul-land, my mythological landscape. An imagined peril enchanted each of its four corners: Duchess, "the killer-dog from the war," prowled her spooky woods on the shortcut to school. Big Sandy, our sledding hill, harbored "bums from the railroad" and the bones of Steinhauser's rabbit—buried there, we kids knew, by Duchess and her pack. A shuttered, silent house haunted a nearby hill. A witch crouched in an old tarpaper shack on the way to Hoff's store.

Inside these boundaries, all was secure and magical. With delicious fear, we hung by our knees from branches of trees in the witch's grove or ventured out from the circle of a porch light chanting, "Starlight, moonlight, hope to see the ghost tonight." In childhood's timeless summer, I curled into the shade beneath August-red sumacs. And three houses down the block, peculiar old Agnes listened with shining eyes to all my stories.

When, despite my desperate protests, we moved away, the unity of my life shattered. Surrounded by places empty of meaning, I claimed a dead tree as my back-yard tower and crouched among its naked limbs—an exiled queen—lowering a basket on a rope for my sisters to fill with whatever I required.

Amputated, stripped of its bark, that tree was an eyesore. Dad cut it down. "I *had* to," he explained years later. "The neighbors would have wondered why we didn't put you away."

For weeks, I pined for Agnes and my old home. And then, one dead afternoon, I began plaiting a clover chain. Jan and Ginger gathered a heap of the longest stems and watched my compulsive braiding. Days later, the chain enclosed the entire yard. Its first dried, brown flowers braided into last green stems completed my fragile loop. With no consciousness of meaning, I had secured myself and this new place within a magic circle called *home*. And in time, life opened to new friends and possibilities.

A child adapts to a new situation more easily than do the very old. Uprooted against their will, according to *their daughters'* understanding of necessity, our parents want desperately to go home. But they *need* the care this good place offers. And in time, with our love and frequent visits, we believe they will find a new and better life in the Tower.

☙

Journal | *Being*

I DON'T EVEN HAVE A WATCH," Dad complained yesterday. Rummaging around a bit produced two watches from his top drawer. Both electronic and displaying the wrong time. One was uncomplicated, so I set it and gave it to him. The other had four buttons, many functions, and no instructions.

"I'll figure it out," he said.

Today, the simple watch is nowhere to be found, and the complex one beeps insistently from his wrist.

"Turn it off," Mama begs, but he can't hear it, and the beeping continues.

Moving was the "least lousy alternative," but, without memory or purpose, my parents are sojourners adrift in the day. Each morning, as though abducted, they look out on an alien environment. Strangers minister to their every need but the one most pressing: to go home. Dad uses the handlebars of his stationary bike for a clothes hook and rejects the exercise room. "I don't want to get in shape. I have nothing to get in shape for."

He tells Ginger, "We aren't happy here. If I had my druthers, I'd live on the golf course, near a lake so Mama could swim."

When she gently reminds him the Tower is what they can afford and they need a place where everything is done for them, he asks, "What do you *mean*?" She lists off the meals, the housekeeping, the shopping, the whole system that includes helping Mama take a shower. Yet again, with Mom and Dad we tour the many resources available. Dad learns how to operate the elevator, use their own TV to buzz people into the building, open their locked mailbox, make meal arrangements. He has to master the system in order to stay in this place—where he is unhappy.

༎

CARRYING IN GROCERIES, Joe and I run the gauntlet of old women stationed by the elevator. The chorus of a Greek tragedy, they reveal their sorrows as they mark our visits: "What do you have there? Will it make us young again?"

"My son wanted his girlfriend to move in with him, so I had to move in here."

"Are you having a party or bringing in yet more stuff?"

"It's just groceries," Joe explains.

And one murmurs, "That's nice."

Loneliness, bitterness, and regret are palpable in this "Heartbreak Hotel."

"Life must go on; I forget just why," Mama often used to say, quoting the last despairing line of Edna St. Vincent Millay's *Lament*. These days she says simply, "Life must go on." *She* seems to have forgotten why.

A few days ago, Ginger brought Mama a box of old pictures to give her something to do. But today a wastebasket holds torn scraps of a photograph of her beloved Auntie. Did Mama see a once-loved face as blank and meaningless paper? Or, unable to read her own handwriting on the back, did she rip it apart in grief and rage?

After supper, the four of us cross the hall to the plant room to watch the sunset. As lights appear in the dark neighborhoods below, planes take off and land at the airport far to the south. Mama is entranced. People are playing Bingo upstairs in the dining room, and we hear each number as it's called. Someone yells, "B-12!"

"Be whatever age you are," Dad quips.

Later, Joe and I take Mama upstairs for a little exercise. We hold her, unsteady, between us and circle the empty dining room. And then high in the Tower, in the dark lit only by the lights of the city, Mama becomes an oracle, her voice hoarse, ghostly: "*Do what you want to do now!*"

Mama, whose consistent advice had been *Oh, stop worrying about yourself and go out and do something for somebody* now tells me this. What does she wish she had done? Is her urgency borne of the knowledge that she can no longer choose? Her mind works—and doesn't work. How does she forget Auntie's face and yet command us to stop wasting our lives, to pursue our deepest desires? It haunts me. I am not doing what I want to do. I don't even know what I want to do.

～

Cityscape

April 1998

A FEW WEEKS AFTER THE MOVE, a picture postcard arrives in our mailbox— the Minneapolis techno-skyline, its towers of finance rising clean and logical into the purple sky like a backdrop for *The Tonight Show*. The message:

> *Please come visit again soon. You're welcome any time.*
> *This postcard will remind you of our wonderful view.*
> *See you soon.*
> *Love, Mom and Dad (written by Jan)*

Gray and ghostly disappearing in clouds, glinting pink and golden in reflected sunset, or sparkling in the night like an alien universe of stars, the changing moods of the city—though spectacular—do not yet resonate for Mom and Dad. Sitting on their suburban balcony, surrounded by flowering plants and visited by geese and songbirds, is their idea of the heaven left to them. On the twenty-second floor, in the muffled drone of traffic, they look down on the tops of trees.

"Where are we?" Dad asks Joe on our next visit. "Those buildings out there— What *are* they?"

"That's downtown Minneapolis," he says. "The tallest one is the IDS Tower, and that white Teflon baggie down there is the Metrodome, where the Twins and Vikings play."

But Dad just squints at them until Mama says, "I was standing by the window wondering how I could jump out."

Dad flinches. "You *know* what it feels like to have someone you love do that. You can't *do* that to me!"

Stunned, she stares at him. He had never before taken such talk seriously.

∾

BACK HOME, A CALL FROM JAN DESTROYS SLEEP. Dad had phoned to tell her the Tower is not the place for them.

"It's too regimented. We don't like the activities and people telling us what to do all day. We want to go back to White Bear." And then he said, "We've lived too long."

Last summer in White Bear Lake, after supper chit-chat and dozing in front of the TV, Joe and I took Mom and Dad out into the lovely moonless night. Because they could not see well, they accepted our guidance in blind trust as we walked four abreast in the middle of the silent street. Mama was giddy with the thrill of venturing out into the dark, its velvet mystery and freedom and hint of danger. In a Dracula accent, she uttered a line from an old vampire movie: "We're night people, you know."

From their apartment high in the Tower, my parents are unlikely to elevator down to street level and find their way through security doors into urban glare and din.

∾

Such Stuff As Dreams Are Made On

May 1998

D AD CALLS FROM THE TOWER AND, when asked how he is, answers, "*Where am I? I'm on top of a skyscraper.*"

"I know."

"Oh, have you been here?"

"Many times."

"We're really down. We're lonely."

The herbal supplements we're giving them—ginkgo biloba for memory enhancement and St. John's wort for anxiety and depression—are not helping. If only there were some comfort to carry him forward into the next day, but each moment is a separate universe unto itself, surrounded by an abyss.

He is like the young man who, to eliminate seizures, had the medial temporal lobes of his brain surgically removed. Unable to remember what had gone before, he lived thereafter in constant bewilderment.

"Every day," the young man said, "is alone in itself, whatever enjoyment I've had, and whatever sorrow I've had." To him it felt "like waking from a dream."

"We are such stuff / As dreams are made on and our little life / Is rounded by a sleep," says Prospero in *The Tempest*. Our consciousness is an electrochemical flow, transitory as waves on water or crystal patterns on a frosted window. Impressions of a moment can be forgotten in the next, just as delicate filaments of dream may dissolve with the morning's alarm. In this constant flux, we struggle to know what is real. To create meaning. And when the processes of memory, fragile at all times, are impaired, the way in which we know the world is "melted into air, into thin air."

 GRASS IS GREENING, cardinals court in the trees, clouds of pink and white blossoms line the city streets. But Mom and Dad are last year's dead leaves blown about. Nothing can melt the winter of their discontent. Earth's life force, budding anew, seems to mock them.

"I look in the mirror and I don't know how I got this way," Mama announces one night. "I don't know how that can be me."

There *is* a sense of unreality to it all, almost as if she and Dad have vanished and these vague changelings have taken their place.

After each doomed attempt to compel my parents to be happy, I come home drained—without corrected papers and clear lesson plans—to play catch-up at school until our next trip to town. But *I* can go home. My sisters live just ten minutes from the Tower and get daily calls that invite micromanagement.

With some alarm, Ginger tells me the staff is concerned. Graded, now, on social adjustment—like school children—Mom and Dad have sunk to "C" level from their "A" classification when they moved in. Instead of embracing the opportunities of the Tower, they sit and wait for us to arrive. If they are unable to make a life there, they will have to move to a nursing home. A nurse and a social worker meet with my sisters to create a plan.

"We'll make it work," they say, and decide we should stay away for a few weeks. That will help convince Mom and Dad they need the place and are lucky to have it. Though we hate to think of them alone, we agree to stay away.

Surrendering our parents to the staff's judgment does little to ease our minds. Even at home, fixation on their problems casts a pall over my life. Nothing seems real. It is as though I can see through to the howling void at the heart of matter. And *meaning* is nothing but a hologram projected upon an essentially empty reality—a hologram that can flicker, falter, fade— And when it does, the significance of the things of this world crumbles to dust.

THE ADJUSTMENT PERIOD FINALLY OVER, we are advised to visit less often and let the staff care for Mom and Dad. Our absence will convince them of their need for the staff. Things do improve. We are told our parents get out several times a day and are adjusting. Jan discovers Dad's apartment door-entry card abandoned in the sunroom, and she still gets harrowing calls at work. But one day Ginger finds Mom and Dad outside sitting on a bench talking to people.

"I hate it here—it's a nice place," Mama tells her.

❧

THE GOOD TOWER STAFF wants everybody to be happy. If Mom and Dad are not happy, there is something wrong with *them*. They must take antidepressants and go to the day program in order to integrate into the place. No matter that the day program—with its artificially perky staff dressed up as Easter bunnies while residents slump over tables spread with paper chicks and eggs—looks like a kindergarten for zombies. Any attempt to make people happy is laudable, but how must it feel to be expected to participate in such things?

"Are we *that* bad?" Dad asks, and refuses to go again.

Distressed, but unable to reveal a cause, Mama comes home early.

One day, Mama voices words she may think will please us. "We're happy here. This is a nice place."

And Dad says, "We're almost as happy as if we had our right minds."

❧

Journal | *Hope*

May 14, 1998

L UCAS, A TALENTED ATHLETE and one of very few black kids in our small-town school, announces, "I'm *on* today." He aces the vocab test and later offers to read aloud. He may be letting me know what he can do. The last time I asked, he'd politely declined, but here he is reading *The Jilting of Granny Weatherall*, deep in the dying mind of an old woman:

> *Tomorrow was far away and there was nothing to trouble about. Things were finished somehow when the time came; thank God there was always a little margin over for peace: then a person could spread out the plan of life and tuck in the edges orderly....*

After class, Lucas stops by my desk. "Hey, some kid just told me I'm a brown-nose. I *have* a brown nose. So what's with that?"

With this perfect exit line, he saunters off. And there's no guarantee he'll be in class tomorrow. Minutes later, during my free hour, our Brit principal confronts a student out in the hall:

"So if I asked B. J. whether you two had a fistfight yesterday, he'd say no?"

"Yah, me and B. J. are friends."

"Oh, like Brutus and Cassius?"

"Huh?"

Once the boy scuffs down the hall, our leader wanders in, shaking his head. "Is he one of *yours*?"

"Not yet, but—though your literary reference was lost on him, I enjoyed it."

He sighs. "So, *what* grade are they in?"

Without waiting for an answer, he slips out the door. This moment, at least, is alive with laughs, and *tomorrow is far away and...nothing to trouble about.*

℘

Nevermore

We think of the key, each in his prison
thinking of the key.... —T. S. ELIOT

June 1998

LIVING A SORT OF HOUSECAT'S LIFE in the Tower, my mother sits and watches and waits. Cared for and fed, she does nothing purposeful. Mama had filled her life with good works, offerings to the vengeful god of her depression that commands, "Oh, stop worrying about yourself and go out and do something for somebody."

And now, unable to remember the good she has done, she is left with the frustrated urge.

"Everything is done for us here," Mama complains. "We don't do anything for anybody. What's next? I wonder if I'll go to heaven."

"I'm sure you will."

"I don't know if *I* would," Dad says playfully. "I haven't always been so good. St. Peter would meet me at the gate and say, 'You *did*? You *were*?'"

"Oh, don't worry," I tease. "They don't keep records that long."

We laugh, but they belong in *Waiting for God*, that bitter Britcom about assisted living.

My sisters have begun to fall apart when talking to friends. Jan wishes we had added more services and left Mom and Dad in their condo. There, they would be home, the place where they belong, where their eyes sweep over known objects laden with memories that anchor them in the tides of change. Home, safely home, cushioned within routines and an illusion of independence.

We do not know how to live. We blunder through our days, and afterward think we know what we should have done. To keep our parents safe, we moved them into a world of strangers and systems that prove, finally, incomprehensible. Imprisoned in old age with nowhere to go, nothing meaningful to do, they wait for their "wonderful kids" to solve their lives. Being together is what they want, yet even with family they sit quietly. A photograph caught them on Jan's couch, dull eyes staring straight ahead, clasped hands bridging the gulf between them. Horrified by that picture, Dad said, "That must have been taken ten years from now."

Last winter, preparing for the move from White Bear Lake, Mama sent Dad and Jan to the basement to pick out a few tools to take along. In seconds, Dad panicked, his breathing growing labored and distressed. Afraid of stroke, Jan led him back upstairs. She chose tools and arranged them in an elaborate new toolbox. At the Tower, she showed it to him and put it away—where it was immediately forgotten. Later, Dad complained he didn't even have a screwdriver. From then on, the toolbox sat out in plain sight—a sort of trophy.

Our friend, Ed, recreated Dad's old workshop in Jan's basement. He painted the walls and floor, set up machines, hooked tools on pegboard, spread sawdust around, and hung a sign from the ceiling: RALPH'S WORKSHOP. When Joe took him down to see it, Dad marveled. "I had a router like that."

"But that's *it*."

Dad had used his old workshop to build napkin holders, bookshelves, a cabinet and speakers for his hi-fi, clocks for all of us. He painted and fixed everything around the house. But this workshop, like Mama's shelf of hand-painted plates, is a monument to lost identity. A museum display. Not quite a gravestone.

എ

A Rooted Sorrow

July 1998

I AM BECOMING MAMA'S MEMORY. I tell her the stories she once told me. The names of old friends, the details of pranks, the fine points of her life story have dropped away. Only a lacy framework remains like the skeleton of a winter leaf. Full of emptiness.

"Really?" she says. Or "Oh, yah." Sometimes she asks, "How can you remember that?"

How can she forget? But forgetfulness is not a choice; at least we cannot prove it is. Brain cells die, synapses clog—and whatever their cause, these are physical problems.

So much of what made Mama who she is has come undone. This is my grief. My work is to be present with her and find what joy is left to us.

Sometimes I entertain my parents with stories from our family history book. Dad especially loves hearing his own stories again and breaks in with the very words recorded in our oral interviews. But today, Mama's pleasure in hearing is mixed with grief—and a stunning disorientation:

"I've been thinking about my life, and I can't remember anything about my childhood."

Our sense of self depends on memories, and Mama is losing herself. I pull out the big ring binder of family stories.

"Well, a lot of your memories are recorded here. From early on, you were outgoing and loving. When I asked Honeybun about your childhood, she said, 'I saw Lois when she was first born, and I've loved her ever since. She was good, happy; everybody loved her. And she loved everybody.'"

Mama's eyes fill up, and she sighs. "I wish I could go see Honeybun."

"So do I, Mama— Do you want me to read more about your childhood?" She nods, a half-smile on her lips. "You were a very active little kid. This is what you told me in your own words":

> Whenever my mother was going to take us anywhere, she would get me cleaned up. And I was to sit on the chair until she got everything else ready because, invariably, I would find some way to run up the hill and fall down and have a bloody knee or something—just before she was ready to leave the house. And from that I gather that I was kind of rambunctious.
>
> Mama said when I was two and three years old, I used to wander off. One time I wandered all the way over to Rice Street, which was a good mile away. Everybody was running around looking for me. The police or the neighbors brought me back. I don't remember getting spanked, but I remember being scolded.

"I don't remember any of that," Mama whispers in alarm. She seems to be searching for some clue, some thread that will pull back what she once knew by heart. "Read more," she says.

> One time when I wandered away, my mother was out in the neighborhood looking all over for me. Somebody must have told her they'd seen me going into a house with some little girls. Mama knocked on the door, and she later told me, "I came into the kitchen and there was the black mama and all kinds of little kids and then you with your blond hair sitting at the table eating fresh bread."
>
> And this mother took me in, see, because I was lost.
>
> After that, my mother tied me up in the back yard. I could run around in a harness that was hooked up to the clothesline. Like a dog-run! That's true! And that was what she had to do with me. It sounds terrible! But she was busy in the house, and I'd take off.
>
> I think I was three years old or so. And why I ran away, I don't know. You know, little kids start walking and they don't pay attention to where they're going.

∽

MAMA ALWAYS MOVED THROUGH THE WORLD with a marvelous extroverted ease, speaking to strangers, making friends, joining groups, volunteering, connecting. That was her nature, but it was also a strategy that worked when her young life was insecure. Money problems forced her family to move again and again, which meant different neighborhoods and new friends. In 1921, when she was four, her father's first breakdown split the family apart for a time. Yet she betrayed no emotion as she told the story:

> My mother didn't start working until after my dad had that first nervous breakdown. And that was just before I went to kindergarten. I think it was when the railroad workers were trying to get representation and they all went out on strike. My dad was an oiler and did not want to strike. I don't know just what it was that brought on his breakdown, but I think it was connected to that conflict.
>
> When my father was in the Northern Pacific hospital, my mother broke up housekeeping. She put all of her furniture in storage, and she and my brother went to live at Auntie's house. I went to live with Aunt Tina and Grandpa Christensen. I don't know how long that lasted, but at that time I went to kindergarten and maybe part of the first grade at J. J. Hill School.
>
> I don't remember any worry about living there. They doted on me. Grandpa used to hold me on his lap and tell me all these wonderful stories about fighting the Indians. I don't know how much fighting he actually did— he built forts—but he told me all kinds of stories that, until I grew up, I never realized were true. When he came to this country from Copenhagen in 1862, he couldn't understand English. He thought he was signing up for a job as a carpenter, but he was joining the army!
>
> When I was at Grandpa's house, they had—the one joy of my life—a wonderful dog. A spitz, I think. That dog let me do anything I wanted, and I was always putting doll clothes on him and pushing him all over the neighborhood in a buggy. I treated him like a baby. I remember Aunt Tina laughing when she'd see the dog in the basket with a bonnet on.

Over the years, Mama frequently described her own mother's hard life— cleaning railroad cars, doing domestic work, raising two kids after her husband's breakdown. And moving.

When my brother, Edward, was here a couple of years ago, we went all around and tried to find the houses we remembered living in. All of a sudden we started to laugh. We wondered why we moved so much, because we moved to many, many, many places. All on the East Side. And he said, "I guess it was cheaper than paying rent."

Mama characterized her own life as happy, though shame and long-standing fears about money had troubled her youth:

When I was in high school, my mother would leave a list and go to work. After school, I would call Schacht's store downtown St. Paul to order groceries. They'd deliver. I'd always talk to the same man.

One time he said, "Lois, I'm sorry, but I can't take an order until your mother pays some of this. Tell her that."

I was shocked, and that erased my memory of whether we ordered from there again. But I vowed *I'd* never charge groceries. And I never did.

છ્ર

RECENT RESEARCH CONCLUDES EARLY STRESS, such as abuse, neglect, or the loss of a parent, may contribute to memory loss. The study was done with rats, but that does not stop humans from extrapolating its results to ourselves. Raised in cages with insufficient nesting materials, the young rats seemed normal at first, but later showed signs of memory loss. Communication among their brains' hippocampal cells, which are important for long-term memory and spatial navigation, was impaired, and electrical activity within those cells deteriorated with age. The brains of humans in the early stages of Alzheimer's disease exhibit this same impairment. Other studies demonstrate the effects of stress on the brain. The fight-or-flight response to stress releases adrenaline—which stimulates the body for emergency action—and cortisol, which keeps the brain in crisis mode. Chronic stress produces an overload of stress hormones that can increase atherosclerosis and damage brain cells.

People differ in the amount of stress hormones they produce and in the ability of their bodies to eliminate them. Genetics and early physical or emotional trauma may influence these levels. Studies suggest early trauma may program people to overrespond to stress. And aging can increase the duration of stress-hormone production in the body.

In what seems a vicious circle, the causes and effects of stress and aging hopelessly interrelate. Not only can aging increase stress but new research shows extended periods of stress can also hasten aging. As elevated levels of stress hormones begin to atrophy the hippocampus, memory loss can result.

When a CT scan revealed some atrophy of my mother's brain, the doctor said it could be Alzheimer's. We do not know if current research throws light on Mama's memory problems. Or if insecurity as a child, or grief and remorse after her father's suicide, damaged her brain. Or whether careless food choices and insufficient exercise, together with a rather isolated and meaningless retirement lifestyle, took their toll. Any attempt to identify causes may be a useless undertaking, or it could point out methods of prevention. In a scientific sense, the human brain is just beginning to know itself.

> *Canst thou not minister to a mind diseased,*
> *Pluck from the memory a rooted sorrow,*
> *Raze out the written troubles of the brain,*
> *And with some sweet oblivious antidote*
> *Cleanse the stuffed bosom of that perilous stuff*
> *Which weighs upon the heart?*
> MACBETH, V, III, 40 –45

ↀ

Happy Birthday to Me, All Right

If you were the devil and you were trying to invent a disease,
you would...invent Alzheimer's.

—DAVID SHENK, *The Forgetting.*
Alzheimer's: Portrait of an Epidemic

October 18, 1998

THE COFFEE POT IS COLD when Joe and I arrive at the Tower apartment. Mama doesn't want to take a shower, but needs one. She is unsteady on her feet and complains of a sore leg, yet stares at her walker, calling it a horrible thing. Ice cream and coffee perk her up a bit, but she does not want to be a bother. Or to go anywhere, not even to Ginger's for my birthday party.

"I'd feel worse if you didn't go, so you're stuck."

She looks at her wedding picture on the wall and asks, "What happened to me?"

Whether or not that is a real question, I answer, "Life happened to you."

Reciting my cheerful little résumé of her pleasures and accomplishments—a hopeless attempt to argue away grief and too much like an obituary—makes no difference at all. Mama hates what she has become and has forgotten what she once was. Around the tenth time she hears what the dinner is celebrating, she says, "I'm ashamed that I forgot your birthday."

"Mama, it's no shame if you can't help it."

"Why am I like this?"

"Some people get this way when they get old. It's not your fault."

Right or wrong, I have never said "Alzheimer's" to my parents. And, of course, we do not know for *certain* why she is this way.

Once many years ago, we kids were particularly naughty on Mama's birthday. On the phone, she complained to a friend about her "horrible kids."

"Happy birthday to me, all right," she grumbled, and it got to be a family joke. Today, I mutter it to myself.

"Don't get old," Mama tells me.

"What should I do, die right now?"

"No," she says. "Just keep pretending you're young."

That may have been my parents' strategy. Nevertheless, they are leaking like old helium balloons, going soft and shrunken, drifting just above the ground.

Mama has always had a sense of karma. When I was nasty as a kid, she cursed me. "You'll get it all back. You get back what you give out in this world."

Our parents gave out love and care, but that is not all they are getting back. Perhaps their own avoidance betrayed them—the unwillingness to consider an unpleasant future, the innocent trust that life will continue on unchanged. Perhaps the laws of karma are not cumulative: each decision has its own consequences, and a good life is no insurance. But, for good or ill, the anxious desire of their daughters to help them is also part of our parents' karma.

∽

THE STAFF HAS DECLARED MOM AND DAD have an alcohol problem! Dad met one aide at the door saying he had a hangover and asked her to come back later. He invited another to have a drink with them, promising, "We won't tell anybody." But the brandy Jan bought for them ten days ago is only down two inches. Was Dad's talk of a hangover a veiled bid for privacy and independence? An attempt to be a bad boy in the stifling Sunday school atmosphere of the Tower? Even if real, was that hangover the consequence of a need to feel "good" once in a while, when precious few pleasures are left to him?

Maybe Dad's offer of a drink was simple conviviality—a desire to be a neighbor instead of a patient. Both of my parents were community people, active in East Side organizations, church, PTA. Mama visited shut-ins and nursing home residents and worked in the kitchen for any number of church events. Dad ushered, served on the church board, and delivered Meals on Wheels. Mama got him involved to such an extent people joked about giving him an award for the "most volunteered husband."

"Doing something for somebody" had been Mama's strategy against depression, but belonging and connection are central to Dad's character. When he says, "We've lived too long" or "We're lonely here," the sterility of his current existence stands in stark contrast to the rich and affectionate community life that fills his stories:

All the men, well, maybe not *all* the men and boys in the neighborhood, played ball on the corner lot of Brainerd and Burr streets. It wasn't a very big lot, but we played with a real soft ball so it couldn't be hit too far. And didn't make any difference what age you were—if you were able to hold up the bat and throw the ball, we invited you in. We had a very good time playing one-a-cat or, if there were a lot of fellas, we chose up sides. After the ball games were over, we'd go sit on the back steps of Frank Cohen's grocery store. And after talking over the game, someone would say, "Well, let's sing a song." So we'd sing all the old familiar songs, like *Sweet Adeline* and *Down By the Old Mill Stream*, all the old favorites. And some of the fellas were evidently up on their music because they would harmonize and sound like a regular barbershop quartet. There was Eddie Olson and Mac Olson, Rube Paulson, Hinie Theline, Art Theline. All ages from ten, twelve, up to forty, fifty years old, sitting in a group. It was wonderful. No difference of religion, age— Frank Cohen kept his store open till nine, but we sang songs until fairly late at night. When he closed, he would come out and stand in the doorway and listen to us singing or talking. And then sometimes he'd go around and count noses and, if there weren't too many, he would go back in the store and come out with ice cream cones. He called them some Russian name for ice cream—

❧

JOURNAL | *Halloween*

October 24, 1998

M AMA HAS BEEN PLACED—alone—in the nursing home next to the Tower, and Dad, Jan, and Ginger are overwhelmed. This was the weekend to catch up on schoolwork, and Joe is gone, but I have to drive to Minneapolis. On the car radio, Bob Dylan sings, "What good am I?" It is not enough to recognize the pain of others, he says. Unless we help, we are no good at all.

Carrying a ceramic angel and a soft stuffed bear, I take Dad to see Mama where the halls are hung with orange and black streamers, dangling bats and spiders. Dad recoils in disgust at a green-faced witch, but does not acknowledge the man pulling feebly on the handrails to drag his wheelchair along. An anxious woman begs me to take her down to breakfast. Another calls insistently for a change of pants. Blank and staring at a clamoring game show, or curling fetal and open-mouthed in a narrow bed, each mortal in this place is a herald of future loss.

It's Halloween in the house of horrors.

My mother's room, despite smeared pink woodwork, is sparse and grim. The frail lights of her little ceramic Christmas tree in the window provide the only cheer. Mama hugs the fuzzy white bear we brought, but doesn't notice the angel. Distraught, she clings to Dad, and they both break down.

"Why am I here?" she wails.

"Mama, you got so depressed that Daddo asked for help."

"This is a horrible place!"

She tries to bargain with me, essentially promising to be good if she can go home. I keep repeating, "I don't have that power. I can't make that decision."

"Who's going to stop us?" Dad asks.

To change the subject, I tell him Ginger will take them to the lake soon.

"Good," he sighs. "We can both jump in."

"You can't do that. We'd all feel terrible."

"Suicides don't consider other people's feelings."

When we return to the Tower, Dad cannot figure out how to use his entry card. He doesn't remember he's lived here since the end of February or what floor number to push in the elevator.

Once inside the apartment, he asks, "Where's Mama? Has she gone to bed?"

"Oh, Daddo, you've just forgotten. Mama's being taken care of for a while in another building—"

"Am I normal?" he cries with a wild look.

Trying to comfort him, I begin reading the Twenty-third Psalm, but it calls up his memories of a World War II bombing raid.

"*This* is the hardest time of my life," he claims. "But I'm less able to bear it now. Mama has always been the strong one."

We sisters need to meet with the staff. We are all looking for a good solution. They are well-meaning people, and we appreciate them. But I keep hearing their unspoken commands: You *will* participate in the program. And you *will* be happy.

ও

JOURNAL | *Here*

October 25, 1998

D AD DOESN'T ANSWER MY "GOOD MORNING." He seems catatonic in his chair until he moans, "Why is Mama gone?"

"Mama was depressed because she couldn't do anything."

"But, my car is— I couldn't—"

"No, it's not *you*, Daddo. She couldn't cook anymore."

He nods.

"And she needed help taking a bath. She couldn't write her name, read, cut her meat—"

"Oh, that's terrible!" he cries. "Where was I? She didn't tell me. She kept all of that from me."

Has he lost his memory in order *not* to know these things? *Folie à deux.*

⁘

THAT EVENING, IN THE DINING ROOM of Mama's nursing home, the friendly supervisor seats Mom and Dad with another couple, and everything is smiles and hellos as I leave to talk with Jan about this latest trial.

"Ginger and I think it's insane to treat Mama's depression by moving her into a depressing place away from Dad!" I say.

"The Tower has rules," Jan replies. "You have to be able to live independently with services. Mama was classified as above 'E,' which means she's at-risk. We put these people in charge of our parents. They are responsible. They can't ignore obvious warning signs. They have only their own observations to go on. They can't rely on us or Mom and Dad saying they are fine. If Mama is so depressed as to be a danger to herself or others and they do nothing, they are liable— And as *you* once told me: 'Whatever way it happens is wrong; there's no good way to do it.'"

At 6:00, the dining room staff greets our return with much relieved laughter. They'd become concerned as the supper hour ended with Dad and Mom still at table. And after Dad explained his daughter had dropped them off, they became suspicious. People actually abandon family members in such places! And at times it's not too hard to understand why—

We all walk Mama back to her room. And when we leave, I have to essentially pry Dad away from her. Then, slumped and shuffling, he lets me guide him to the elevator, where two male aides stop us. They assume he's a resident they've somehow missed putting to bed. We laugh it off, but my mind replays two questions from earlier in the day:

Dad, in horror and disbelief, staring down the nursing home hall of funhouse mirrors, asking, "Do we belong *here*?"

And a concerned nurse, calling me out of Mama's room to suggest, "Why don't you bring your father over here, too?"

∽

IN THE TOWER, even holding Dad's hand, Mama was miserable. When it was time for the day center or her hair appointment, she'd close herself in the bathroom, crying, "You can't make me!" Or she'd take off her clothes and lie down in bed. Intimidated by the huge dining room with its dressed-up strangers, she'd refuse to go to dinner. "They'll bring it down."

Dad had been calling Jan in despair. "What's going to happen to us? I can't take care of Mama."

And he had *asked* the staff for help.

During her weekend in the nursing home, Mama has gone from stamping her feet and crying, "I won't stay here!" to agreeing to follow the program. Though it hasn't been easy, the staff says she eats and gets physical therapy and doesn't cry—until Dad visits. But what haunts me is the vision of Mama alone in that desolate room, with her name penciled in on a signboard near the door and iron-on nametags already on her clothes.

∽

JOURNAL | *Reasonable*

October 26, 1998

W ITH A SUBSTITUTE TAKING my classes at school, I am home trying to catch up on work, but all I can think about is Daddy in the Tower, forlorn and unresponsive as time drags on. And Mama, bewildered by the thick accents of some caregivers, waiting for someone who loves her.

On the phone, an Alzheimer's Foundation advocate says the staff doesn't have power over our decisions. It is not an acute situation, so Mom and Dad should be allowed to be together. When I call Dad at the Tower, his breathing is labored and stressed.

"We're working on a solution, Daddo. Just hang in there."

"You mean I shouldn't jump out a window?"

"Not yet. Don't let the bastards drag you down."

He likes that.

Preparing to talk to the public health nurse who made the decision involves putting on my most reasonable, warm, and diplomatic persona, but her voicemail says she's out of the office till tomorrow. Heart beating wildly, in a rage with no outlet, I know in my guts what it is to be powerless. A professional can say, "I make the decisions," even when the Patients' Bill of Rights promises "reasonable advance notice of changes." It says we should not be required to "surrender these rights as a condition of receiving services." We have the right to "take an active part in creating and changing the plan and evaluating care and services," and to "refuse services or treatment."

We are to be "told in advance of any change in the plan of care," but, on a weekend, without warning, they take Mama from Dad and isolate her in a barren room. No clause says all your rights go down the tube if somebody decides you're in danger. They are supposed to come up with a plan in ten days; meanwhile, Dad is getting worse. And Mama is sitting there in misery. No drugs have been given for her depression. She feels punished.

"What did I do wrong? Why am I here?"

One nurse is a Pollyanna. "They'll adjust. They'll have to grieve awhile, but they'll adjust."

Later, the Tower social worker, who had been talking with Jan when I phoned her earlier, calls me back. It is a time to try to be reasonable. "On what basis did they make the decision? I wasn't there when it happened."

She doesn't know, but Dad said he couldn't take care of Mama anymore. Mama wouldn't go to the day center, had less mobility, was just sitting there doing nothing. They were drinking. And there was a room available.

"I want you to hear this," I say. "My parents do *not* have a drinking problem. The only access they have to alcohol is what we give them. The bottles have hardly changed in three weeks. They talk about it, joke about it, rarely remember to do it."

"Well," she says, "an aide smelled alcohol on them. And Lois was wobbly."

Mama is *always* wobbly! And one drink, even one bender, does not an alcoholic make. And since when is "sitting there doing nothing" grounds for internment?

Though only reasonable words actually pass my lips, every argument is met with "Uh-huh." I am being managed, but do learn it was the public health nurse who pulled the services from the Tower and transferred them to the Hall. She decided Mama was not safe, so Mama had to move. That she can consider Mama's current situation *safe* is staggering.

At mention of the Patients' Bill of Rights, the social worker says, "You can get an advocate."

She admits the Hall has a skeleton crew on weekends. She agrees both parents need to be evaluated for depression. She didn't know Mama wasn't getting antidepressants, but thinks she will adjust. She isn't as confident about Dad.

"This happens once a week here," she says. "We have to give them time. And maybe we'll find a room for him next door."

"My mother's condition is not acute and doesn't require a nursing home," I argue. "She is supposed to have a treatment plan in ten days. Why should she sit there miserable until then?"

"Because the county arranged it."

෫ා

TONIGHT, GINGER CALLS TO TELL ME ABOUT HER DAY. When she asked a staff member how Mama was doing, he said she'd been crying.

"My parents want to be together," Ginger told him. "Mama keeps saying she wants to leave this place."

"It would help if you'd visit more often."

Angry at what was no doubt a stock answer, Ginger shot back, "We've been here around the clock all weekend!"

The staff says we can move Mama back to the Tower if someone will live there with them! That cannot be a serious suggestion. We all have our own work to do. I could move in again for a week or so to try to get Mama into the routine. Or we could move them to Jan's temporarily, or find a different facility in a hurry. Or somehow get the staff to see it our way with or without an Alzheimer's Foundation advocate.

Ginger took our parents, her kids, and the dog to the lake for ice cream this afternoon. Happily enjoying the peaceful scene, Mom and Dad totally forgot their current sorrows. At suppertime, she brought them into the nursing home dining room and found a table for two. When the waitress came, Dad ordered the first entrée. Thinking he was in a restaurant, he pulled out his billfold.

"I've only got $20. Is that enough?"

"It's already paid for," Ginger said.

"Did you kids?"

"No, you paid for it."

And then he realized where he was and started to cry. He'd been so pleased as he sat down at table.

Later, Dad called Jan. Alone and desperate in the Tower, he'd been drinking. Jan brought him home with her for the night.

ᏬᎧ

JOURNAL | *Alone*

Ah Love! could you and I with Him conspire
To grasp this sorry Scheme of Things entire,
Would not we shatter it to bits—and then
Re-mold it nearer to the Heart's Desire!

—EDWARD J. FITZGERALD,
Rubáiyát of Omar Khayyám

October 29, 1998

YESTERDAY, AGAINST THE ADVICE OF STAFF, Ginger took Mama out of the Hall. Breaking free from that juggernaut of care required courage. At the same time, without the help of an advocate, she convinced the public health nurse our parents have to be together and a different plan has to be made for them. Mom and Dad are back at the Tower, and I'm staying with them again for a time—trying to correct a paper or two between Mama's questions and Dad's depressive remarks. My sisters are drained by their efforts, but Jan brings a good supper.

Later, Ginger arrives to talk about the following day's meeting with staff. We decide to move to the plant room across the hall, but Mama is instantly suspicious, fearing we are planning to separate them again. All our protestations are futile. It's clear *she doesn't believe us*. Because we let it happen before, she thinks we're powerless against the staff.

I hold her anxious face between my cupped hands. "Mama, I will not lie to you. You've got to believe me. You and Daddy will be together."

We hope, tomorrow, to establish a normal routine with Mama at the Day Center. We don't know what services will show up in the apartment, but I'll stay here, and Jan will bring groceries. For now, it's enough Mama isn't isolated in that forsaken institutional room. She told us she's always been afraid of being confined alone. Dad is in a deep funk—depressed and anxious and unable to remember why. Afraid of the dark, he holds on in our goodnight hug and only reluctantly lets me go.

☙

JOURNAL | *Control*

October 30, 1998

EVOCATIVE OF OUR LITTLE ISLAND in a swirling tempest, the wind keen-ing around the Tower is too much objective correlative. We need music to muffle its dismal moan and the hiss of traffic far below. Any sound beyond the endless litany of questions: *Aren't you supposed to be at work? Are you losing money? Who's going to stay here tonight?*

When, after much button-pushing and misdirection, the *Pops Classics* finally resounds from Dad's old stereo, Mama whispers, "Oh, that's beautiful."

But Dad is bewildered. The music creates a place in which his soul is laid bare. "Where are we? Do we live *here*? Can you play something a little livelier?"

A psychologist told Ginger that suicide is a real danger at such times, that people get creative about it. We don't dare leave them alone.

"If this was *Brave New World*, I'd be gone," Dad says. "Just walk into the ovens." After a pause, he adds, "Humans ought to come with an off-switch."

❧

SITTING AROUND A BIG TABLE at the care providers' meeting, we're offered a questionable scenario: Take Mom and Dad to a psychiatrist for evaluation, then admit them to Fairview Senior Care for an undetermined length of time, paid by Medicare, to be detoxified from gingko biloba and St. John's wort and stabilized on antidepressants. Finally, they'd be moved into a nursing home. The staff advises us to "do what's best for them," and "let go of them."

"We're *not* going to let go of our parents!" Ginger insists.

We tell them we'll think about our options. We give a month's notice at the Tower and ask for services until the move. Then we sisters take Mom and Dad to a doctor who just happens to be the ex-husband of a dear friend of mine. This connection seems beyond mere luck. In the midst of medical plans, rules, and procedures, this doctor is human—even getting Dad to laugh. And he levels with them about the place into which they'll be moving.

"You'll have less freedom, but your needs will be met, and if you don't like it, you can leave."

Huddled close to Mama, clasping her hand, Dad asks, "Will we be together?"

The doctor smiles his wide smile, spreads out his arms like Zorba the Greek, and declares, "Yeah, all three of us!"

As our laughter breaks the tension, he launches into a joke about a guy who'd been very bad in his life. After he died, he was amazed to find himself in a beautiful place with everything he'd ever wanted—mansions, golf courses, pleasure boats, beautiful angels serving cocktails and gourmet meals, and all his old lost friends gathered around to raise a welcoming toast to him.

"What's up?" he asked St. Peter. "This place is a paradise."

"Your *wife's* here."

Dad doesn't get it. Without *his* wife, heaven wouldn't be paradise.

The good doctor thinks it was crazy to put Mama in the Hall. He thinks, too, the plans for the Fairview program and the psychiatric evaluation are crazy.

"The two biggest robbers of freedom in this country," he says, "are the cops and the nursing homes."

When he learns Dad hasn't had any herbal remedies today, he pulls out a sample of an antidepressant, writes a prescription, and tells us to return in two weeks. And when I ask him about the staff's prohibition of alcohol, he says, "A half a drink a day is okay. The cardiologists have one, so they recommend it for their patients."

He is compassionate and soulful. He is on the side of people, not the machine.

℀

SOON AFTER WE RETURN TO THE TOWER, the social worker calls to learn the doctor's opinion. She doesn't seem to like what she hears—that Fairview and the psychiatric evaluation are unnecessary.

Some victory— Now we're looking for a double room on a dementia ward. Dad continues to be disoriented. His only defense may be to retreat in mind from the shock his body remembers. The antidepressants will take a while to kick in. Meanwhile, his guts rebel in hiccups and gas. And his breath comes hard, as though a great weight presses on him.

"What will happen to us now?" he moans.

We'll find a place where you can be together and get the care you need.

"Where?"

We're still looking.

"Not White Bear?"

No.

"I've been praying to leave this place," Mama whimpers. "We're going home!"

I so hate to correct her.

Dad tells us he doesn't want to commit suicide because he doesn't want to leave Mama. Throughout the years, he's rarely spoken about the war, but now he keeps telling war stories—the building next to his billet got hit and eight guys died, a buddy sitting next to him in a jeep killed by a sniper. He can't understand why he stayed calm then, but is losing control now.

"I'm not the captain of my ship anymore. What happened to me?"

After we walk Mama over to get her hair done, he slips back into believing she is gone.

Jan goes home after supper. While we watch TV, Mama murmurs, "I'd hate to leave this place—"

"Why would you say *that*?" Dad blurts, suddenly alert and anxious.

"I don't know, I just felt it."

"Why do you look so sad?" he asks me. "Do *you* know anything about it?" I pretend ignorance. *Now* they like the Tower! As well they might: it's palatial compared to anything they'll have again.

ℰↄ

JOURNAL | *Discovery*

November 3, 1998

JAN TOLD ME WHILE MOM AND DAD are staying temporarily with her, Mama sometimes thinks it's her own house. But can't find the bathroom. It doesn't matter Jan's stucco two-story Tudor, with its stained-glass lamps and dark Oriental rugs on oak floors, bears no resemblance to any house Mama ever lived in.

Last night, Jan made a nice anniversary supper for our parents. She read their story about the crazy bet that began their loving life together, then led them in a recitation of the wedding vows they'd made fifty-eight years before.

At "till death do us part," Mama said, "we did."

Ginger and the kids came to Jan's for supper on Sunday. Their dog, Maggie, provided some amusement. The big golden retriever was ridiculously intimidated by one of Jan's cats. Though Lulu is *some cat*. Transfixed by a CD of old songs, Mama smiled to herself. Dad watched his offspring play Scrabble. One laid down an obscure word they had to look up, but Dad knew the meaning—the fruit of his years of daily crossword puzzles.

"This is what I like," he said several times. "I grew up in a big family, and I like to have people around."

That idyllic scene was not typical of our parents' days at Jan's. When my sisters went out to evaluate nursing homes, their friends filled in for them. Steep steps and bad weather kept Mom and Dad inside, bored in front of the television, waiting to be fed and served coffee, and more coffee. They had nothing to do and could do nothing for themselves.

❧

MOST SCHOOL DAYS ARE ROUTINE, uneventful, even productive. It's the weird stuff that makes it into my journals. Yesterday, Louie, that sly-eyed rascal, asks me if I've corrected the vocab tests. Of course I haven't.

"Well, I want you to know I sacrificed a point for a pun."

That evening at home, I grade test papers to Andean music. It feeds the rest of me something vital while that tiny, dry part with the red pen rules each answer *correct* or *incorrect*. On Louie's test, a smiley face marks number six, where instead of spelling "wiseacre," he's written "smart ass."

I should thank him for a good laugh, but write, "Is this a confession?" My red pen takes off a point—but refrains from adding the definition of "pun." Or "synonym."

Today, Louie defines human life as "halfway between diapers and diapers."

"Louie! That's wonderful!"

The classroom is seven rows of blank stares.

"He means we begin life in the diapers of infancy and end wearing the adult incontinence products of old age."

Some gasp. But they all think *that's* funny—

I want to tell them life is a gift. That all the powers so freely given us will be taken back. *Life* will be taken back, sometimes all at once, sometimes in a slow bleeding away of all we are. But they will discover that for themselves.

For me, it's not only that my parents are declining. That breaks the heart, but it is the way of the world. What grabs hold and squeezes my life out of alignment is the violation of their sovereignty, the role reversal—parenting my parents, forcing them to do what they don't want to do because they no longer know what is best. They always knew what was best. I don't know what is best.

Tonight, though recognizing the difficulties it would create for everyone, Jan calls late proposing to keep Mom and Dad at her house with help from Ginger and home healthcare workers. Every third weekend Joe and I would stay with them while Jan went elsewhere. Ginger had pressed for this plan, but I ask Jan if she's sure she wants to take it on. And don't encourage it.

☙

JOURNAL | *Crushed*

November 4, 1998

TONIGHT, JAN CALLS TO REPORT A MIRACLE for Mom and Dad: adjoining rooms connected by a private bathroom in a dementia unit adjacent to the Tower. Carpeted and nicely decorated, the sunny corner room with windows on two sides will be their living room. The other their bedroom. The unit has about twenty-five people, a sunroom, and a whirlpool. A godsend.

We all suffer over the prospect of actually walking them into that new "home." Jan asks about my schedule, but it's the end of the quarter. Five classes of papers to correct, final grades due. It would be the fourth weekend in a row in Minneapolis—and it's too soon to ask the district for family leave again.

Jan can't understand. "If Mom and Dad died would you still have to get your grades in? You only put your parents in a nursing home once. I've been missing meetings and am constantly apologizing at work. Ginger had to cancel a class she was supposed to teach."

Fearing my sisters' anger and needing their love, I sink into sleep. Minutes later, I wake with a jolt, believing myself in a coffin crushed by some terrible weight.

⅌

Lois and Ralph at Jan's—1998

Journal | *Fear*

STAFF FROM BOTH BUILDINGS have promised help on moving day. Mom and Dad are allowed to keep some furniture and their double bed, but we have to buy a rubber sheet. Because cloth upholstery is forbidden, the unit will provide vinyl wingchairs.

Only eight months ago, we sorted mountains of their stuff to select what we thought they'd need in the Tower. Now almost all of that must go. Mama's plate rail of hand-painted dishes. Dad's toolbox and big stereo cabinets. We'll divide up what we want for ourselves and get rid of the rest. King Lear is howling on the heath again. Maybe Mom and Dad will settle in and bask in the security of total care. Or maybe they'll just die.

ↁ

"WHAT HAPPENED TO ME?" Dad asked the other day at Jan's house. "Did I have a stroke?" Though he shows no physical impairment, he's been flattened. He eats little and, cuddled together with Mama, sleeps till noon. That may be due to exhaustion from his recent trauma or difficulty adjusting to antidepressants, but Dad sees no reason to get out of bed. We all fear for him.

"Talk to somebody," Mama tells him. "It helps."

When, later, Mama says she wants to die, Jan reminds her of that wise advice: *Talk to somebody*. But Mama says, "I've always been able to tell *other* people what to do."

Nothing can ease her anxiety about where we are going to put them. No amount of explanation stays in her mind.

"Nobody tells us anything," she moans.

And though Mama tells Jan how much she likes staying at her house, Jan overhears her ask Dad, "Where can you take me that's not here?"

ↁ

RALPH

Purple Hearts
Dementia Unit

November 12, 1998–September 25, 2000

Journal | *Layers*

November 12, 1998

Because mama is worried about what they'll think of her in the new place, Jan dresses her up and applies some blush and lipstick. Dad is so weak he can hardly get into the van. That may be due to the antidepressant Paxil, but being moved to rooms he hasn't even seen can't help.

From the front seat, Mama keeps calling, "Are you there, Daddy?"

To sustain himself, and Mama, he tells stories of their courtship all the way. Then, as they drive into the courtyard, Mama shouts, "Not this place!"

I lunched over and inconsolable, even with Dad holding on to her, she slams her walker against the sidewalk and cries. She has not forgotten her desperation in that blank lonely room within these walls.

Mellow within his shield of antidepressants, Dad follows Mama into the elevator and then down the corridor. When he sees a box on the wall marked EMPLOYEES ONLY, he quips, "Do they make them that small?"

"It was horrible," Jan tells me on the phone. "Even with all the help. But the staff members were great. They had moved the furniture, made up the bed and turned it down. They brought coffee, but Ginger and I were distraught to think Mom and Dad had been actually installed in that place. To me, it looked like the nursing homes where Ginger and I as kids sat out in the car waiting while Mama visited old people. Old, cramped buildings with layers of grief like scum on all the surfaces."

I've got to go there tomorrow. My sisters are wrecked.

∽

JOURNAL | *Alarm*

November 13, 1998

SCHOOL WOULD HAVE BEEN EASY TODAY, compared to the dread of actually walking into the dementia unit. As Jan and I leave the elevator on the second floor, we release the orange panels that camouflage its door. This simple deception is enough to keep the residents confined. A notice in the hall informs us TODAY IS FRIDAY, NOVEMBER 13. THE WEATHER IS COLD AND WINDY. At the far north end of the floor, a sign on the locked exit reads: THIS DOOR IS ALARMED. *I* am alarmed to think of what might lie beyond that door.

Three women in wheelchairs near the nurse's station stare vacantly. Hunched over his walker, a frail man concentrates on taking one baby step after another. We ask an attendant for Lois and Ralph's room and are directed to the far end of the hall.

Mama's hair is fixed. She talks happily about a program they'd been watching till she had to go to the bathroom. Dad is quiet but calm. With a view of the courtyard and busy street, their cheerful living room contains remnants of their furniture—a little mirrored chest of drawers, an end table and lamp, a few family pictures. And through the open doors of the bathroom that connects their two rooms, we can see Dad's dresser and their own bed.

Talking a bit, we tour the ward together. Visit the sunroom with its blaring TV and dozing residents. Mom and Dad seem at peace. It's as though on some level they know they need this place and feel safe in it. Not so bad for Friday the thirteenth.

"Are you going to stay?" Mama asks.

"No, there's no room."

"It would be nice to have a house," Dad responds. "This place offers no opportunities for exercise."

We don't remind him he never used the exercise equipment at the Tower.

"Daddo was heartbroken about not playing golf," Mama says.

The ward is warm, quiet, pleasant. A friendly and concerned staff checks on our parents, meets their needs. We can't know whether an advocate could have helped us find a better solution, but it could have been far worse.

During supper at Jan's, we share our impressions of the day. Jan says when she visited Mom and Dad a few hours after I did, they'd forgotten my visit. Dad told her, "Nancy will have to do something weird next time so we'll remember."

How weird would that have to be?

What's *really* weird is realizing our parents are actually in a nursing home and all we have to do now is visit them.

"I'm comforted to know Mom and Dad were content today," Ginger says, "but I'm just devastated by this whole process."

Later, we drink wine and watch some inane movie on TV rather than talk about our parents.

☙

JOURNAL | *Lemonade*

November 15, 1998

DIVIDING THINGS AMONG US, we sisters worked in the chaos of the Tower apartment all day Saturday. In White Bear Lake, only eight months ago, we sorted through mountains of stuff and thought we'd pared it down to essentials. Now most of this will go, too. Once we've done what we can, we don't visit Mom and Dad. We accept an invitation from David and ReNae to have a comforting supper aboard their houseboat on the Mississippi.

This morning, Joe and I finish our work in the Tower apartment and take a few things to my parents. Their room is hot, stifling. Mama slumps in a chair with her blouse half off.

"Oh, I can't believe my eyes!" she cries. "This was a terrible day. I'd been praying you'd come!"

It's obvious she, too, needs antidepressants. Especially here. We open windows, and a cool breeze freshens the air a bit. Dad is down but cushioned by the pills. And nothing can sort out his confusion.

"Where are we now?" he asks. "I liked where we were before. There are people here who don't know where they are."

"I want to be someplace where we don't get help," Mama pleads.

"Mama, you both have memory problems—and that makes help necessary. That's hard, but you have to try to make the best of it." Then I offer the old cliché: "If life gives you lemons, make lemonade."

"But you've got to have sugar," Dad argues.

"You've got to find the sweetness inside of you. I know it's there."

And then another resident from the dementia unit wanders into their room, babbling and looking from face to face for some response. As she stands before us with one shoe on, swaying, humming a bluesy tune, Dad is embarrassed—we all are—and no one knows what to do until Mama welcomes her.

"It's so nice of you to visit us and sing for us. We're still unpacking. Won't you come again later, when we're settled?" The woman stands there humming and swaying for a long, uncomfortable moment until Joe gently takes her arm and escorts her down the long hall to the nurses' station.

This, then, is where my parents will spend their days, rediscovering what their lives have come to each time they encounter the dementia of fellow residents. It brings to mind a story one of my parents' friends told them during a visit to the Tower:

The singer Andy Williams stopped by a nursing home one day and a resident called him over to talk awhile. Andy wondered if the man recognized him, so he asked, "Do you know who I am?"

"No," the man said, "but if you go over to the desk, they'll tell you."

At home in Litchfield, unable to concentrate on anything for long, I put away Mama's hand-painted dessert plates. For years, she tried to give her treasures to the three of us, but we were reluctant to take them. Today, we simply divided them among us.

Mama always said, "If you fight over my stuff, I'll haunt you."

We didn't fight, but she haunts us anyway.

෨

JOURNAL | *Escape*

November 16, 1998

THE MOST DANGEROUS GAME, by Richard Connell, occupies my ninth graders today. After reading this story about a human being hunting other humans for sport, they consider the question: "What is civilized?"

Not that there's any simple answer. To put one's parents in a safe facility where all physical needs are met—while not ideal—is regarded as civilized. But it might be kinder, when they can manage no longer, to leave them in some pleasant place with a blanket and two days' rations.

Yesterday, I asked Ginger to call the doctor about antidepressants for Mama, but she doesn't think Mama needs them.

"Simple pain avoidance, Gingo. If you have a headache, you take aspirin."

"I usually don't," she said.

It's not as though Mama is trying to accomplish something that requires all her remaining wits. She is just suffering. It would be like administering "soma"—the drug that pacified the inhabitants of *Brave New World*—as she sinks away. But Ginger is opposed, and Jan is ambivalent. I could have called the doctor myself but don't want to go against my sisters.

Mama wants to escape from the nursing home, talks often about dying. What might she do?

"The child of a suicide will naturally think of death," Kurt Vonnegut points out, "the big one, as a logical solution to any problem."

∾

Journal | *Chronic*

T ODAY, IN AN EMAIL, Jan so well expresses our current predicament:

> *They are not going to understand what has happened to them. They aren't capable of it. I plan to talk to someone, one of those support groups or the Alzheimer's society, about a more effective way of handling their mindset than beating them over the head with the facts of their situation and their dependence and then having them not remember any of it the next time they look at us and ask the same questions: Why can't we live by ourselves? Can't we find a better place than this? Why can't we live by a golf course?*
>
> *The only thing they accepted was when, at my house, we created an illusion of their independence—doing all the necessary tasks without their knowledge. And when we did that, Mama still wanted Dad to take her "anywhere but here." That was as good as it gets.*
>
> *In the nursing home there is a chance that they might get to know people or at least accept what that life is and be content. They will be cared for and safe. But the alternative is that we take them in, and lose our lives in order to make ourselves feel less guilty while they remain confused and unhappy. And their care and safety and the response to Mama's inevitable increasing needs would be in our hands. We don't have the background, knowledge and skill to handle it. All we have is guilt and loving feelings.*
>
> *It's sad and awful. And, like you, I feel terrible and uninterested in other things. But I am going to try to focus on my whole life and do other things that make a difference to people. Life goes on, as Mama always said. On and on and on.*

℘

IN RECENT YEARS, the efficacy of the medical response to dementia has been questioned. Robert L. Kane, a specialist in long-term care and aging at the Minnesota School of Public Health, and his sister, Joan C. West, an adjunct professor at St. Joseph's College, whose experience with their mother's Alzheimer's brought into harsh focus the problems of elder care, characterize Medicaid regulations as "hastily put together, draconian, medicalized—"

"The medical establishment operates in a world of acute illness, but Alzheimer's is chronic," they argue. "It is not a single battle, but a long-time process."

As their mother was moved about among different facilities, each dedicated to a specific medical need, her condition rapidly worsened. She could not adapt to changes. Kane and West believe such treatment-caused deterioration is common and unnecessary: "Managing chronic illness should be like landing an aircraft: a smooth glide, not a series of abrupt transitions."

❧

JOURNAL | *Catch-22*

November 21, 1998

PICKING THE BONES OF OUR PARENTS' sojourn in the Tower makes us feel like vultures. We send loads to various charities and still the place is not empty. Compulsively, I winnow out pens that work, match up scattered earrings, sort through boxes of cards and letters and old photos. What can they possibly still use? Dad had so wanted the stereo cabinet he'd built brought to the Tower. Obsolete, it stands out on the curb behind the building waiting for pickup—Mama's bad dream come true. We can't let them see that. The women who monitor the elevator don't laugh at us for moving all that stuff out again so soon.

Later, in their ward, Mom and Dad sit like zombies in front of the day room TV. Since they aren't eating yet, I disturb them. Immediately, Mama cries, "Take me out of here! I can't stay here!"

She shivers and shakes. And Dad says, "I'm afraid Mama's going to have a breakdown." Holding on to them changes nothing.

"They took me into a room and put something in my ears," Mama whimpers, as if reporting an alien abduction. "They asked me a lot of questions—"

"Were they hard to answer?"

"Yes."

"It's okay; you didn't have to answer. They were just trying to find out how to help you."

She tells the story again

"I want to go back high up," she whispers. "The people who live here don't know who they are. I can't stay *here*. I'll die."

And Dad asks, "Is this *it*?"

I flee to the nurses' station, where shelves are stuffed with thick ring binders, one for each resident. Most bear DNR in big letters: DO NOT RESUSCITATE. The nurse explains they irrigated Mama's ears and asked evaluation questions.

"My sisters and I don't agree about antidepressants, but it's really important that Mama get them," I say. "Her father had two nervous breakdowns and finally committed suicide. Mama fought depression all her life, but she's losing that battle now."

"I'll inform the other nurse," she replies. "Have you talked to a doctor?"

"I live out of town and only visit once in three weeks. My sisters take care of medical issues."

"Your parents are such quiet people—"

"Mama wasn't quiet. She was the life of the party. She lit up the room, did all sorts of community work, won a good-citizen award, baked things for people. She's quiet now because she knows she is no longer what she was."

Hoping that message has done some good, I return to the day room to get my purse and say good-bye. The meal has been served. Dad fumbles with his bib. Mama stares at her plate. I lift a forkful of mashed potatoes to her mouth.

"Is that num-num?"

"No."

"The food's good," Dad says, "but I don't have an appetite."

I promise to come the next day but don't want to ever enter this place again. We're caught in a perfect Catch-22: If Mom and Dad could understand why they need to be here, they wouldn't need to be here.

Clattering into chairs and walkers, I escape back to Jan's house for another family dinner sans parents. It's too soon to take them to our houses, the staff says. They'd have to go through the whole horrible entry shock again. Meanwhile, they can't accept the nursing home—which is not surprising—but would they be happy anywhere? When they stayed at Jan's, Mama asked Dad, "Where can you take me that isn't here?" High in the Tower, they threatened to jump from the windows. Even in White Bear, Mama repeatedly asked us to find another place.

"Mama, I love you. Jan and Ginger love you. We all love you," I told her today, but her response was bitter.

"That doesn't do me any good now."

ↄ

JOURNAL | *Test*

November 29, 1998

A T A CARE CONFERENCE, the nursing home staff tells my sisters that Mom and Dad can stay in their present situation until they reach the absolute last classification level. The staff will test them once a year. Dad, who'd answered half of the questions, is a "B." Answering only five or six out of thirty classifies Mama as an "E." No wonder she was troubled immediately afterward when I visited her in the day room.

The staff reports our parents have been to church, eat well, are pleasant to deal with. They participate in some activities, refuse others. They need a regular schedule because that helps memory-loss patients. We can give them vitamins, we can get the doctor to prescribe antidepressants, but anti-anxiety pills can worsen Mama's physical balance problems.

Since no alcohol is available, they can see Mama indeed has balance problems. Jan tells them what's apparent to us when we visit—Mama's constant weepiness, Dad's depression and inability to deal with her.

༇

JOURNAL | *Least*

December 6, 1998

NOW THAT THEIR OWN PHONE has been installed and programmed with our numbers, Dad seems to have forgotten how to call the staff. He pushes the Janet button at all hours. Adrift on the waters of the present moment, without anchor or rudder, he sometimes calls her three times in one afternoon. The lasting emotional effects of these calls are especially difficult for her at work.

When I answered Jan's home phone the other day, Dad thought he'd called the wrong number. He was agitated and confused about everything. "What is this place? How did we get here? Why are we here?" Fundamental questions, usually approached by myth or religion. No answer I'd give would satisfy him.

My parents don't know they are on medical assistance and that it costs more than $5,000 a month for them to live in what Dad calls his "cell." He used the same term for the Tower, where he had much more freedom.

We sisters think this double room is satisfactory—the least lousy alternative.

❧

JOURNAL | *Flight*

December 20, 1998

ON WEDNESDAY, Jan takes Mom and Dad to the doctor. She'd hoped to get a medical power-of-attorney signed but accomplishes only some preliminary work on it. Jan remembers the doctor, my old friend, as considerate and respectful throughout the full hour he talks with them.

"How are you adjusting to the nursing home, Ralph?" he asks.

"I'd rather live on a golf course."

"Wouldn't we *all*?"

That smiling response is so much better than, "You can't afford it."

When the doctor asks about DO NOT RESUSCITATE forms, Dad declares, "When my heart stops, that's it for me."

"Me, too," Mama says.

"Lois, have you been sad lately?"

"No," she replies, but in a bit begins to tremble and weep. At that, Jan almost breaks down but holds herself together to show strength. The doctor hands her Mama's prescription for Paxil, the antidepressant and anti-anxiety drug Dad is taking.

"Lois, Ralph—I'm going to ask Jan some questions now," he explains.

Even so, Dad feels left out, simply a witness to a discussion of his fate, and he asks Mama, "Do you feel like a bug on the screen?"

☙

JUST BEFORE DINNER AT JAN'S THIS WEEKEND, Dad hunches to the table, where he pulls out a chair for Mama, eases her into it, and with difficulty pushes her closer to her plate. Weak and tired, Mama tries to drink her fruit cup until Dad gently takes it from her hand. Later, Ginger brings her a plate of cake and ice cream. When I hand her a forkful of cake, she turns it upside down in her lap. She spills ice cream on her dress. She has started taking Paxil, which cannot yet have reached its full effect but is taking its toll. Watching my parents' halting movements, I flee in mind back to Phalen Park's ice rink, maybe forty years ago, when as one body, hands clasped together and each with an arm wrapped behind the other's waist, they swept past me on their long-blade skates.

The Old Smoothies

L OIS CHRISTENSEN AND RALPH PEARSON met on an ice rink, and their skating style mirrored their relationship. With long strokes on long blades, sailing on ice to *The Skaters' Waltz*, they seemed weightless, transcendent. Mama said she and Dad skated as if they were one person, as if they were "joined at the hip."

Actually, they *were* joined at "the Hipp." The Hippodrome skating center in St. Paul was the scene of their courtship. Skaters of all sorts—hockey players, speed, figure, and long blade—used that facility on the Minnesota State Fairgrounds. At night, an organist provided melody and rhythm for pairs of skaters as they flew around the rink. Mama thought it was heaven.

"I never wanted to do anything else but skate. I wouldn't have had much to do with Daddy if he hadn't wanted to skate every night. And I do mean *every night.*"

"She was the cheapest girlfriend I ever had," Dad said. "One season ticket at the Hipp, and she was happy all winter long."

"We were highfalutin' in our day," Mama laughed. "And in later years, friends used to call us 'The Old Smoothies.'"

Orin Markhus and Irma Thomas, figure skaters of the *Ice Capades*, were the actual "Old Smoothies," but my parents, too, were grace on ice. For both of them, love of skating started early and lasted long. Mama told me:

> When I was a girl and got cut bad skating, my mother was frantic: "Oh, why do you go skating all the time? You're getting hurt out there!"
>
> But I looked down at all this blood and said something that made her really mad. I said, "Mother, it was worth it."
>
> Because I loved skating, see?

I can never remember not having some kind of skates. At first, I had some that clamped on to my shoes, and they would fall off in the middle of the ice. It was terrible! I think I was ten years old when my father bought my first pair of shoe skates. I remember coming out of the warming house and gliding onto the ice with that secure feeling of my ankles being tight to the shoe and not having to worry about my skates falling off. That was when I fell in love with skating. Right there at Dunning Field [in St. Paul]. I went every night.

Dad played hockey three times a week and skated all the other nights, including weekends. He often said he was "practically born on skates." When he was a kid, he and his East Side buddies not only formed their own hockey team but created a place to skate.

We didn't have any playground supervision like they have nowadays where you could go and have some older person tell you what to do. We had to make up the stuff on our own. Little Olson's Pond down off of Desoto Street was just about the size of a hockey rink. And we kept that clear almost all winter. *Kids* did that. And we built a little warming house on one side. There we organized our first hockey team: the Bulldog Athletic Club. I organized it.

The first shin guards I made myself. Got some old canvas and put little slats of wood down and then put some cotton in back of 'em. The kids thought I was a sissy: *I* had shin guards.

Dad's hockey progressed from that early club, through junior and intermediate leagues, to Johnson High School and Hazel Park teams and beyond. He was good, and he had a box full of sweaters with insignias such as ACE HIGH OILS and EAST SIDE POST 358. Later, he played on a semipro Central League team from White Bear Lake. But it was the Depression. Those teams paid little, and at that time he and his sister, Marguerite, were the only ones with jobs in a family of six.

After they married, my parents' skating was interrupted, first by my birth and then by World War II, when the Hipp was converted into the largest airplane-propeller manufacturing plant in the country. Mama said:

I didn't go skating when I was pregnant and after I'd had Nancy. The year Nancy was born, Ralph came home, and he waited until we were in bed and then he told me: "The Hipp opened tonight." I cried and cried because it was the first time I hadn't been there on opening night. Nancy was a little tiny baby, and I was nursing. He knew I wouldn't go. Not with nursing every four hours!

After the war, my parents skated again. And all through my youth, as I scratched away on the figure skates they scorned, they slashed past, covering the length of the Phalen Park rink in about six strokes.

Well into retirement, Mom and Dad met old skating friends at Aldrich Arena in East St. Paul. "If you can walk, you can skate," Dad said, though their almost-airborne glide on ice belied their careful steps on pedestrian surfaces. Then in 1988 or so, it all ended. Mama fell on some stairs, and her ankle stayed swollen. When she could not lace her skates tight and had to be held up that last time skating, part of her seemed to give way.

Now Mom and Dad shuffle slowly down long corridors of wheelchairs and walkers. At times, they pass a big glass case where nesting pairs of bright-colored birds spend their lives, raise their young, chatter and flit among dry branches. Mama loves those tiny birds, talks to them with little chipping sounds and, every time she sees them, wants to release them from their perfect cage.

ಌ

Santa Lucia in the Dementia Unit

December 20, 1998

To celebrate santa lucia for Mom and Dad, Jan and I meet Ginger and her kids in the nursing home lobby. Soon Alia's friend, Annika, arrives with her mother, and we all wait for residents to return from church service. Our two lovely little Lucias in long, red-sashed white dresses, their blond braids crowned by artificial evergreens and electric candles, hover nervously above trays of bakery coffee cake. Our homemade kringler is against regulations.

Finally, the residents assemble in the sunroom. Some watch the loud TV; others, already asleep, curl forward in their wheelchairs. A few, however, present sweet faces when our procession enters, and Mama's eyes shine as she holds Alia's big Lucia doll on her lap.

Though the staff has not yet brought plates and coffee, Ginger begins. She turns off the TV, and in the sudden silence a few eyes look her way.

"Good morning," she calls out and introduces herself and the girls. "Santa Lucia is our family tradition, and we want to share it with you today. In Sweden, the eldest daughter in the family—wearing a wreath of candles on her head—serves coffee and sweet buns in the darkness of an early morning before Christmas. And we've brought some sweet rolls for you."

She doesn't mention that, according to tradition, the young girl chosen as the Lucia Bride also visits all the hospitals and nursing homes.

Then the coffee arrives and, in the clatter of cart and trays, Ginger switches on the Santa Lucia song in Swedish, a language none of us can understand.

My parents' faces glow with pride as the sweet young Lucias so carefully serve this group of familiar strangers. Some of our guests smile and thank the girls. A few sing along; others stare at the black television screen. One man lets his face go slack and his head sag onto a shoulder. Another struggles to get the last crumbs of coffee cake into his mouth.

"Is this what people do here?" a woman asks. "I'm visiting from Ohio, so I don't know." Denial may be a more comfortable home than a dementia unit.

❧

BECAUSE NATURAL TREES are against regulations, the little Christmas tree for Mom and Dad's living room came in a long box. Assembled and shaped, it looks almost real. Before hanging each ornament, I show it to them.

"Oh, I thought I'd never see those again," Mama murmurs.

"If we can't go to Christmas," Dad says, "Christmas comes to us."

"You'll go to Christmas at Jan's."

"Today?"

"No, today is Santa Lucia. We always bring that to you."

After the tree is decorated, an aide pops his head in the door to call them for lunch, and we reach for our coats. But Mama pleads, "Don't go—"

And, close to tears, Dad declares, "The only thing that would be better is if you took us with you when you go."

"We'll get together Friday for Alia's birthday."

Staying upbeat doesn't fool *them*, but it helps me fight off despair.

"I stand by the window and want to go *out*," Mama announces. "But we're old so we can't." She says "out" with such fervor.

Earlier, sorting their ornaments, I found a Post-it note stuck in the bottom of the box. It is one of many such messages Mama sent into a future she could not know.

> *1989 Christmas*
> *One of our very best!*
> *We were all together,*
> *And Alia was our joy.*
> *Grandpa's dollhouse*
> *was a wonderful gift—*
> *we are blessed!*
> *Mom*

In 1989, Alia was three. Mama was seventy-four and still driving. Dad, who'd just turned a robust and clear-minded eighty, had assembled an intricate Victorian dollhouse from a thousand little pieces of cedar. Even with Mama's first signs of confusion and forgetfulness, they were saying, "We saved the best till last."

⁊

JOURNAL | *Christmas Eve*

December 24, 1998

A S JOE AND I ARRIVE ON THE AFTERNOON of Christmas Eve, Mama bubbles over with joy. "We're going out! Oh goody, goody, we're going out! Oh, I'm so happy!"

In the lobby, Dad notices Mama's ID bracelet is too tight on her swollen wrist. An attendant cuts off this plastic strip that identifies her as #352 LOIS PEARSON and provides a contact number to facilitate her return if lost. At the desk, I have to give my name as the party responsible and note a phone number and an estimated time of return—checking my parents out like library books. When the cold hits us through the open door, Joe offers to get the car.

"No," Mama insists. "I want to walk. Oh, it feels so good just to breathe!"

Outside, she fills her lungs with fresh air, then adds in a conspiratorial tone, "Dad and I tried to go for a walk the other day, but we only got to the corner. Then they came running out and brought us back. 'We're responsible for you,' they said. 'Don't do that!' I don't know if they thought we'd run away—"

In the twilight, the cedars in front of Jan's house are already bright with colored lights. We help Mama climb steps luminous with ice candles. At the door, she stops to admire the wreath bedecked with dried flowers and red velvet ribbons. Inside, the air smells of Swedish meatballs. Spruce boughs and ribbons adorn the mantel and wall sconces. The tree, hung with strings of tiny blue-and-yellow Swedish flags and ornaments Mama made, glows in the window bay. It feels like Christmas.

Because most of the cooking is done, there's time for Mama to take a shower. For that we need the bathroom with a sit-down stall. Following behind, with hands braced against her hips, I guide Mama up the stairs. "Step up. Step up again, and again." Since she lost sight in the eye that had cataract surgery, her balance is worse. Each parent now has one blind eye.

Then begins the process of taking off her clothes, lifting each foot as she enters the shower stall, settling her down on the bench.

"I never thought I would be this way," she says.

Unable to stand water hot enough to warm the stall, she shivers. To speed things, I crowd in with her and, when my clothes get soaked, strip them off.

Naked, I hand her soap to wash herself, but don't ask her to wash *my* back—and, rinsing with the hand-held showerhead and toweling her dry, remain the helper, the one in control.

Again and again, Mama laughs at her clumsiness and weakness, her need for help, adding, "It's no fun to get old." And, "I remember when I worked at church. All the old ladies I'd visit! Now I'm one of them. So I know how hard it is for you."

"It's not hard."

But of course it is. Not physically. This is my *mother* I am helping climb stairs, prompting her every move. And whenever we go out, dressing her, giving her pills, and I hope without irritation in my voice, answering again the same heartbreakingly surreal questions:

Is this a special occasion, someone's birthday?
Where are we going?
Are we staying overnight?
Did I used to live here?
What time is it?
It's not too late, is it?
Even as Dad tries again to orient himself:
Whose house is this?
Where do we live?

ॐ

LIFTING A SPARKLING GLASS OF POTENT CRANBERRY PUNCH, Uncle Bob recounts all the things he never does anymore:

"I have this great Swiss steak recipe that I haven't made for *years*," he says. "It's the same with my meatloaf. I just never cook anymore. And it's been ages since I skied or skated. I just abandoned skates, skis, poles, everything, when I had to move—just *days* before I was leaving for Rome. Never replaced any of it. And of course, I stopped swimming forty years ago when my legs got like toothpicks."

Sometimes he reminds me of J. Alfred Prufrock—although he no longer has even enough hair to part behind. But Bob has always been a favorite uncle. In younger days, tall and handsome with wavy brown hair and a sophisticated manner, he regularly traveled to New York for the theater season, and to San Francisco,

France, Italy, and Greece. His tastefully decorated place in South Minneapolis contains thousands of books and records. "Almost wonderful" is his highest praise. And the few lively transcripts he's shared from his sixty-year cache of journals fire my curiosity about his life.

Suddenly, all is bustle and hugs as we greet relatives we see once or twice a year. Cousin Karen, Graham, and their kids arrive from Owatonna bearing shopping bags heavy with gifts, a canister of delectable cookies, and a casserole of rice pudding wrapped against the cold.

We call Honeybun in California, and Mama cries and wishes they were together for Christmas. A little later, she says, "We should call Honeybun."

"Well, Mama, you've already talked to her—"

"Why don't I remember things like *that*?"

At the table, candlelight glows through glasses of red wine and goblets of ice water. All sorrow is for a time forgotten in the spell of family and food and tradition. The obligatory Christmas meal of Swedish meatballs and sausage, bruna bönor, scalloped potatoes, fruit soup, and rice pudding with lingonberries is, as ever, wonderful. As we raise our glasses to toast the holiday, Mama raises a fork. Then a spoon. Even when Dad points to it, she can't see the wine glass in front of her. He has to lift it toward her.

"Skål!"

Looking off into the distance, Bob adds softly, "To absent friends."

Over coffee, we pass the tray of delicate cookies—spritz wreaths, shortbread stars, pepparkaka, cream wafers, and a dozen other kinds. Then the children present *The Night Before Christmas*. Alia recites almost from memory, while Ian acts it out with props, stealing the show. Grinning, he can't remember his only line, so Alia provides it:

"Merry Christmas to all and to all a good night!"

Bob asks Alia to read Tom Hegg's *A Cup of Christmas Tea*, saying, "At first I didn't identify with the old lady in the story, but now I do."

She reads well, but Bob, who at eighty-six has never admitted his need for hearing aids, misses most of it.

⁑

JOURNAL | *Christmas Day*

December 25, 1998

W E USUALLY SPEND CHRISTMAS DAY at the farm of Joe's sister, Shirley—a jolly party with kids and games, tables laden with food, and stacks of presents under the tree—but Mom and Dad are emotionally fragile, and my sisters are stressed. Instead, we join my family at Ginger's house. There, Christmas unfolds in its traditional ways.

"The candlelight glinting on the cut-glass goblets is just exquisite," Bob declares at the table, then laughs. "And I am the arbiter of such things."

With tall candles and Yule wreath, Ginger's table is fire and ice. Bob's sterling, Mama's goblets, Grandma's china and linens—all inherited as our old ones divested themselves of their treasures. We value these things, not only for their beauty, but their connections with our family story. Seen in an antique shop, they'd be empty of all that. And we cherish some only as reminders of love. On my kitchen shelf at home, Pierre, the fat yellow cookie jar chef, is ugly—and precious beyond measure: Mama kept it filled, and after I broke it, Dad glued its head back on.

After supper, Mama shows us her fingers laden with huge, clunky rings, and her hoop earrings—all junk jewelry, except her wedding band and diamond.

"My fingers are getting thin, and these rings are loose," she says. "I'm afraid of losing them."

"The only one that's really valuable is this diamond," I say.

"Take it," she replies.

"Are you sure?"

"I want to have the pleasure of giving it while I'm still alive."

To prevent theft, the staff had said, we should take our parents' valuables away and replace them with replicas. We've had some concern about Mama's diamond, but taking it seemed a violation. For years, Mama has tried to give us her things. But, aware of how little she has left, we've resisted.

This time I try on the ring, but it's too small. It fits Ginger, but she quickly offers it to Jan. When it doesn't fit, Jan hands it back to Ginger, and with lips trembling, Mama says, "I'm so happy to give my ring away."

Later that evening, Dad calls to Mama, "Come and sit by me."

Holding hands on the couch, they cling together like children stuck atop a Ferris wheel, with nowhere to go but down into what looks alien and small. And the warmth of that loved hand, the familiar face smiling, however tentatively, are the only things that seem real.

"We never should have left White Bear," Ginger hears him say. "We were happy there."

෴

BACK AT JAN'S, LATE INTO THE NIGHT, Mama begs Dad to come to bed.

"I can't hear you," he calls out to her and continues gazing at the Christmas tree with me.

"I like this time of night," he says. "It's peaceful. It all comes together."

Sitting there in the quiet afterglow of the family celebration may be a respite from the frailty and forgetfulness of old age, from being put to bed early and gotten up and dressed according to an institutional schedule. And from Mama's constant need for him.

෴

JOURNAL | *Sweets*

December 26, 1998

WHEN IT'S TIME TO TAKE MOM AND DAD back "home," Jan arranges a plate of Christmas cookies for the staff.

"I wouldn't have thought of doing that," Mama tells me.

"Oh, but you always did before. Jan does it because you did."

We carry the plate to the nurses' station, and though Mama doesn't really respond to the nurse's hug, she's delighted to present the cookies.

All during my youth, whenever Mama mixed up a batch of something sweet, we'd automatically ask her, "Who's that for?" And she'd pretend to snarl at us.

Awhile ago, my Uncle Carl's daughter, also named Lois, told me, "Your mom used to bring cookies for my dad after he had his stroke. She and your dad would go to church on Sunday, and then they would stop in to see us. She knew he liked sweet stuff, so she was always bringing him something."

❧

JOURNAL | *Fountain*

January 17, 1999

WHEN I ARRIVE IN THE DEMENTIA UNIT, Mama acts as though she's been saved from drowning. A few minutes later, she says, "This is a nice place. They're nice to us here, but I wish I could die."

Would death be better than the cryogenic death-in-life of the nursing home, a life in which she has no function? Kind aides take care of everything—checking on her, dressing her, making sure she eats and drinks, keeping records of every activity and concern, trying to amuse her, bathing and giving her "groin care."

Her only power lies in the "No" that results in emptiness. The phone connects her with her daughters or their answering machines, but nothing she says changes anything. She asks, "Is *this* where I live?"—perhaps in the hope someone will say, *No, this is just temporary while we prepare your home on the golf course by the lake, while we procure the elixir from the Fountain of Youth.*

❧

JOURNAL | *Marriage*

February 5, 1999

B ECAUSE THE NEED CANNOT BE FAR DISTANT, today—Mama's eighty-third birthday—I begin to write her eulogy, digging through the family history and the many loving entries from their fiftieth-anniversary scrapbook. It's important to do it right, because it reverses, at least in mind, the dissolution. It reconstructs the mother to remember instead of this ghost, this shell. And conveys her essential nature that has always reached out and embraced the world. She still does that. She sees water and wants to swim in it. She sees inline skaters and says, "I wish I could do that." She hears that Joe's nephews were roaring around in the mud on four-wheelers and says, "*I'd* do that."

But nothing illustrates her humor and love as well as the letters she wrote from San Diego. In 1980, when Joe and I were writers-in-residence for the Southwest Minnesota Arts and Humanities Council, Mama wrote:

> *When people ask me what you and Joe do, I just say you are poets in residence— they don't know what that is either, but it usually sets them to thinking and they don't know what to ask next! People in our age bracket tend to measure success by how much you make—due, no doubt, to our built-in insecurity from the Depression—and sometimes in the middle of the night when I wake up and can't go back to sleep because my list of worries won't let me, I can think of more damn things to fuss about.*
>
> *It is the same idea as when you were out—heaven knows where—and the sirens would wail, the clock would show 2 AM. Like when you were a baby and got to wheezing and your chest would be tight and you sounded like a frog, I would be sure you wouldn't last until daylight! Must be something that happens to women along with the first birth pain! Anyway at 2 AM, I'm not worth the powder to blow me up!*
>
> *Daddo, on the other hand, did not have those birth pains; so, he says—those kids all have a good education, they are young, they are resourceful, they will be all right. And he is right, of course. (You are still kids!)*

On the occasion of our fifth anniversary in 1980, Mama considered her own good marriage:

Odd how looking ahead 5 years seems like a long time, but when you look back, why the years just flew! Doesn't seem long ago at all we sat and cried at the church! True tears of joy, they were. So—our best wishes for the next five, and then the next!

Daddo and I are looking toward the 40th—just think, and I think we have saved the best for last as far as many things go—we certainly are free from most of our concerns now—it is a good time of life for both of us and every day I appreciate it, you can be sure of that.

We say what happens next can't change what we already have had. When Flo used to get frustrated with her life in the nursing home, we would sit and talk about her trips she'd taken with my mama and that would always make her feel better and get in a happy mood again. I learned a lot from her.

ↄ

Journal | *Birthday*

February 7, 1999

AT HER EIGHTY-THIRD BIRTHDAY PARTY, Mama spills food into her lap and onto the floor, smudges her napkin with chocolate, forgets the occasion though we tell her again as we read each card, open each package. To "Happy birthday!" she replies, "Happy birthday to you, too." We raise no glasses in toast, but cut her meat, butter her roll. Next time, one of her daughters will sit next to her and help her eat.

Leaving for home, I kiss her, and she says, "Take me with you."

"No," I laugh, in the old joking tone we've always used.

She laughs, but it's no joke.

Take me with you. The depths of helplessness in that statement. It's my mother saying it, not the old woman hoping to break free with our traveling Poetry Outloud troupe—her shadow dancing about the wall as she flings herself into the ragtime rolling from Bill Holm's piano. *Take me with you. Take me where life sings and dances.* It's my mother saying it, not the old woman in the Marshall nursing home, grabbing at my clothes from her wheelchair. *Take me with you, back to the real world, back to my real self.*

"I miss the things I used to do," Mama said at the dementia unit when we picked them up today. "I'm not doing anything here."

In a TV episode of *Da Vinci's Inquest*, a detective asks a resident what it's like to live in a nursing home and is answered with a question: "Have you ever sat in a waiting room for five years?"

&

JOURNAL | *Joke*

February 25, 1999

A T OUR PARENTS' THREE-MONTH CARE CONFERENCE, Jan is told they have adjusted. They are, in fact, the "stars" of the dementia unit. Everyone likes them, values them, and is so impressed by their relationship. They participate in eleven to twelve activities a week and have gone to chapel. They lead the conversation in the day room. They play Bingo—both on the same card and, maybe with help, have won. And, indeed, when Ginger peeked through the window, they were smiling and seemed to be enjoying themselves.

The activity leader asks Jan to encourage Dad to join the men's group.

"Ralph told me some of his war stories. He would be a good addition. And there are so few men here."

Dad has been reclassified as "A" and Mama as "D" instead of "E." Moving actually improved both of them. They'd qualify for the Tower again. But Jan feels the Tower was a mistake—and if we'd chosen that smaller residence we considered first, they could still be somewhat independent. That may be true, but it's not what we did. Dad refuses to join the men's group because he doesn't want to leave Mama. The two of them have taken over two chairs outside their door at the end of the hall.

"It's a little like their old balcony in White Bear," Jan tells me. "The staff says if a resident wanders down there, Mama takes hold of an arm and walks him or her back to the nurses' station."

"So is Mama territorial, or is she guarding her man from those other old ladies?"

"They're doing better than we are," Jan says as her voice breaks.

Can it be that as fundamentally well-adjusted people who know how to enjoy their lives, they actually *have* adapted? The last time I visited, an alarm went off out in the hall, and Dad and I both jumped.

"What's that?" he asked.

"The door to the other wing has a sign on it that says: THIS DOOR IS ALARMED."

"I should ask them what it's afraid of," he said.

"Yes *do*. They'd like that."

"Yah, I don't suppose they get too many jokes from the people here."

Unsinkable

MAMA LOVES WATER. When Joe and I spring her and Dad from the dementia unit for a few hours, we usually drive around Minneapolis lakes. "Oh, this is just wonderful!" she croons. "Do people swim here? Can we stop for a few minutes so I can jump in?"

I give her some excuse. "It's too cold," "We're due at Jan's for supper," or "You don't have your bathing suit on."

To this last, she replies, "I don't care."

And it's true. Years before, she stripped down to her bra and panties and jumped into the icy water of a quarry because she just couldn't stand not to. And not too many years ago, she went skinny-dipping in the middle of the night at their friends' lake place in Cumberland, Wisconsin.

"I'll take you swimming this summer, Mama, I promise."

A story from her childhood may begin to explain Mama's love of water. When she was five, her family spent a summer on a lakeshore farm in the hope that hard work and getting out of the city would help her father recover from his first breakdown. "I don't remember anything about that lake except that my mother was nervous about it because she couldn't swim," Mama said. "I think that made me want to swim."

For my parents' golden anniversary scrapbook, Dad's sister, Carol, sent a picture in which she and Mama run hand in hand through the water, laughing, splashing, light in their bodies, graceful as deer. The caption: *Golden Days at Phalen.* In another, Mom and Dad float together in ease and youthful glory.

"Those were the days," they so often say.

Lois and Carol Pearson frolic in the waters
of Lake Phalen

In my own childhood, those golden days at Phalen continue. All summer long, Mama and her friend, Charlotte, pack up all their kids and head for the beach. On Mondays, we have to wait till the wash is on the line, but housework is never a priority. The younger kids dog-paddle in the warm shallows or scamper over hot sand to the smelly bathhouse to buy Popsicles that drip down their arms. Charlotte, slender with flashing eyes, and Mama, fat in her black bathing suit, with forties-style home-permanented hair, lie on blankets—talking, laughing, keeping an eye on us, and tanning dark.

Once fully waterlogged, we kids are confined to the blankets. Penny and I, our towels set apart from the rest, are responsible for the younger ones as our mothers breaststroke out past the diving raft. Beyond the boundaries within which kids splash, cannonball, and dunk each other, out in the middle of the lake, they float free. "This is the life," they tell each other.

Not "Mama," not "Mrs. Ralph A. Pearson," nor PTA secretary, Martha Circle president, good neighbor, community volunteer—at Phalen, she is "Just Plain Lois." Weightless, fluid, cradled, unlimited, she enters her element. She bobs in perfect buoyancy, arms outstretched and toes pointing at the sky.

When nervous lifeguards lurch up in their rowboats to check on them, Mama laughs and calls out, "Do we look like we could sink?"

∽

SCORNFULLY, MAMA TELLS ME about going to Phalen with a friend who "didn't know how to swim worth two hoops":

> I'm out there in the middle of the lake, and she's walking up and down on shore wringing her hands and beckoning to me. I thought something was the matter with her, so I swam in, and she said, "You can't be out in the middle of the lake! What if you should drown? I can't swim. I couldn't come out there. I can't stand watching you!"
>
> And I thought, that's the last time I go swimming with you.

∽

GINGER AND ALIA VISIT MOM AND DAD in the nursing home. When they talk about things they love to do, Mama is suddenly intense. "The only thing I still want to do is get in that water."

Later, Alia insists, "We *have* to take Nana swimming."

The next Sunday, Mama hears the plan and cries, "Oh, goody-goody!"

She gives me a look that really connects. As I put my swim shoes on her feet, she hums *The Skaters' Waltz*.

Once Mom and Dad, Ginger and her kids, and Joe and I reach Lake Nokomis, we park as close to the beach as possible, but have to trudge across a busy street. Mama pushes her walker tentatively. Dad steps cautiously in splash shoes. You don't see the very old in bathing suits in public. Cars stop to let us cross the road. People smile benevolently as at a family of ducks.

Each step difficult, unsure, Mama pushes her walker down the boat landing to the lakeshore. Then, one on each side, Joe and I help her struggle over stones, slowed by the resistance of the water itself. Finally, we sit her down with a great whoosh, and her feet float up, swollen ankles lifting like water wings. She is weightless, unsinkable. I tow her like a little boat into the deep water, and we play, bouncing and splashing, giggling like girls.

For hours afterward, my parents are happy. They have done something real. After eating Jan's fine dinner, they sit in the fading glow of the day with drinks in their hands and family around them. Over and over Mama croons, "I just *love* it."

This is the picture to remember: Mama floating free, for a time, of her slow, heavy body and the dry hours of the nursing home. Free of the weight of years.

જ

One for Grandma

"A child is a bell of mindfulness, reminding us how wonderful life is."
—THICH NHAT HANH, *The Long Road Turns to Joy*

UNTIL GINGER, AT AGE THIRTY-FOUR, gave birth to Alia, Mama's three daughters had not produced a grandchild. This winter-solstice baby brought light to all of us, but especially to Mama. And everyone in the family shared her joy. Ginger told me that once she, Alia, and Ned moved back to the Twin Cities, our cousin Lois said, "I'm so glad you're back here for your mom and dad. And that they can enjoy that little one. I tell you, she used to tell my dad, 'You're so lucky to have those grandkids.'"

"Mom takes Alia every Thursday," Ginger told her. "They're good buddies. Alia looks forward to Thursday. We call it 'Nana Day.' And she goes over there and spends the whole day. I pick her up at ten o'clock at night, and they're still going strong."

In 1992, the birth of a grandson, Ian, was new delight, but Mama could not master his name. To the list of her friends' names that Dad had hung by the phone in White Bear Lake, he added another spelled phonetically: EE-ANN. Still, Mama called him "that little guy." She adored him, but when his toddler energy overwhelmed her diminishing abilities, she gave up taking care of him—with great and lasting regret.

But tonight, at a family party, Mama fails to recognize her grandchildren. She gazes with wonder at seven-year-old Ian telling his sly jokes. And her admiration is mixed with disbelief when Alia stands shyly before her. How can this tall and lovely girl be her little playmate? This stranger, who does not remember her preschool days when she was the joy of her grandmother's old age:

On their White Bear Lake balcony, Ralph and Lois with granddaughter Alia

All those years that I wasn't a grandma—and I never expected to be one—had a purpose. When my friends were all having grandchildren, I don't think I would have had the time to enjoy Alia as I do right now. She's in a very good stage now, and if she gets a little bucky sometimes, I just ignore it. We play hide-and-go-seek and I have a couple of places she comes to right away because she knows I hid there before. One time she came to Ralph and said, "Boppa, I can't find Nana."

I was lying down on the far side of the bed near the wall. It didn't occur to her to come around there.

I don't talk to my friends about any of the things she does because it sounds like I'm bragging. There's no describing the games we play, because she's a different animal every time, and I get changed from one thing to another—sometimes without being told. She'll say, "You're the mama, now." Or "You're the grandma, now." Or whatever.

But a week ago, I had to give birth to a bunny. She wants me to pretend I'm giving birth. I have to set the bunny up underneath my blouse so I have a big tummy and then she wants to go into our bedroom, and that's where I give birth to the bunny. She says, seriously, "Now I'm going to leave the room."

If it's a dolly, she comes and picks it up just like it's a newborn. It's been a puppy dog and— What was it the other day I refused to give birth to?

After Mama's inevitable struggles with her daughters, especially with me, she found a beautiful and enlightened way to be a grandmother. With Alia, she let the storms of childhood pass like weather and offered complete and forbearing love:

Have you noticed that the peanut butter we buy is packaged in glass now? Alia was not going to eat it because, "That's not the peanut butter we have at *our* house."

And I said, "Yes it is."

"No, it isn't."

So I had to explain to her that I had checked and this is just new packaging. Then I said to her, "If you don't want to eat it, it's all right."

I never argue with her. If she wants to be stubborn, I let her be stubborn. I say, "I'll just wait till you get better."

She's just fine. We got that all straightened out. She comes around every once in a while when we're sitting there doing something and she says, "I love you, Grandma."

Just as she had done with her own children, Mama shared her love of water with Alia and delighted in her response:

> One time I took Alia to Phalen Lake and I said, "Do you want to walk in the water?"
>
> She wanted to walk in the water, so we took off her shoes and stockings. I carried them, and she walked out as far as she could in her little short dress. When she wanted to go farther I said, "Oh, your mother doesn't know I'm doing this, and Grandma will get in trouble."
>
> But later she said to me, "I want to go back to that place where we walked in the water."
>
> That was not the first time. When Alia was only two years old, I took her to White Bear Lake, and when we got out where it was fairly deep, I bounced her up and down to see if she was afraid. *She* wasn't afraid of the water. When I held her in water right up to my chest, she didn't care. I said, "You're one for your grandma."

❧

A Crack in the Armor

*Without the fiery embrace of everything from which we demand
immunity, including depression and failure, the personality continues
to seek power over life rather than power through the experience of life.
We throw the precious metal of our own experience away, exchanging
it for the fool's gold of a superimposed image, an image of what our
experience should be rather than what it actually is, the final element
in the act of creation.*

—DAVID WHYTE, *The Heart Aroused*

Autumn 1999

SURROUNDED BY FAMILY CHATTER, Dad is an island of silence. He sits next
to Mama, bemused perhaps by realizing this is his ninetieth birthday. And
the relatives, even his sister, Carol, from San Diego, have gathered at our cousin
Karen's. It's time to give him my gift—a big ring binder of memories.

"Daddo, I've made this book for you. It's called *The War Years: The Pearson
Family Remembers World War II*. It's full of the war stories you told us."

He takes the book, looks at two of its cover photos: Mama, young and beautiful, holding two-year-old me, and Dad himself, in uniform overseas, leaning on
a jeep named "Nancy."

"It's full of love and courage, Daddo—and longing for home. It's got some
pictures you took in England and France, and newspaper clippings Mama saved
while she was keeping the home fires burning."

Stunned, Dad shows no sign of comprehension. He holds the book. He doesn't
open it.

❦

"LIFE GOES AWAY SO FAST," Mama says, as we sit in front of the nursing home watching the fountain, its splatter almost drowning out the pulsing thunder of passing boom-cars. As several children from yards across the street spill out into the constant stream of traffic, she frowns. "Somebody should be watching them," she says.

She is watching them.

"Maybe you're their guardian angel, Mama."

"I never thought I would be like this," she muses.

"I'm sure it's hard."

She agrees. As a nurse hurries by, Mama looks after her. "I used to walk like that."

❦

NORSE MYTHOLOGY RECOGNIZES the inseparable union of life and death. Forever half-dead and half-alive, Yggdrasil, the world tree, is fed and *fed upon* in the heaven of the gods, on the earth, and in Niflheim, the underworld of the dead. There, the dragon Nidhogg gnaws at the very root of life, trying to loosen all that holds firm. Yet even in the darkness of that world beneath the worlds, life renews itself. Yggdrasil is nourished by springs that flow from deep wells of the spirit.

But I have lost my way to the spirit wells. My parents' misery is ever-present, an eerie background music. The ultimate end of it all mocks every act. Life has sprung a leak, an emotional hemorrhage. At times, the world seems somehow less than physical—even virtual, a projection of cyber-manipulated images that dissolve as the abyss opens again.

In order to continue teaching high school—a job never easy—I encase myself in a sort of armor. Though my soul is on a sojourn in the underworld, I bury grief beneath layers of work or escape into TV's fantasy at home. And that effort blocks all replenishment. Again, that nerve on the left side of my face has begun twitching, continually, like a downed power line sparking in the dust. Not the ideal way to meet teenagers, though out of kindness, inattention, or embarrassment, they don't mention it.

According to medical reformer and educator Dr. Rachel Naomi Remen:

> The expectation that we can be immersed in suffering and loss daily and not be touched by it is as unrealistic as expecting to be able to walk through water without getting wet. This sort of denial is no small matter. The way we deal with loss shapes our capacity to be present to life more than anything else. The way we protect ourselves from loss may be the way in which we distance ourselves from life....
>
> We burn out not because we don't care but because we don't grieve. We burn out because we've allowed our hearts to become so filled with loss that we have no room left to care.

At home, the twitch interferes with meditation, my long-practiced discipline. It destroys sleep. And yet, ragged from fatigue, I tell Joe, "A crack in the armor could let me spill out over the floor."

"You have to have faith."

"Faith?"

"That you *won't* spill out over the floor."

Without armor, facing not only grief but students seems impossible until a voice in a dream says, *Go soft and open. We are all one.* Hoping desperately to relax and focus on the kids, be really present for them, my litany becomes, *This is my practice. These are my children. I have nothing to fear but fear itself. Go soft and open. We are all one.*

Without armor, I try to embrace my parents *as they are* and to savor this bittersweetness. Perhaps we do not die from sorrow if we let tears flow. If we let ourselves soften and swell, and our hearts open.

A few weeks later, Ginger teases Dad. "What are you going to be on Halloween?"

He grimaces, gestures toward his ravaged face. "Isn't this scary enough?"

℘

FOR THANKSGIVING, the Pearson family gathers again at Karen's home. Mom and Dad sit isolated in their island of forgetfulness as the rest of us chat. Clearly threatened by the state of his older brother, and talking a little too loudly, Bob announces, "I prefer death to the sort of life Lois and Ralph have. I don't want to decline and not be able to walk—and become forgetful."

"But you're doing so well," I argue. No one must mention he's eighty-six. For years, he's archly claimed to be "just twenty-three." Until today.

"At my age," he continues bitterly, "Ralph was still driving and just a *little* forgetful."

I try to shush him.

"Oh, *they* can't hear me."

Dad, even with hearing aids, is somewhat deaf, but Mama is not. Still, she gives no sign of hearing him.

Karen invited friends to our Thanksgiving party, a couple with newborn triplets. Everyone is charmed, especially Bob. Once he has taken a sleeping baby tenderly into his arms, his brittle shell melts. Our albums carry snapshots of Bob, who never married, beaming at the baby face of every child in the family.

Gazing longingly at the two of them, Mama asks, "Dad, do you think I could still have a baby?"

"Oh, they're so much trouble," he grumbles. "Way too much work."

"Mama, none of your *daughters* could still have a baby."

When no one responds to this bit of reality, I allow a crack to open in my armor so Mama's dream can slip in.

"It would be a miracle."

☙

Santa Lucia Again

December 1999

A S WE DECORATE THE LITTLE ARTIFICIAL TREE in Mom and Dad's room, I hand Mama a sequin-encrusted felt Christmas stocking. She loves it but cannot believe she made it. It is the same with the little wreaths studded with cut-up costume jewelry, the bells made from plastic communion cups.

"Oh, every Christmas," Dad says, "the dining room table would be full of ornaments Mama was making."

And then memory hits him like a hammer. Clutching his heart, he gasps, "It all came back, the life we had—"

Mouthed platitudes don't comfort him. He knows all of it is lost: Rushing off after supper to play softball with the church league, sitting down to a Sunday roast beef dinner, cutting grass in his raincoat and goofy pith helmet hung with mosquito netting, hitting two holes-in-one, talking late with Mama after the kids are in bed.

For Dad, forgetting may lessen the pain of loss, but his daughters want to hold on to the life we had. Though our parents can participate only marginally, we continue our family rituals. Shortly before Christmas, we bring Mom and Dad to Jan's to stay overnight so Saint Lucia can visit them in the morning.

When Ginger and her kids arrive at 9:30, our parents are still asleep. Wearing a white nightgown with scarlet sash and lit by the candle glow of her electric crown, Alia enters their darkened bedroom with her tray of coffee and kringler. Mama starts awake to strange music, punctuated by whirring clicks and blinding flashes of light. She blinks in fear and bewilderment, her bed surrounded by shadowy forms, their smiling faces flaring, then disappearing in the darkness, to flare again.

"Ralph?" she calls, and his arm automatically reaches out to calm her.

Mama always delighted in this lovely surprise and had been Lucia herself for Honeybun. But now, she doesn't seem to see Alia's face.

We put the cameras away, open the blinds on a gray morning, and pour coffee, serve kringler. Gradually, Mama relaxes. And Dad laughs a bit.

This scene and the recent news that Honeybun lies in a coma throw a pall over our Christmas plans. We choose not to tell Mama about her dearest cousin at this time and stick to our traditions instead. Even manage a little grim humor.

"I leaned the Christmas tree against the window, stuck in a soup pot," Jan tells Ginger. "Do you think anybody will care if I leave it that way? I haven't baked any cookies yet. And I went Christmas shopping, but all I bought was a present for myself."

"Scrooge!" Ginger laughs. "You are going to be visited by three ghosts!"

&

A Christmas to Remember

Even memory is not necessary for love. There is a land of the living and a land of the dead and the bridge is love, the only survival, the only meaning.

—THORNTON WILDER, *The Bridge of San Luis Rey*

December 1999

"THIS HAS BEEN A CHRISTMAS TO REMEMBER," Dad announces. But it isn't Christmas. We have just returned from Alia's twelfth birthday on the winter solstice. Earlier that evening, when Joe and I arrive at the nursing home, Mama waits in her pink vinyl wingchair, dressed and eager to go.

"We don't ever go out, you know."

"Well, not often enough, I'm sure, Mama, but every weekend one of your daughters takes you out."

"No, that can't be true."

"But Mama, I was here four days ago. And last weekend you were at Ginger's. And the one before at Jan's."

Her eyes squeeze closed behind her glasses. "What's the matter with me that I can't remember *that*?"

In order to convince her we love her and visit her, we'd have to convince her she's lost her mind. We usually try not to argue against her truth—loneliness, boredom, isolation, debility, memory loss.

"A friend of ours, I forget who, said to his wife, 'I've seen you working around here. What is your name?'" Dad says, shaking his head uneasily. "Isn't that terrible? To get like *that*—"

Though repeated over the years, details of this story have dropped away.

Mama's face crumples. "I'd probably be the one to forget Daddo's name."

In the corner, amid a clutter of cards from unremembered friends, an abandoned poinsettia is dying.

Mama struggles into the coat Dad holds and croons about how happy she is to be going out. But as we trudge down the hall, dodging the wheelchair hazards, she doesn't sing out her usual, "We're going out! *Out!* Oh, goody-goody!" accompanied by a raised fist. She makes a cat snarl at no one in particular and then pauses to lift a hand from her walker in a good-bye wave to Dolores, their kind nurse. Near the elevator, which is imperfectly disguised by its fence of orange polyester straps, Bing Crosby sings from a neglected TV:

> *Through the years we all will be together, if the fates allow.*
> *Hang a shining star upon the highest bough,*
> *And have yourself a merry little Christmas now.*

❧

DAD HOLDS THE DOOR AS WE HELP MAMA climb the few steps into Ginger's fragrant kitchen. Joe, ever gentle and solicitous, supports her from behind. I go up backward, holding both her hands.

"Okay, now step up again."

She carefully lifts one foot to the next step and then the other.

"Did you ever think I would get this way?" she sighs, and recovers her smile.

We maneuver around the furniture, then install her on the couch in front of the fireplace and a glittering Christmas tree. The room is soft, glowing. Crystal, silver, and cut glass sparkle on the table. Just as in our childhood, electric candles on the windowsills push back the darkness outside.

Ginger and Alia are still dressing, but as soon as Dad sits down next to Mama, seven-year-old Ian cuddles up between them to explain the intricacies of his new monster Transformer. Dad softens and relaxes. Mama beams in contentment and, when Ginger's needy golden retriever slaps a paw into her lap, responds with tentative pats, baby talk, and little air kisses.

Atop a bookcase, stately and serene terra cotta goddesses exhibit the stages of motherhood—birthing with legs spread wide, breastfeeding tiny infants, bearing older children on their backs. Ginger not only home schools her kids but volunteers as a La Leche League counselor out of a primal and deeply spiritual connection to motherhood.

With a quick hello, Ned bustles in to add an armload of wood to the fire, then rushes off to the kitchen to mix Brandy Manhattans for Mom and Dad. As the fire blazes up alarmingly, Ginger sails in, a bit stressed but welcoming in her slim black dress.

"You're early! And I'm late!" she laughs, kissing everyone around the circle and rushing off to put the finishing touches on Alia's birthday meal.

Joe gazes at the fire, content in his thoughts. Now and then, to make conversation, he asks Dad about his long-ago hockey or softball prowess, and Dad warms to telling his stories. When Jan arrives with her pink peppermint "mile-high" birthday cake, Alia comes running. Blond and willowy, she giggles, then swipes a finger through a swirl of frosting and pops it into her mouth. Mama created an instant tradition when she baked this cake for Alia's second birthday.

"Did you make my favorite meatballs, too?" Alia asks, bouncing on her toes.

"Of course!"

Like another mother to Ginger's kids, Jan always finds ways to enhance their special occasions. She is essential. When Alia was little, she asked a friend, "Who is *your* Aunt Jan?"

∽

AS THE PARTY ENDS, DAD MUTTERS, "Well, back to another week of nothing."

And Mama looks hard into my eyes as she slowly pronounces each word: "I don't want to go back there."

"Oh, Mama, I wish you didn't have to go there, but you need more care than any of us can give you."

She presses her lips tightly together and says nothing.

Back at the nursing home, Dad shuffles after Mama like a ghost. He carries her walker to the door, takes off his hat in the elevator. At intervals, Mama can't see him and calls out, "Ralph?"

"I'm here, Lois," he says each time, patting her shoulder.

As we move down the long hall to their rooms, Mama says, "This is a nice place, and the people are nice, but they're not our own."

The heartbreak in that statement takes away my breath. But they are together in this "nice place," I tell myself again, with every physical thing they need. They sleep in their own marriage bed. They love each other and their family. They enjoy our gatherings and any chance to get out. And even though they never remember anything we do with them, it could be worse.

"You're one of the faithful ones," a resident told Jan. "I see you here often." Jan doesn't feel like a faithful one, but of course she is. We all are. After our good-byes, I stop at the nurses' station to tell Dolores that Ralph and Lois have returned. She is concerned about them.

"They feed off each other," she says. "When one is upset, the other one gets upset, so I separate them sometimes. I let Ralph sit in his chair and read and take Lois to the sunroom."

⁊

THIS SEASON IS HAUNTED by *Christmases Yet to Come*—the specter of my parents' ever-increasing diminishment of function and connection. The ornaments Mama made over the years lie in their boxes. Quickened by memories, too many of them are vampires that thirst for life's blood. Once, in White Bear Lake, Mama was gluing whiskers and google-eyes with wire glasses on to furrowed halves of walnut shells. As usual, I teased her about her crafts. "Oh-oh, what are those?"

"Mouse hats," she hissed.

"What?"

"Mouse hats," she repeated in mock indignation. "And you're going to have them whether you want them or not."

Each mouse had a little hat: lacy caps for grandmas, berets for grandpas. She had attached yarn tails with little bows, then hair clips to hold them to evergreen branches. I do still have them.

Months ago, high in the Tower, Mama told me, "Do what you want to do now." And though it is—and isn't—what I want to do, finally I hang Mama's ornaments on the green and dying branches, mouse hats and all.

⁊

A Right to Mourn

January 2000

MAMA DOESN'T KNOW THAT, in her family, she is now the last member of her generation. Her cousin Honeybun died December 28, and her only brother, Ed, died January 15. Jan plans to tell her because "these deaths are part of what Mama's life has become. She has a right to know, a right to mourn. On some level she can assimilate this knowledge."

Ginger says she bases her decisions on practicality: Does it work? But how can we know if either of these approaches provides a reason for telling Mama? Will she remember or feel pain for a while and then forget?

My decision-making is grounded in pain-avoidance, for Mama and myself. Are we arguing over her right to know or her right to suffer? Nothing is served by telling her of these new losses, I believe. Just as we should medicate for pain and depression, we should protect from excruciating knowledge. I told Jan she may do as she wishes, but I'm not going to be there.

After Jan tells her about Ed, Mama brings it up herself a bit later, saying she wishes she had been able to go to the funeral. The following week, Jan tells Mama about Honeybun and shows her a sweet sympathy card from friends. Mama's lip trembles. She doesn't want her dessert. After a while, Dad tells her to eat it, and she does.

❧

A WOMAN IN A DEVOTED MARRIAGE had a stroke that put her in a nursing home. A few years later, her husband was admitted to a different floor of the same facility. When the woman died, the family decided not to tell her husband for fear grief might kill him. The staff kept the secret for two months, then unknowingly a new nurse offered him condolence for his loss. Though he hadn't seen her for so long a time, he had been waiting for his wife. Two weeks after learning of her death, believing they would be together in heaven, he died.

Much is wrong with the decisions and regulations that separated this loving couple. For maximum efficiency, without regard for human feeling, they were classified according to medical needs that placed them on different floors. But it was literally a matter of life and death. A husband and wife should be free to comfort each other in their final difficult days.

The man's family shielded him from pain they thought he could not bear. Though motivated by love, their decision marginalized him, barred him from sharing his sorrow with people who loved him. Months after the communal coming together of his wife's funeral, he mourned her alone.

Dementia may require a different approach. Other than suffer a few moments and then forget, what can my mother do with the knowledge of her loved ones' deaths? And yet, no simple answer is possible. Jan justifiably questions whether people should be protected from all suffering when she asks, "Was Mama's mourning for her family members one authentic real-life moment, even if forgotten?"

෨

Journal | *Rhinoceros*

April 23, 2000

A NNE SEXTON SAID TEACHING A DIFFICULT CLASS "is kind of like having a love affair with a rhinoceros." I do try to love my ninth graders—but they don't make it easy. The moments of my days at school feel a bit too much like trying to fix my parents. When I told Jan my eighth hour is the class from hell, she quipped, "What are they, exchange students?"

That *does* seem a possibility.

All semester, trying to make the perfect seating chart has been like playing chess with lighted firecrackers. Where to move Ruthie so she won't chatter and mouth off? How, in finite space, to blockade Jonah? And how to keep Arnie away from everybody—and the detention that would bar him from baseball? Is there anyone here who won't pick on Paul for talking to himself? To say nothing of Angie and Brad and Tim— Whatever computer dumped this bunch into the last class of the day had it in for me. And we're reading *Romeo and Juliet*.

On Wednesday, Tammy waves a tattered worksheet. "Can I have a new one? Jonah ate mine."

"It's just nibbled around the edges," I say. "He didn't eat anything essential."

Later, Jonah reads the part of Benvolio. Based on behavioral evidence, that ability had been doubtful. But I am actually able to praise him—which may have damaged his self-esteem. The next day, he refuses to take the part and, with a sudden wrench, splits the book open like a cadaver.

"How old *is* this book?" he sneers.

"All of three years—"

I take the broken paperback out of his hands and give him an old anthology. "So where are we?"

As the class waits for me to find the page, a few hum the *Jeopardy* theme song. After we've read aloud to the point where Romeo is banished for killing Tybalt and Juliet vows death will take her maidenhead, it's time to assign a journal entry: Do you believe in true love?

Jonah doesn't have his notebook, so he snatches a torn triangle of paper from the floor. "I'll use this."

"Here," I say, holding out a clean sheet.

"Oh, I'm not going to write much."

"No, take this. Besides, you might want to eat that other piece."

A few nearby snickers indicate another violation of my personal code.

Today, it's time to counteract the romantic notion of suicide-as-solution. "If anyone in this play had made a smart decision," I tell them, "it wouldn't be a tragedy. It's full of bad choices. Take on the identity of one of the characters—Romeo, Juliet, any of the Montagues or Capulets, the nurse, the prince, the friar—then describe your problem in a letter to *Dear Abby*."

They groan and reach for their folders.

"Ask Abby what you should *do* about it. After that, pretend you're Abby and give your character some good advice."

Jonah's Romeo is a caveman: "Me Romeo. Me bad. Me kill—" And the answer he writes for Abby excoriates him. Jonah seems quite proud of that work. It's almost the only thing he's done this quarter, except fail—gloriously—several vocabulary tests, filling in the blanks with his own outrageous words. Spelled creatively.

Through it all, the left side of my face twitches relentlessly, but Jonah is the only one who mentions it.

"What's the matter with your face?" he blurts, as the class shuffles out into the hall.

"My neck is out, and it puts pressure on the nerve."

"Oh." He scrunches his face to mimic mine, turns on a heel, and scuffs off.

As I leave, late and loaded down with papers, the sky is luminous with cross-hatched brushstrokes, but all I see in them is Jonah's *Dear Abby* letter, smudged with mistakes he might never erase.

⸎

It's Good To Get Out

May 2000

AFTER ONE HELL OF A WEEK, it's a great relief to get out of town and visit my family. Due to stress, or a chiropractic adjustment stress made necessary, shingles had erupted on the back of my skull and neck. I couldn't sleep at all. Outrageous pain left no place to lay my weary head. When the left eye swelled, a doctor prescribed an antiviral drug. For a virus lurking in my body since childhood. The pain, piled on top of grief, guilt, and powerlessness, made me feel as oppressed as Job. The only benefit was missing two days of my class from hell. Does a neck go out because a life is out of alignment? The day before shingles struck, I wrote in my journal, "This grief about Mom and Dad has ripped me open, opened my soul."

⌘

LEAVING THE DEMENTIA-UNIT ELEVATOR, Joe and I walk past Ruthie sleeping in her wheelchair and greet a new woman who stares through us. Then, turning the corner, we see them sitting alone at the far end of the hall: my parents, as blank and empty as the others. I wave. Mama peers at me till Dad cues her. "It's Nancy!"

Her hand fluttering ineffectually at my shoulder, she chokes out, "Oh, this is just so— The thing I— Oh, you don't know how good this is. I was so down, down at the bottom. Oh, thank you."

Long hugs and a cheery act help. But Mom and Dad don't remember Jan visited yesterday—though she signed her name on the guest sheet we hung on their wall. For proof, maybe. What would it be to live every day lost in the fogs of dementia? To passively wait for someone from the real world outside, while staring down that hall into the underworld of the dead?

A wheelchair haunts one wall of their room. Mama glares at it, and Dad explains, "They're using that sometimes now."

When we decide to go for a ride, Joe gestures toward the chair, but Mama will have none of it.

"This is a nice place," she says. "Only thing is, we never get out for a walk. They think we'll run away." As we pass the window, she pauses to gaze at the busy street. "Here is where I stand and look out," she says. "And now I'm *going* out."

Dad shuffles behind Mama as she inches her walker along. On our way out the door, he says, "You might not be able to get us back in."

We drive to the lovely green parkland of Lake of the Isles. It is the same place and the same conversation every time—a Möbius strip rerun of brain connections that still work.

Dad asks what lake it is, and adds, "If it was Phalen, I'd recognize it."

In any weather, Mama exclaims, "Oh, look at that water! I want to get in it. Do we have time?" or "I'd just jump in, if I were free."

So much has changed since the day eight years ago when we all celebrated Father's Day in Litchfield. The plan was for my parents to stay overnight so Dad and Joe could play golf the next day. Dad had given up his club membership because he couldn't afford it, couldn't leave Mama, and was frustrated with his game.

After the others left, we four sat on the front porch to watch a glorious storm. In a poem, Joe caught Mama's hand-clapping delight at the scene:

SO WET

Behind dark front-porch screens,
the four of us sat appreciative as
the afternoon sky blackened
and thunder cracked and
cracked again, then rumbled,
and the windows behind us
trembled and rattled a little, and
with first spatters and sprinkles,
damp-earth smell rose in the air.

"Oh, boy!" said Nancy's mama, Lois,
who always felt herself a fish
out of water and, lacking a lake,
would surely strip and swim
in a puddle or a bucket. "Oh, boy!"
she cried, as a white wall of rain
roared down before us and
deep thunder spoke to our bones.

A wild wind tore at the limbs
of our front yard elms, and lightning
rippled and danced somewhere
above the falling white wall.
And then, then something
strange was coming hard down
our street, two of them, teenage boys,
fully clothed and fully drenched,
racing, laughing, calling to each other
and perhaps to the gods of the storm.

Mama Lois loved them and in sweet
benediction spread her arms wide.

"You can only get so wet!
Only so wet!" she cried.

❧

MAMA LOVES THE WIND, the fresh air and sun. And on this glorious day
at Lake Calhoun, while Dad and Joe wait on the grass, she and I walk along
the shore. She speaks to all the dogs and geese. And while we wait for inline
skaters to whoosh past, she says, "I was like that once and faster than they are.
All these young people, they don't know. They should enjoy it now before
they get old."

To the passing joggers and skaters, she whispers, "Make the messt of it—"
Then, correcting herself, "Make the *most* of it, people."

She is like the parrots in Aldous Huxley's utopian *Island*, trained to wake the inhabitants to the present moment. "Here and now, boys!" they call. "Here and now!"

As we ride on around the lake, Mama sits in the more accessible front seat with Joe. In back with me, Dad talks about roller-skating at the Coliseum "BL— Before Lois."

"Daddo, you did that seventy years ago!"

"How old *am* I?" he asks.

"Ninety."

Dad tells about the old Harley he'd bought for $60, BL, and the tinge of regret he feels because he never opened it up all the way. And about a trip to Canada he almost took with his friend Milo. Every now and then, Mama pats Joe's hand. "Oh, this is so fun! Thank you!"

So that we can continue on down to Lake Harriet, we circle half of Lake Calhoun again. Each time Dad notices gulls on a sandbar and asks what they are. Each time he tells the roller-skating story and the motorcycle story. And asks what lake it is.

"It's so nice of you to come and take us out," Mama keeps saying. "It's good to get out."

When Joe adds, "But then it's good to go home again," Mama is silent.

After we've left my parents in the dementia unit, I complain, "They repeat the same things over and over."

"Yes," Joe says, "but they're good things."

⁓

Purple Hearts

If you want to learn life you must simultaneously learn death.... Look at yourself. You are fading away from moment to moment.... We have to live right in the middle of dangerous situations. If we live in that way life becomes very beautiful.

—DAININ KATAGIRI,
Returning to Silence: Zen Practice in Daily Life

July 2000

DAD SITS ALONE, his chin resting on his chest, when Jan and I visit the nursing home one evening in late July.

"Hi, Daddo," we say, and he snaps awake.

"Nancy! Janny! How good to see you!"

He clings to me and cries the way Mama sometimes does. They've just lowered the antidepressant dose that had made him too lethargic to eat. I sit down in Mama's chair, and Jan pulls up a footstool.

"Where's Mama?" she asks.

"I don't know."

Jan goes into the bedroom where the attendant, who is just putting Mama to bed, gets her up again. Mama is vague. Sitting next to Dad, she lifts her head and squints at the table lamp. With the panic of a diver separated from air supply, she calls out, "Ralph?"

He reaches across and takes her hand. "I'm right here, Lois."

Things are bad. It's hard to be upbeat and cheerful when I want to scream.

Then Dad starts talking about the war. Ever since we moved them to the

Ralph smiles from a bridge overlooking a Luxembourg viaduct;
Ralph with the jeep he named Nancy.

nursing home, they've been comparing it to World War II, the other hardest time of their lives.

"We got through three years of separation during the war. And we can get through this, too," Dad frequently reminds himself.

"I dreamed about the war again," he says, "and I woke up, heart pounding. Still in it." Even with memory loss, the old traumas remain.

"Guys were dying all around me, and I never got a scratch," he tells us, closing his eyes, back there again. "So I never got a Purple Heart."

"They should give Purple Hearts for this place," Jan says.

The nursing home *is* a wound for them, for all of us. Not that the place is bad; what tears at us is our parents' need for it. Dad refers to a story he has told and retold about the war. It shows what he is made of:

> Falmouth, England, was way down toward Land's End. A big naval installation there. The barrage balloons the English had up over the city and the docks hadn't been moved, I bet, since they were put up. The Germans acted like they had a map. They'd come zipping down and go right between them and up again. Strafing as they went.
>
> Antipersonnel bombs would float down to about thirty feet above the ground and then explode. Flying particles all over. I was just plain lucky I didn't get hit. We had no protection at all. We were out in the open, lying in a hedgerow. The bombardment lasted about half an hour, one big hit after another. Planes coming over and strafing and dropping antipersonnel bombs. I finally got fatalistic about it. I thought if something's going to hit me, it isn't going to be in my back. After I'd said the Twenty-third Psalm to comfort myself, I turned over and looked up at the biggest display of fireworks I ever saw. I've never been interested in seeing any fireworks since.
>
> One fella in our group was a braggart—always blowing his top about how good he was. During that air raid, he got so scared he cried like a baby and threw up. He had no inner strength to hold him up, I guess. When it was over and we went back to our billet—which hadn't been hit, luckily—he was deflated. We didn't hear him bragging after that.
>
> The next day, we found out that just a quarter block away from us, eight soldiers had been killed. There was a direct bomb hit on their house. Guys were loading them into an ambulance, and blood was running down the street. Not a very nice thing to remember. Maybe the Twenty-third Psalm brought me through.

Now, in his final years, Dad is mustering the same courage, the same good-humored endurance. Only rarely has he faltered. Once he complained bitterly to Ginger, "I have three daughters, and not one of them will take us into her house."

When Ginger tearfully explained how much she had wanted to do it and how it broke her heart that Mama needed more care than any of us could give, he comforted her—ever the good father.

Thinking Dad might want to read some of his stories or look at the pictures he'd brought home, I pull out the World War II book made last year to celebrate his ninetieth birthday. He takes the book as though he's never seen it, then focuses on one of the cover pictures: himself, in uniform, leaning casually against a bridge railing high above a distant aqueduct. Smiling, handsome, and strong.

"That's Belgium, but was that really me?" he asks. It must seem a different incarnation. Opening the book to a photo of his family—sitting around the kitchen table, smiling, drinks in their hands, before the war, before any of the children were born—he begins naming the dead.

"There's Elmer and Carl and Marguerite. And my mother—" He closes the book and holds it shut with both hands. His breath comes heavily.

"I'll look at it another day," he says.

Why did I think he'd want to look again at images that haunt his dreams, the faces of loved ones lost?

The aide returns to put Mama to bed, explaining, "This is my last job of the shift and then I can leave." In the bedroom, we hug Mama goodnight. Her eyes fill up, and she whimpers, "Thank you, thank you."

As we kiss good-bye, Dad pulls back, looks into my eyes and says, "Appreciate your time."

Thinking he means he appreciates *this time* spent with him, I mumble, "It's my pleasure."

"I mean, appreciate the time you *have*."

He is an oracle speaking from a world where all possibility is lost.

On the walk toward the elevator, I feel young, light on my feet, alive.

Katagiri is right. Life is beautiful *because* it is fading away.

છ

Papa's Visit

GATHERING FAMILY HISTORY IS, among other things, an attempt to connect with the dead. Within a story, lost relatives seem almost to materialize and then—as if caught in a faulty sci-fi starship transporter—disperse. And yet some sense of them remains. One such is my grandfather Paul Pearson, saved by his children's stories from becoming nothing more than a name, a date, a haunted face in old photographs. Dad remembered him with affection and compassion:

> My father came over from Sweden when he was, I think, nineteen, knowing no English. He drove a team for a while. And went to night school. He learned to speak pretty good English. The only trace of accent he had was that the Skåne people roll their Rs like the Scotch. So when he said my name, it was "Rrralph."
>
> My father was supposed to be the disciplinarian in the family and, I mean, it was almost ridiculous. He never *touched* us. He had a razor strap—he shaved with a straight-edge razor, you know. That strap was two leathers, and he would snap it. It would make a lot of noise, and that was supposed to scare us. My father never made much money, but he was jolly and friendly—a very popular man. He worked for A. Peterson & Co., which sold workingmen's clothes. When he got home, all the kids would flock around, and he'd say, "Look in my pocket." He'd always have a little bag of peppermint candies in there. But, you can imagine, with six kids it wasn't easy. I don't think he ever made more than a hundred dollars a month.

In the early twenties, before the Depression, Paul Pearson lost his savings when the Broadway Bank folded.

"In those days, there was no Social Security," Bob, his youngest son, said. "And he lost what little money he had in the bank. The bank went broke and, whatever he had, he lost it."

My dad believed the strain of that financial loss, coupled with the later loss of his job, was "just too much for Papa":

> The company he had worked for was going broke. The poor guy had worked long hours all his life and then had nothing to show for it, except a family that he couldn't support.
>
> One day in 1924, Papa was missing all day long. Then, late in the afternoon, somebody found him on a little railroad bridge out by Wheelock Parkway. Just sitting there. Had sat there all day. And for a long time, he didn't know who he was or anything. At least he made no sign.
>
> He was never the same after that. There was no putting him in a home or a hospital; he just stayed home. I think he came out of it enough so that he knew everybody, but he never thought that any good could happen anymore. He'd look in the kitchen, in the breadbox— There'd be lots of things in there because my two older brothers were working and we were getting along, and he'd say, "No bread in the breadbox."
>
> He'd just— It kind of bothers me to think of it even now.

Sitting beside Dad, listening, Mama added:

> "Well, what bothers you is when you're young, you don't understand all the pressure that life can bring. Later, you wish you had been more understanding and could have helped. And that's the way I feel, too, about *my* dad—"

Bob, who was only twelve at the time of Paul's breakdown, missed a father's attention.

> "My father was very aloof and quiet, and I don't think he liked me very much. I don't *know*, but I know he didn't pay much attention to me. He

wasn't interested in anything I did or said or wanted to do or anything. He just didn't care— Well, it may be that he didn't care about *any*body or *any*thing."

Shortly before his wedding in 1940, Dad discovered his beloved Papa was still present inside the impassive shell he presented to the world. The family was talking about the big day, and as always, Papa was just sitting in his chair, silently reading the paper. Dad's older sister, Marguerite, asked, "Well, Ralph, what are you going to wear on your wedding night?"

When Dad answered, "The tops of my pajamas," his father laughed so long and hard he almost rolled out of his chair!

എ

IN 1944, AFTER YEARS OF SITTING IN SILENCE, Paul Pearson had a stroke that left him paralyzed and unable to speak. Notified while in the service in France, Dad wrote this letter of sad regret:

9 July 1944—England

Darling Lois

All I can think about now is Pop. How good he was to us kids, how hard and faithfully he worked to bring us up in a good way, how quiet and even-tempered and understanding he always was. I write this all in the past tense because from what you told me I figure that there is very little hope of his recovery. I've prayed hard that he would be all right and that I would be able to see him again, but for all I know, being so far away, it may be too late now.

Sometimes this being so far from home and family and so helpless in times of trouble nearly drives me mad. My only comfort at these times is my religion. My faith will bring me thru all right and anything that He wills, I will be able to stand.

I have wonderful memories of my father, all the things he did for us—and always thinking of us first and never of himself. He loved to go fishing and to work in his garden—and what wonderful gardens he had until he had that break-down. Better stop this or I'll break down myself—

Years later, Dad recounted a wartime visit that had comforted him:

I forget the name of that French town; it might have been Laval. We had come into town, and I'd been working nights, long hours and everything, and I got tired and got sick. I was running a temperature, and the group I was with—there were five or six fellas that were handling the RTO duties there—didn't want to lose me, so they took over working my shifts. I had a room with a feather bed. A private room. And they came up and fed me for a few days till I got over this thing.

On October 13, 1944, I was still weak and in the bed. I had been sleeping, and I woke up. My dad, when he woke me in the morning to go to school or to work, he would tweak my toes. And lying there that time, I had the distinct feeling that I'd had my toe tweaked. I looked up, and there was my dad standing there.

"Don't worry, Ralph," he said, "everything's going to be all right."

I don't know. A few days later I got a letter from home telling me that was the day he died. That's the only experience I've had like that, but that was definite. I *know* I was awake.

Dad never doubted his father had stopped to tweak his toe and say good-bye. But Mama carried no such comforting image of *her* father; her bitterness about his suicide continued unabated. During hard economic times, both of their fathers broke down under the pressures of unemployment in a society without a safety net. As a result, my parents experienced heartbreak that darkened their lives. Perhaps fear of breakdown led them to create a secure environment for the family they established together. But whatever the cause, their undying love for each other proved a healing balm for early wounds.

※

A Long, Long Way

July 31, 2000

JAN ASKS UNCLE BOB WHAT HE WANTS to eat for his eighty-eighth birthday party. He drawls, ever suave, "Surprise me."

Once Ginger has delivered him to Jan's living room, Bob sits silently, sipping a gin martini, abstracted perhaps by this milestone in his life. He doesn't speak unless someone asks him what he's reading or when he's going on his next cruise. Once, though, he announces, "There's too much air in this glass," and holds it up for a refill.

At dinner, Bob talks to us but not to our parents. He is clearly appalled at what has happened to Mama and has little in common with Dad. Though they shared a room as boys, Dad's passion was sports and Bob's was theatre, movies, and books. Dad told me he used to dump his hockey gear in the middle of their room just to provoke his younger brother. And Bob, unable to stand the mess, would put it away. Slim and elegant, he holds to his careful no-second-helping regimen that always leaves room for dessert.

Mama fiddles with her spoon and fork, but mostly eats with her hands. I pick food out of her lap as unobtrusively as possible. She doesn't seem to notice.

After the toasts, the cards, the *Happy Birthday* song, and Bob's favorite whipped cream pie, Mama sits alone. I try to get a cat to sit with her, and when it struggles free, lay my head in her lap.

"I'll be your kitty, Mama."

With vague gentle fingers, she pets my hair as she did long ago. My tears wet her knees.

"Nice kitty," she murmurs.

Then, as I lift my head and meet her eyes, her shocked laughter explodes.

Some time earlier, because of Alia's and Ian's fascination with the Harry Potter books, Jan began to read them. When Harry's mother used the power of her love to protect him from the evil wizard even though she, herself, was killed, Jan thought of Mama. She and I know while an evil wizard is slowly killing *our* mother, her love has built a firm foundation that continues to support us from within.

Over and over tonight Mama shows how little she understands who is present and what is happening during her visits. "I love to come here and listen to them talk," she says, "even if I don't know who they are." She makes little signs with her hands and mouths meaningless syllables, "Ya yam ya ya."

"We don't have that where we are," she says. "All the people there have problems."

Within a few hours, she has moved from a despair that whined, "I'm a mess. I'm terrible," to laughter and fascination and the belief that the *other* residents of her ward have problems.

When it's time to take them back, Dad holds my hand tight all the way.

"A few years ago," he says, "I was where Joe is, driving people home. Things change— Now I don't know where I live, we've moved so often." Then he slaps his jacket pocket in alarm. "Here I am without my keys or billfold! 'Course there probably isn't any money in it—"

"You've got everything you need," I tell him.

"When we get there, can we get in?"

"Yes, we'll ring the buzzer, and they'll open the door for us."

As we enter the Hall's circle drive, he asks, "Is *this* where we live? Boy, I'd never be able to find my way home."

Once the elevator shuts behind us and sinks away, we walk down the long empty hall of closed doors.

"It's so quiet here," Dad whispers.

We joke about how funny it would be to come home drunk and singing in this controlled and proper place. And Joe asks, "What would you sing?"

"*It's a Long Way to Tipperary,*" Dad says, and softly we sing that rowdy old song of love and longing, on down the hall to their rooms.

It's a long way to Tipperary,
It's a long way to go.
It's a long way to Tipperary
To the sweetest girl I know...

Unable to remember all the words, we skip to the end of the refrain:

It's a long long way to Tipperary,
But my heart's right there.

☙

What the Heart Demands

> *The process of living itself is a form of violation.... We are born*
> *half-strangled and choking for air, grow up invaded by sickness, are*
> *battered by mortgages, unwanted bills and difficult circumstances as*
> *adults, and in old age must prepare for the ultimate violation and*
> *indignity of the hospital deathbed.*
>
> —DAVID WHYTE, *The Heart Aroused*

August 2000

PERHAPS MOST OF US PRETEND THAT WE, and those we love, will pass unscathed through life. Certainly I've tried to deny the depredations of time. Other people's parents had problems, not mine, who were bedrock: health and stability personified. My parents, long-valued pillars of church and community, were supposed to live to a healthy, clear-minded ninety or so and then wink out. They had to be immune to all that flesh is heir to—slings, arrows, outrageous fortune, the whole bit.

Their waning threatens my own illusory immunity, as well. And stimulates grim one-liners: "If *I* get Alzheimer's, I'll kill myself—*if* I can remember."

"Despite everything you have achieved life refuses to grant you, and always will refuse to grant you, immunity from its difficulties," David Whyte writes.

History and the daily news abound with proof of this truth. And remind us there is no happiness without sorrow, no pleasure without pain. On television, a man with devastating medical problems says, "When all the good things happened to me, I never asked why, so how can I ask why the bad things happen to me?"

It is almost absurd to ask dully, uncomprehendingly, why *me*?

Why *anybody*? Life happens. In part at least, our lives depend upon blind luck.

In grief over the death of a close friend, Jan recently read this: "Anything that can happen to a human being may happen to me, and I accept the truth of this."

"I get this same message from various places," she said. "I guess it is my lesson right now."

And—mine. But I have neither time nor capacity, at present, to adopt a world-view that accepts such vulnerability. Work overwhelms me—lessons and grad standards to prepare for two new classes, one of them advanced. And in just weeks, the school year begins again.

The conflicting demands of work and family become painfully clear at the time of our parents' next care conference: I can't afford the half-day it would take to travel to and from Minneapolis to attend a half-hour conference.

"Why did you say you'd go?" Jan complains. "I could have scheduled my work around it. You should call Ginger. She's angry because she'll have to go alone."

On the phone, Ginger rejects teleconferencing the meeting as unnecessary. "This is important—and it's more the principle of it."

Jan's next email calls for solidarity in our family and describes developments that are the very opposite of what the heart demands:

> *Thought I'd send you an update. I was disappointed and mad because you bagged the care conference, but Nano, there is much more to deal with than hurt feelings. We can't avoid communication. We all need to be in this together. The care conference was awful. Ginger went by herself and there was one difficult question after another. She was in tears telling me about it. The staff wants to switch out their double bed and use two hospital beds because it is difficult to get Mom out of the double bed without disturbing Dad. I think she is also waking him when she needs help. They are losing everything—even sleeping together after 60 years....*
>
> *Mom's care level is between an "E" and an "H" now. She needs more help and Dad tries to help her. The staff says they feed off each other. If one is sad or anxious, so is the other. Mom has been falling fairly often. Once she lost control of her bladder and they found her on the floor—she apparently slipped in the urine. So far, she hasn't been seriously hurt, but they want us to think about contingency plans—what to do if Mom falls and breaks a hip, etc.*
>
> *They are considering moving Mom and Dad to a room closer to the nursing station so they can get more help. A device on Mom sounds when she tries to get*

up out of the chair but it can't be heard from very far. Seems useless to me. They want to keep her mobile as long as possible; they don't want to use a wheelchair.

Dad is depressed and not eating. He doesn't want to go down for meals. He goes back to bed and then Mom does too. They sent him to a doctor who wants to put him on Ritalin, which apparently helps. They also sent him to a psychologist who said his antidepressant dosage should be much higher. I'm not sure where it all is at this point. Gingo has been dealing with the medical stuff—

We have been stopping in to see Mom and Dad—we haven't had them out since Bob's party. (I don't know what we should plan for Dad's birthday.) They haven't asked about going out with us, but talk a lot about escaping.

Dad said, "If it weren't for Mama I would leave. I wouldn't tell anyone where I was going."

"Not even us?" I asked.

"No," he said. "Because you would just put me right back here."

I brought cookies on Tuesday but he only ate one bite. He has to be bad if he doesn't eat cookies. On Friday I stopped at 1:30 in the afternoon and they were sitting in the dark. It was like a tomb. When I went in and turned on a light, Mama seemed to come to life again. Dad seemed better—he at least ate one cookie—but he cries a lot. He likes to hold my hand and get hugs.

When Ginger saw them yesterday, Mom was in bed. Ginger sat on one side and Dad on the other. He was very affectionate—stroking Mom and telling her he loved her. Ginger said they need a love seat; the chairs are too far apart. They didn't want to go eat, but one of the care workers brought their meals to them. Ginger said Mama's breathing was quick and shallow. Other than that they were well.

Sorry for all this bad news, but things are deteriorating. After you have a chance to read it, give me a call. I hope you are planning to come in soon—is it this weekend? I need you. Love, Jano

∽

NOT LONG AFTER, sitting with Dad at Mama's bedside, Jan again witnesses her despair.

"I'm just terrible," Mama moans. "I don't remember anything. How did I get this way?"

Ginger had recently answered that question truthfully.

Dad is sweet and tender. Almost in tears, he strokes Mama's legs and tries to remind her of who she has been and what she has given. "You've done so many wonderful things you couldn't possibly remember them all," he says. "You've forgotten more good things you've done than most people ever do in their whole lives."

Dad believes that and, even at ninety, gives Mama credit for his virtues. "She said I was wonderful so many times I started to believe it," he told me. "If I had a bad thought, I had to wipe it out because I remembered that she thought I was an angel."

Such devotion brings to mind an incident in *Cider with Rosie*, a *Masterpiece Theatre* production based on Laurie Lee's memoir of English rural life after World War I. Together for fifty years, an old couple sit in their cottage holding hands. When authorities decide they can no longer manage on their own, they are brought to the workhouse. Men to the men's side. Women to the women's side. Allowed to see each other twice a month. As they are led away to separate quarters, the two old lovers stare back at each other in dumb anguish. Robbed of their hearts' demand, both die within days.

My parents are together, I tell myself. It could be worse.

&

A Perfect Place

*"I believe that in [nursing homes] in America, really every year,
thousands and thousands of people die of a broken heart."*
—DR. WILLIAM THOMAS,
What Are Old People For? How Elders Will Save the World

August 2000

YEARS AGO, WHEN DAD CALLED JAN AT WORK, he'd ask, "Is this Janet
Pearson, Rising Young Executive?" But now, his pleading, sometimes angry
message on her voicemail is likely to be, "Janny—" There follows a pause with
labored breathing and then: "Can you come here? We need help." After checking with the nurses' station to learn all is well, Jan is left wondering what kind
of help Dad means.

One day, as Jan recalls, Dad phoned her at home and to say again the words
we dread: "I have three daughters, and not one will take me in. I could live in
your house."

"I have to go to work—" she tried to explain, but he hung up, not realizing she
meant that if he lived at her house, she would not be at home during the day to
take care of him. A short time later, he called again, and Jan said, "The last time
you called, you hung up on me, and I can't take that."

"I'm sorry, I don't even remember calling before," he said. "But what use is it
now? All I want is to go for a walk, and they say *no*." (He made that *no* sound
petty and tyrannical.) "I've been free all my life. Now I'm a prisoner here. Why
should I still be alive? Can you buy me poison?"

"Oh, Daddo," Jan replied. "I don't have the power to fix it."

"Well, then you aren't any help. I gave you a roof over your head when you needed one—" Then, ashamed, he moaned, "I'm not *like* this. This isn't *me*. If I wander away, that's where I went—to die. I suppose you want to hang up now, so you'll be free."

"This will bother me all night. I won't be free."

Dad wouldn't remember what he'd said, but his daughters have yet to forget.

Around that time, Mama, too, pushed the phone button that calls Jan. Confused and helpless as Dad crashed around in their room, she pleaded, "Will *you* talk to him?"

At least they have each other isn't enough anymore.

☙

THE ROMAN EMPEROR MARCUS AURELIUS wrote words that in the face of Alzheimer's seem ironic: "Does the light of the lamp shine without losing its splendor until it is extinguished; and shall the truth which is in thee and justice and temperance be extinguished before thy death?"

Sometimes the answer is *yes*.

And the ancient Taoist sage Lao Tzu teaches us "the Way is gained by daily loss, loss upon loss until at last comes rest." But if the mind—which can learn acceptance, resignation, peace, and the concept of the Way—is lost, then the body simply deteriorates in slow animal misery, and the heart rails against even its protectors as keepers of the prison. The safe, humane nursing home becomes a place of torment.

Willing to risk any suffering to escape the Hell of Sartre's *No Exit*, Garcin shouts, "Open the door! Open, blast you!... I'll put up with any torture you impose. Anything, anything would be better than this agony of mind, this creeping pain that gnaws and fumbles and caresses one and never hurts quite enough."

For Garcin, "Hell is other people." His *mind* defines his experience. And only mind can open the doors of Hell. In Milton's *Paradise Lost*, though banished from Heaven, the mutinous Lucifer nevertheless finds sanctuary in his own mind, declaring:

The mind is its own place, and in itself
Can make a Heaven of Hell, a Hell of Heaven.
What matter where, if I be still the same.

But my father is *not* still the same, and he sometimes knows it. He cannot shout:

Hail horrors, hail
Infernal world, and thou profoundest Hell
Receive thy new possessor.

He can, however, rally a couple of old guys and try to break out.

"Lois is waiting for you." That simple sentence is enough to foil his escape. Mama is the bait in the trap, their love the tie that binds.

❦

A NINETY-YEAR-OLD FRIEND of ours sends a cry of distress from a nursing home in Colorado he calls "the Twilight Zone, America's Medical Gulag for Old-Age Cases." He writes he is "trapped in this hellhole" because his daughter wants him "warehoused," even though "the *Gauleiter* here says he agrees I am too intelligent to stay among the patients, many demented with heads horizontal on one shoulder." Use of the term *gauleiter*, the Nazi title for governor, reveals despair that turns to hope by the end of his letter. He's been told he may be released to a better place and "later maybe freed to Sweden," where he'd lived for years among friends. He never answers my responding letter. Months later, I learn death has freed him.

Dwelling with strangers who are so obviously mentally disabled is a major source of distress for my parents as well. Looking with horror into blank faces that become mirrors of his own, Dad asks incredulously, "Are we *that bad*?"

And Mama cries, "I can't stay here, I'll die! These people don't know who they are."

When she says, "I want to go home," the staff says, "*This* is your home."

But my father insists, "No, this is just a place to stay."

The dementia unit is set up for physical care and efficiency according to well-defined and legislated practices. It has all the necessary facilities and a staff that genuinely cares for the residents. They do their best to create a nurturing environment with plants and pets and activities, but the *system* is wrong. Good nursing homes everywhere humor, palliate, baby, and, especially, control their residents. Even Dad's Brandy Manhattan must be approved, poured from a bottle kept in the nurses' station and administered like medicine.

My father's rebellion arises from his confrontation with the sterility and meaninglessness of this long-term care existence. He has lost *himself.* Life has been reduced to waiting while his body uses up its reservoir of health, waiting while his genetic clock—which has betrayed him by grinding on inexorably—runs out of time.

By equating old age with illness and "medicalizing" it, our society all too often compels people "for purely economic and political reasons, to live out their lives within the sick role, tended to in medical facilities," writes reform advocate Dr. William H. Thomas. When my parents entered long-term care in the Tower, they were forgetful, not sick. But moving, itself, contributed to their disorientation. Intimidated by the vastness and impersonality of that place, Mama cried and stripped off her clothes rather than go to meals in a dining room full of strangers.

Her inability to adjust forced their move to the dementia unit, a lifestyle as unnatural and sterile as the sealed biosphere of the "boy in the bubble." Born with no immune system, he lived his brief, unhappy life touched only by gloved hands that reached to feed and care for him. A nursing home—or any institutional world—may feel as remote as a space station circling out beyond the atmosphere of the human earth.

In order to endure the dementia unit, my parents have to be drugged. They are given the antidepressant Paxil—an artificial cure for an iatrogenic affliction.

಄

IN AUGUST 1998, WHEN MOM AND DAD still lived in the Tower, our family took them swimming in little Lake Manuella near our home in Litchfield. Delighted, Mama said, "Dad, when we go back, let's live by the water."

Regretting he'd never been able to give Mama such a place, Dad talked about living in a small town with a lake for Mama and a golf course for him. "Not *necessarily* Litchfield," he added. That night I wrote in my journal:

If I could design the perfect place for them, it would be a nursing home by a lake with a golf course nearby. They'd have their own large bedroom with chairs and TV. There'd be a dining room for all residents, a living room, a porch and deck, an exercise room, walking paths and gardens. There'd be about ten or twelve people in the place. It would be like a large family. They'd have cats or dogs, music and tai chi. Instead they're locked in the Tower. (Rapunzel, Rapunzel, let down your long hair....)

Such places did in fact exist, but they were neither near at hand nor affordable. In recent years, however, a movement to humanize elder care is taking shape in this country. Clearly built on a social rather than medical model, a growing number of alternatives to standard nursing homes base long-term care on the idea elders will thrive in *family-sized* houses.

The Green House Project in Tupelo, Mississippi, for instance, emphasizes "autonomy, dignity, and choice." Its design makes central the ancient pleasures of smelling good food cooking and sharing meals with known individuals around a family-sized table. Residents determine their own daily routine, menu, and activities. They can volunteer for chores that help keep the household running. Not surprisingly, residents report more dignity, privacy, meaningful activity, relationships, and autonomy. Significantly, they also show less depression, incontinence, and decline in their ability to feed themselves.

With support from nurses and therapists, nurses' aides manage these facilities. In their daily work, they "blend the roles of caregiver, homemaker and friend." By streamlining jobs and shifting resources, "green houses" cost no more than nursing home care. They accept Medicaid for low-income residents. Fundamentally, these homes recognize and try to meet the emotional needs of human beings. As William Thomas, founder of the movement, says, "In long-term care love matters and institutions can't love."

The Green House movement is expanding. In 2008, the Leonard Florence Center for Living in Chelsea, Massachusetts, received funds to construct ten houses of ten-bedroom units each. Barry Berman, executive director of the Chelsea Jewish Nursing Home, said this project "will create an important, new compassionate model for how we deal with our frailest elders and those with serious life-changing illnesses.... We want to celebrate elderhood, instead of having people dying of a broken spirit."

St. Mary's Hospital in County Monaghan, Ireland, carries autonomy and choice a step further. They've found a unique way to prevent residents from being literally "bored to death": a licensed pub on the premises. There, according to Assistant Director of Nursing Rose Mooney, patients "just love the crack of the banter and people in and out." Bar staff monitor how much liquor they serve.

"We shouldn't allow [social life] to just stop dead when people come into a care setting," Mooney says. "If enjoying life for older people means having a half and a whiskey or a small brandy, well, that's what they should be entitled to. Many's the good night has been had—and day—in the bar, let me tell you."

When most men and women work outside the home, we shouldn't be forced to choose between home care and institutions that apply a medical model to our elders' daily lives. No setting can solve all problems of old age, but surely our elder care can be "nearer to the heart's desire." Home-like natural affections and pleasures that make life worth living must replace the controls and restrictions that imprison and infantilize. Old age is not an illness; it is a stage of life. It is the future toward which we all are moving.

❧

Valley of the Shadow

September 2, 2000

D AD IS BRIGHT AND CHEERFUL WHEN WE ARRIVE. "Oh, it's Nancy and Joe!" he calls out to let Mama know what's happening. The staff has gotten them dressed up for Dad's ninety-first birthday party at Jan's. Mama is wearing her teal pants suit and lipstick, and Dad looks nice, though his whiskers bristle. This is the first time we've used the wheelchair for Mama. She accepts it without comment.

At the elevator, the woman who hummed the blues for us the day after Mom and Dad moved in anxiously clutches her hands together. She meets our eyes, pleading in garbled syllables. We consider looking for one of the scarce weekend staff members, but she doesn't seem in danger.

"I'm sorry, I can't understand you," I say, patting her bony shoulder. When the elevator opens, Joe wheels Mama inside. We let the door close on the woman's anguish and drop away into our own.

At Jan's, Joe maneuvers Mama's chair to the foot of the front steps where, with help, she will have to climb to the door. I step up backwards, pulling the walker she holds; Joe follows behind to keep her from falling.

"Okay, now step up. Great! Now step up again."

At the fifth step, dismayed, clearly exhausted, she sighs, "Again?" And there is one more yet to go. Each such trial seems epic, as we focus on the moment, the task at hand. Inside, we guide Mama across the living room and help her sink into a chair. While Jan finishes putting the meal together, I make Dad the stiff Brandy Manhattan he's waiting for and bring Mama juice in a glass too heavy for her to hold. After pouring her a smaller one, I catch one of Jan's cats for Mama's lap. It soon struggles free.

In a while, David and ReNae—who are almost relatives—arrive, then Ginger, Ned, and the kids, and the room fills with cheerful talk. Everyone wishes Dad a happy ninety-first. When he shakes the ice cubes in his empty glass, I pour him another drink. It is, after all, his birthday.

Mama can't bring a triangular corn chip to her mouth and must be fed a bite at a time. Although she usually watches our parties with bemused delight, she suddenly comes alert and announces, "I'm no good for anything."

"But, Mama, you were *wonderful!*" I say. "You made cakes and fudge for everybody. Do you remember when you asked Uncle Martin whether he wanted a chocolate cake with white frosting or a white cake with chocolate frosting? He said, 'Yes,' so you made him a 'Yes Cake'! Half of each!"

She stares at me, showing no sign of recognition.

"And back in the seventies, Mama? You got a Phalen Area Good Citizen Award for doing their newsletter and volunteering for any number of community projects. They had to practically close down the East Side when you moved to California! You were a great wife to Daddo and a wonderful mother to us girls and the world's best grandmother to Alia and Ian."

"Really?" she says, sadly. "I don't remember any of that."

"But *I* do, Mama. I do."

Around my parents, performance mode works best—telling stories, joking around. And that may be why so many nursing home workers take on that perky quality. To fight off the despair and sorrow of the residents. And their own.

"Something happened to me today," Mama moans.

Her nine-year decline happened just *today!* Surely, she noticed the past tense of my catalog of her good works and achievements. The woman who did those things is as good as dead. Only an impulse to give and a desperate sense of uselessness remain.

"I want to go home," she whispers.

Dinner is almost ready, and her absence would spoil Dad's party.

"Why don't you just lie down for a while? That'll make you feel better."

In bed, rubbed and patted, she relaxes into sleep. Two glasses of wine don't blur my recognition of this ending. Hiding in another room, I can't stop crying.

The table holds Jan's striking arrangement of red and pink roses, and the buffet is loaded with Dad's favorite foods: Swedish meatballs, horseradish mashed potatoes, green beans, salad, corn cut off the cob for his fragile teeth. Dad is tipsy and unsteady, and I did it to him. He's quiet and doesn't eat much. And doesn't ask for Mama.

Returning with a plate to the dark bedroom where Mama lies still—her forehead cool and damp, her breathing labored—I try too hard to sound cheerful. "Mama, here's some of Jan's good meatballs, Auntie Marguerite's recipe."

"I don't think I can eat," she murmurs.

"Well, try a little. It's really good, you know."

She slowly chews one meatball, one bite of a roll, but spits out the mashed potatoes. Her eyelids droop into sleep.

At the table, Ginger sets down a gorgeous apple torte with four flaring candles, and the singing begins. Our family always harmonizes the *Happy Birthday* song and howls like wolves after each line. No one remembers how it started, but wine helps. It could be the voice of the death that each birthday moves us toward, a cry of existential anguish, or just a lupine comment on the quality of our singing. This time, the group's howling is not wholehearted—but mine is. At my great yowl, the others give me strange looks.

Dad has to blow four times to extinguish his candles. As he struggles to open packages, he doesn't seem to recognize the truffles as candy and sets the mystery novel aside. He still reads at night after Mama goes to bed. But once when we visited, he laughed and said, "I only need one book." Then, with a quick gesture—as if wiping words from his brain—added, "It just goes shoooop!"

He hugs Jan's bottle of mixed Brandy Manhattans as if it's a lost friend. And when he sees her big container of oatmeal raisin cookies, as always, he purrs, "Oooh, coo-kies!"

Cheerful, loving, and sweet, Dad seems unaware of Mama's absence and expresses none of the anger and depression of a few weeks ago. The increased dose of antidepressant is doing its work. When it's time to go, we begin our strange parade down the steps: Joe on one side of Mama, David on the other. I follow supporting her from behind. Once Mama is safely seated in the wheelchair, David pulls it backward to the curb, where we lift her into the car. As we drive back to the Hall, Mama says, "That was a nice time."

"It was a good weekend," Dad says. "But now it's over."

The party did seem long, but it lasted only four hours.

Once we are back in their room, Dolores, who has come to put them to bed, asks brightly, "How did the birthday party go?"

"Not well," I mutter, grateful for the understanding in her eyes.

Pulling Dad's presents from their carrying bag, I give him my card again. Its first page holds the Twenty-third Psalm that has been his comfort for so long.

"That protected me from the bombs. Made them miss me," he says. His arms rise in a shield over his head. As he begins to read, Dolores stops preparing the meds to listen. Dad's voice is the only thing in the world.

> *The LORD is my shepherd; I shall not want.*
> *He maketh me to lie down in green pastures:*
> *he leadeth me beside the still waters.*
> *He restoreth my soul:*

Mama looks up, connects. We are all transfixed.

> *He leadeth me in paths of righteousness for His name's sake.*
> *Yea, though I walk through the valley of the shadow of death,*
> *I will fear no evil: for thou art with me;*
> *thy rod and thy staff, they comfort me.*

Dad closes his eyes and continues, reciting now from memory. His voice is sure. The anxiety and grief of the day retreat to the far corners of the room.

> *Thou preparest a table before me in the presence of mine enemies:*
> *thou anointest my head with oil; my cup runneth over.*
> *Surely goodness and mercy shall follow me all the days of my life:*
> *and I will dwell in the house of the LORD forever.*

⁕

JAN AND I WONDER whether we can take Mama out anymore. Our thoughts of the coming holidays are filled with dread.

"With Mama's shallow breathing and swollen ankles, her heart must be weak," Jan observes. "Maybe she won't be alive at Christmas."

"We, and she, won't be that lucky," I whisper.

The vital, focused Mama of past years flashes into mind, then vanishes, leaving such emptiness. My face contorts, and my fists clench in the primal, inborn fear response to falling. The primate baby swings under the mother's belly, clutching her hair, close to her milk. The newborn human, briefly able to hang by tiny hands, instinctively arches its spine when threatened with falling. And I am falling away from my mother, my father, clinging to them even as they slip my grasp.

We sisters have been trying to keep normal family life intact—birthday parties, Christmas plans—when Mama is dying. We have to let go of our traditions and focus on *what is really happening*. Mama is precious and lost, and nothing can fix her but death. My mind knows she should die now. It would be better for her, for everybody. Yet my heart cries, *I want my mama*. That ineffectual hand fluttering at my sleeve, patting me from depths of confusion and despair, is all that is left of her.

I must let this passing be what it *is*.

◈

Journal | *Efficiency*

September 17, 2000

Two mornings in a row, I wake in a struggle with nature, trying to improve on nature. The dreams are forgotten, except for a vague sense that trying to stave off my parents' inevitable dissolution is opposing the very way of the world. I have been blaming nature for their decline. The slow deterioration of their bodies and minds seems such senseless cruelty. But nature didn't cause it. Nature knows an easier way out. In spite of medicine's ancient vow to "do no harm," we, in our pity and kindness, have perfected a slow and continuing torture, ensuring the victim lives on until the body totally breaks down. Even then, unless specifically refused, machines breathe, pump blood, drip nourishment in, and drain it out again. It feels just too close to the bizarre sequence in *Catch-22*, in which nurses remove the urine bag from a mummy-wrapped patient, hang it on an IV stand, stick a tube into a vein in that same patient's arm, and run it all back through again. *A perfect system.*

In accordance with our parents' wishes, my sisters and I signed their DO NOT RESUSCITATE, DO NOT INTUBATE FORMS. But the big DNR codes on the spines of their ring binders in the nurses' office prevent only heroic measures. Meanwhile, we're *protecting* Mama till there's nothing left of her mind, her dignity, and sense of self. Just a quivering, helpless shell, ashamed and constantly apologizing for her uselessness. Yet, how can we let her go?

The forgetfulness of Alzheimer's once seemed to me like the flaccidity of prey species that, shocked in the teeth of a predator, go limp and appear not to feel pain or to struggle against their fate. But even drugged, Mama struggles and suffers. And now the staff tells us that as soon as another woman dies, we should move Mama into a total-care room. If she falls or has an emergency that puts her in the hospital, they argue, such a room might be unavailable. The staff is just planning ahead, and yet I'm unable to suppress an uncharitable paranoia: It all seems too efficient, almost a *disassembly* line—

They want to move Mama before a crisis occurs, but this act of prevention could precipitate one. Dad is Mama's one remaining anchor to the world. "Where's Ralph?" she calls out, even when he's sitting next to her.

And he equally often declares, "The one thing that keeps me alive is taking care of Mama."

JOURNAL | *Question*

September 23, 2000

JUST BEFORE LUNCH HOUR YESTERDAY, his eyes lit with mischief, Alec announces, "Mrs. Paddock, have you ever thought that you carry in your body about a pound of poo?"

Outrageous! The class explodes. And Alec sits there delighted in his tacky 1950s sport coat, just waiting to see what the teacher will do with that one.

This teacher laughs, and her face goes into spasm.

Such weird energy must not be encouraged—or squashed. Somehow I manage to keep from saying, *Well, you are certainly full of it.* After all, who's the adult here?

The need to control what cannot be controlled—whether it's my students' behavior or my parents' inexorable decline—creates a tension that repeatedly squeezes my vertebrae out of place. The chiropractor realigns my neck but can't realign my life. It's humiliating to stand in front of yet another five classes, face contorted, trying to ignore the obvious. And it provides some small insight into what Mama must feel as her mind and her body betray her.

℘

A ROOM HAS OPENED IN THE TOTAL-CARE WARD on the north end of the floor. And Mama has been reclassified as an "I," which means she needs more care than the dementia unit can give her. The staff says it's our decision, but they'll hold that room only so long. Jan calls other nursing homes, but finds no good option. Besides, we know these people and believe they are trying to do the right thing.

When Jan and Ginger talk to Dad, he is very reasonable about the move, saying, "Whatever Mama needs."

For some time, he's been telling us, "Mama needs total care." He knows he can't help her enough. Once, we found the two of them squeezed into their tiny bathroom: he impatient and ineffectual, telling her what to do, she distraught and unable to comply. Tired and miserable, Mama frequently goes to bed early, while Dad stays up late to read. When a morning staff member comes to dress Mama and take her to breakfast, Dad stays in bed. Is he trying to avoid the tedium and strain of her constant calling for him, the pain of watching her deteriorate, the strange loneliness of sitting next to her absent presence?

Dad won't remember this talk of moving Mama. And though it could be a relief for him, what will it be for her? Alone and abandoned, she won't understand, no matter how many times we try to explain. But what else can we do? Medical Assistance has rules ensuring patients receive the level of care they need. Mama needs more than the dementia unit can give her; therefore, she must move. That logic is unassailable—and totally impossible to bear. We will move Mama on Monday at 1:00. All of my attention is poised on that fault line. Driving around town, I twice quelled an impulse to swerve into oncoming traffic. To avoid Monday.

But we must focus on what is important now—care at the right level, medication for anxiety, loving visits, letting this anguish be what it *is*. Let go of the double room. Let go of their marriage bed. Let go of their being together, even though our mantra since moving them to the nursing home has been "at least they still have each other."

Do not grasp at the hope of an easy release—

Loss after loss until at last comes rest.

Alzheimer's happens! Learn its lessons. And try to be alive in the present—even as the vast, well-intentioned machine we sensed when Mom and Dad entered the system grinds on.

෪

D-Day

September 2000

WHEN MY FRENCH FRIEND Nicole and I were talking about our parents' lives during the build-up to World War II, hers in France and Algeria, mine in St. Paul, I said, "I was conceived in fear because my dad was going to be drafted."

"No!" she protested. "You were conceived in passion, in a love that wanted to be together and to have a child of that love."

Nicole is right. Nevertheless, my parents' great love increased their fear that world events would soon force them apart.

Dad was Class A, but he'd been put on call after hay fever made him fail his physical. On-call status kept him from taking a better job. With a salary frozen below a living wage and the ubiquitous pressures of recruitment—such as posters in which a son asks, DADDY, WHAT DID YOU DO IN THE GREAT WAR?—he enlisted. Telling their story, Mom and Dad make clear their years apart were not only a time of longing and fear but a test that confirmed their love:

> "In 1943, when I went out to Fort Snelling to enlist," Dad said, "it was my birthday. My thirty-fourth birthday. 'Cause I remember there was a fella named Youngquist asking me questions and typing in the answers. And when I said my birthday is 1909 and September 2, he looked at me and said, 'This is a hell of a way to celebrate your birthday.'"
>
> "A few weeks later," Mama recalled, "I took him out to Fort Snelling and cried all the way home. On my new coat. I had makeup on, and the makeup ran down." She closed her eyes to see it all again. "I never got it out—the coat was light green, I think. And I don't know how I got home without having an accident, because I cried so hard."

"When we got to Europe in April of '44," Dad explained, "we went in through Liverpool and then down to Bristol. There we learned our duties. We were Regulating Traffic Officers, whether we had any rank or not. We had red-and-white armbands, RTO, and we learned all about the D-Day invasion. *All* about it. Everything except the date. For ten days or two weeks, we went to school all day long. And then we were quarantined. Couldn't go anywhere. We couldn't even talk to anybody." His hands clenched and unclenched in his lap.

"Our letters were censored. And then a month before the invasion, they stopped all our mail. We wrote, we kept on writing, nobody told *us*." He breathed in deeply, then pressed Mama's hand. "I'd get letters from Lois that would say: 'I haven't had a letter for a week.' 'I haven't had a letter for two weeks.' 'For a whole month.' She didn't get a letter until after D-Day."

"There was one time when I had no mail for thirty-one days," Mama said, and her jaw tightened. "And then one morning, I heard a radio voice telling about D-Day. He said American soldiers were in France, and my heart just sank. I thought, maybe he's dead. And I looked outside and saw Charles, who was the son of the old couple next door. He was deferred because he was their only means of support, and he was out there swinging a golf club." She sighed. "He was a nice fellow. And his mother was so nice to me. But here my world had just crashed down—and he was swinging a golf club.

"That January, Ralph's cousin Johnny, a co-pilot in a bomber squadron, had been shot down. I was as bad as Johnny's mother wondering why Daddy had to be the one to go." She leaned her head against Dad's shoulder, then stretched up to kiss his neck.

"I hated it when the actual D-Day did come. June 6th," Dad said. Then, grim-faced, he told the rest. "All that night we were loading men and equipment on the boats down in the harbor. And I was calling the roll. That was one of the worst things I ever did—call the roll for the amphibious engineers going on the boats." He winced, staring off across the years.

"Over half of them didn't come back. They went in first. I was calling off their names. Some of those guys were green in the face. I don't blame them. They had to go in ahead of everything and cut barbed wire, get rid of the mines— Amphibious engineers, they called them and, boy, what they really were was a suicide squad."

Once the mail finally came through, Mama got a pile of letters, including one written just two days after D-Day:

June 8, 1944—England

Darling

You'll have to excuse me for not writing the last two days. I've been pretty busy. I suppose there was a big celebration over there a couple of days ago and I hope and pray that it continues to be something to celebrate over. Maybe we'll be together again sooner than we expect. I hope so. Don't ask me to choose between the two pictures, they're both wonderful. Certainly am happy to have them, but oh how it makes me long to see you and hold you in my arms again. After this I'm never going to let you out of my sight, if possible....

Years later, Dad carefully understated his vivid memories of the aftermath of the invasion:

> After D-Day, there were about twenty of us waiting at the Hillsea barracks in Portsmouth to be put on a boat for France. And as we were waiting, we worked on salvage coming back from the invasion. And that stuff told a lot of stories. Life vests with holes in them, blood, and all that kind of thing. That was—a sad experience.

In a letter of the time, he said nothing of that work.

June 13, 1944—England

Last Saturday nite I was down to the A.R.C. and saw a movie. Wife Takes a Flyer *was the name of it. It ridiculed the Nazis all the way thru and I laughed until my sides hurt. We need a little comedy relief once in a while so I think it did me a world of good. Between reels they played some good music. I was sitting there lost in thought when all of a sudden I realized that Bing Crosby was singing our song,* Sunday, Monday or Always, *and oh, the flood of memories it brought back. I could hardly stand it. Oh! Darling, when are we going to be together again?*

I am sorry you're not getting my letters but, as you probably know by now, I was writing almost every day. They must have been held up as a part of the invasion plan.

From what you say about Nancy, she certainly must be a little honey. My heart aches with longing to be home and have a part in her bringing up. I hope I don't miss too much of it....

One day on the way home from the A.R.C. a chubby little girl about two or three years old with curly blonde hair ran up to me and took my hand and

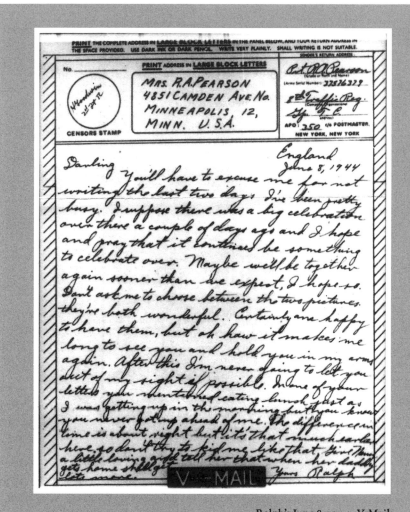

Ralph's June 8, 1944, V-Mail

without a word started down the street with me. I was sort of taken aback, not being accustomed to being picked up by such young blondes. (Don't worry, honey, I am still true to you.) Not wanting to lead her too far from home I stopped and dug down and gave her a stick of gum. She seemed highly pleased and after flashing me a big smile took off in the opposite direction. I walked on in a doubtful frame of mind, not knowing whether it had been my fatal charm that had attracted her or if it was just a new approach in the "any gum, chum?" game.

In almost daily letters, my parents explored the meaning of their separation and the importance of fidelity and home. In late August 1945, Dad wrote to Mama from France, "How good it makes me feel to know that finally the wheels are slowly grinding us toward each other again." A few days later, he shared his dreams of their future family life:

September 1, 1945—France
Just read your VJ day letter over again and it's really wonderful. Honey, it just glows with thankfulness and hope, not to say promises of what our future will be together. I think that even after I've been home a long time that I'll wake up at night and put my arms around you and hold you tight just to make sure it's real and that we are together again. And if for no reason while you're working I interrupt and hug you for a while you'll understand. Darling, I've been starved for you for so long that I can hardly believe that there is a possibility of seeing you again.

October 3, 1945—France
Darling, Darling, Darling—
At last it has come! Yes, honest! Got up this morning and went to work and said good-bye to the other man who left today, then came up to my room to brush my teeth and in a few minutes Jim knocked on the door and said, "Start packing. Headquarters just called and said you should come in as soon as possible." After he shut the door I knelt down and thanked God and as usual in moments like that my eyes let go with a little saltwater. Can hardly believe it. Don't think it will seem real until I see you. You can stop writing now because I'll be moving and chances are my mail will never catch up to me.
Boy! Oh Boy! I've been waiting for this day for a long time. Gus is going to drive me into Reims tomorrow morning. If the call had come a half hour sooner I'd have been on my way now with the other fellow. This is better because it gives

Photos Lois sent to Ralph during the war:
Lois with Nancy in front of the Pearson home,
and a scene designed to encourage homesickness.

me more time to get ready and say good-bye to my friends. Oh Honey, start shaking the moths out of those civilian clothes, I'll jump into them as soon as I get in the door.

Don't get too anxious, Sweetheart, it may take quite a while to get there yet, but anyway I'm started. I'll keep on writing every chance I get and will do my best to call you when I hit the States....

Can you feel me coming nearer to your arms? My anticipation is growing every minute. Man, am I dreaming! All my love forever, Ralph.

cs

FIFTY-FIVE YEARS LATER, in another invasion of sorts, the wheels begin grinding the two old lovers away from each other.

After much negotiation, Joe and I agree to take my parents for a ride while Jan and Ginger and the housekeeping staff rearrange their furniture. Dad will sleep in what had been the living room of their former two-room suite, Mama in the locked total-care ward on the other side of the building.

It is glorious weather. Mom and Dad are happy to see us and eager to go out. On the way down in the elevator, Mama twists nervously in her wheelchair and asks for Dad.

"That's Daddo, right there," I say.

"It's easy for her not to recognize me," he jokes. "We only spend twenty-four hours a day together."

They are unusually alert and enthusiastic on our customary circle of Lake of the Isles, Calhoun, and Harriet. Even Mama, who had pursed her lips and blown a raspberry back at the nursing home. Over and over she asks to "get into that water," despite the wheelchair folded in the trunk. Dad actually comes up with "Harriet" while we round Lake Calhoun. They keep thanking us for taking them out. I feel like Judas.

When we stop at Harriet to watch the lake and the passing people, Mama notices all the dogs, reacts when big trucks go by, and not only sees the inline skaters but mimics the sound of their skates.

"I wonder if those kids know how lucky they are," she says again and again.

We return to the nursing home at 3:30 and sit with Jan and Ginger in the conservatory. We had planned to be positive and upbeat about it, not treat it as the tragedy it is, but no one dares broach the subject. As Mom and Dad grow suspicious, Joe breaks the news. Dad does not grasp it, but Mama does. And she fights back.

"I think this is just terrible!" she shouts. "Just terrible!"

When Dad finally connects, this man who never swears yells, "This is bullshit!"

We blame it on the regulations. We say we are looking for another place. Angry, clear, and articulate, Mama fights for her life.

"I'd rather go to hell!" she sobs, which is exactly where she is when she cannot put her hands on Dad. "I want to die right now! I'll take care of it. I'll jump out the window."

"It isn't high enough," Dad mutters. "I'll have to get a gun."

We tell them they'll be together all day, sit together in Mama's room, eat together, do activities together—but nothing comforts them.

"Night is an important time," Dad insists.

Meanwhile, the staff has moved out their marriage bed. The bed they had shared throughout their sixty years together—the bed in which their daughters were conceived—is placed in storage till an agency can pick it up.

Mama's new room is stifling. Feminine and pink with flower prints and white furniture, it has a locked window looking out on a brick wall. As we crowd in, Jan and Ginger sit facing Mom and Dad but, huddled on the bed in a corner, I cling to Joe and try to control myself. Jan tells me later that during the moving process she had slumped down on that bed with a most disquieting pressure on her chest. But now Jan and Ginger do well, even saying the "A" word: Alzheimer's made this change necessary. At first, Dad thinks he is the one who needs extra help and this room is his. Then the new case supervisor appears and loudly introduces herself. She is ever so cheery.

"My mother isn't hard of hearing, at all," Ginger tells her, but that has no effect on the volume or the cheeriness.

Finally, Mama says she does not blame us. But Dad cannot see why anything has to change. At first, he even refuses a Manhattan, assuming it could not be real brandy in this place. After what seems like forever, we walk back toward Dad's room on the other side of the building.

"I hate that room," Mama says, dragging her feet to slow the wheelchair. Bent and shuffling, Dad breathes so hard on the long trek Jan fears a stroke. We pass the glass cage full of bright little birds twittering and flitting about, but Mama does not notice them.

Rearranged, Dad's room is unrecognizable. We crowd in, and he sinks onto his single hospital bed, continuing to argue against the move. I hold on to him until Mama cries, "Stop doing that to my husband!"

She does not recognize me! I flee into the hall, where Dolores wraps me in her arms and tries to explain why this move is necessary. But there is no logic in her reasons.

"Lois won't eat unless Ralph comes to her," Dolores says. "I can't even get him out of bed unless I tell him, 'Lois is crying for you.' She calls for him, even when he's *there*. And sometimes, she just yells—"

At that, my mind flies back, more than thirty years, to a forlorn voice calling in the darkness of my neighborhood. Night after night, from her own nursing home window, an old woman cried, "Mama! Mama!"

"I think Ralph will adjust, but Lois will have trouble," Dolores says.

"You're probably right. The one thing Mama still knows is Dad."

That stuns her. She confesses there are total-care beds in the dementia unit, but not enough staff to give additional patients that level of care. She does not explain why they chose to move Mama rather than someone else. Or why regulations forbade Dad from moving with Mama.

"Mom and Dad have to be together whenever they want."

"We'll try, but we can't promise because a staff member will have to take Ralph over to see Lois." Yes, a guide to lead him through alarmed security doors to and from Mama's room—and to prevent his escape.

What must it be to work in that place, hour after hour, day after day? The nurses and aides are trying to do the right thing. They *do* care, even though caring must daily break their hearts. It is not their fault the place is understaffed. But the regulations meant to protect Mama may inadvertently destroy her. What would the administrators have done had we refused the move? Did we even ask?

Back in the room, Mama cries, "Ralph, Ralph, we just have to—kill somebody!"

"We'll all still visit both of you," Ginger tells Dad. "We'll still take you to our homes for family dinners—"

Dad blinks and stares at her. Visits and family dinners will not undo this cataclysm. He cannot decide where he will sleep or when he will see his wife. He is powerless.

❦

JAN SAYS JOE IS OUR CHAMPION. As always, we sisters can depend on his strength and compassion. Whenever we are overwhelmed, he steps in with gentle words that re-establish our balance. Back home, with stacks of papers to correct and lessons to plan, I say, "I wonder if Mom and Dad are sleeping."

"We can't be there," Joe says. "They have their troubles, and you have yours."

True, but my parents' sorrow is an illegible message bleeding through from the other side of the page, obscuring the logical sentences of my life and work. For my parents, of course, that bleeding *is* their page. The whole terrible day of the move that parted them felt like the Halloween of two years ago, when Mama was therapeutically isolated in the Hall, leaving Dad alone and desolate in the Tower.

Once again, it is as if conjoined twins have been separated. Twins with one heart.

In a June 20, 1945, letter from France, Dad wrote, "Memories and dreams: what a dull world this would be if we didn't have them." Now, in this time beyond dreams, beyond even memory itself, my parents' world is not only dull but incomprehensible and beyond their control. And their great love, which united them throughout their good lives, has become a wound. Just months before he returned from France, my father wrote:

> *My love for you has become so much a part of me that I don't think anything else matters. I want you so much it hurts. I want to have you close to me forever and ever to share everything with me, good and bad. The good will be that much better and the bad won't be quite so hard to take, with you. I love you so much that even after all this time each day without you seems endless and not worthwhile.*

❦

LOVE ALTERS NOT

The Crack Between the Worlds
Total-Care Unit

September 26, 2000–January 3, 2001

Let me not to the marriage of true minds
Admit impediments. Love is not love
Which alters when it alteration finds,
Or bends with the remover to remove:
O, no! it is an ever-fixed mark
That looks on tempests and is never shaken;
It is the star to every wandering bark,
Whose worth's unknown, although his height be taken.
Love's not Time's fool, though rosy lips and cheeks
Within his bending sickle's compass come;
Love alters not with his brief hours and weeks,
But bears it out even to the edge of doom.
　　　If this be error and upon me proved,
　　　I never writ, nor no man ever loved.

—WILLIAM SHAKESPEARE, SONNET CXVI

JOURNAL | *If*

September 26, 2000

TODAY, MY EMAIL TO JAN IS FILLED WITH PARANOIA about the staff's motivations in separating our parents: "Don't get rid of their bed! Can't we find a better place?" Though she *has* found an opening elsewhere, Jan thinks another move will only further disorient Mom and Dad. The voice of reason, she replies:

> *Dad was calm and lying down when Gingo and I saw him last night. He had been to visit Mom for a while. He was okay but asked for you. He wanted all his daughters there. "I know I'm losing my mind," he said, "but where's Mama?"*
>
> *When we said, "Sleeping," he pointed to their former bedroom and asked, "In there?" and we said, "No, in her room." But he wasn't agitated like earlier in the day. We talked about other things. He seemed happy about the new TV, made some jokes about us walking around carrying the TVs at night and people thinking we were looters. He thanked us for coming and was pleased when I said I'd bring him cookies. Mom was asleep when we brought the TV into her room.*
>
> *I share some of your doubts about how and why this has come down, but I think the caregivers genuinely care; they see this as difficult. But yes, they do need to make it easier on themselves. If two or three people are helping Mom that means someone else on the ward is not getting attention. As to whether they think separating Mom and Dad might be a plus, I don't know. All I know is that they care for them day in and day out. They hear things from them and see them do things that we don't. We think that Mom and Dad being together is the most important thing in their care, but we only have the "idea" of them together; we don't have all the information about their day-to-day lives and what they require from caregivers. I do think that the regs that mandate this have their base in insuring that patients are properly cared for and in avoiding past nursing home abuses. We may think an exception should be made because our parents' relationship is unique, but I'm not sure we have all the information to make that determination— We just are dealing with the impossible in a different way— If we had all the money in the world and could build Mom and Dad a house overlooking a lake and a golf course and could hire 'round the clock care, it would still be heartbreaking....*

&

Journal | *Dissonance*

September 27, 2000

I'VE GONE FROM DOCUMENTING EVERY DETAIL of my parents' decline to not wanting to think about it. Recording it all here is a sort of exorcism. Journals have always been that for me. Once it's written, I can let it go enough to do my work.

Jan told me when she and Ginger visited at about 7:30 PM, Mama was strapped to a chair in her room. She responded when they said, "Mama," but was vacant and just wanted to go to bed. Jan had to get a staff member to help Mama lie down. Her breathing was shallow and cluttered with little sounds of distress or exhaustion. She seemed almost dead.

We did this to her. On that terrible moving day, Mama was more forceful and articulate than she'd been in years. She fought hard to stay with Dad. But now, defeat and grief have opened a deep well of bitterness. Her only solution is to die.

Jan says she's glad we were all there that day. But it would've been far better to have someone tell me about it than for Mama to think I'm some woman after her husband. Or hear her with perhaps a last mothering gesture tell us she doesn't blame us.

Throughout this ordeal, Joe has cared for me. He cooks, shops, washes clothes, listens to my troubles. He rubs my back, drives me to and from Minneapolis, helps me care for my parents. Without him, I couldn't bear up, especially now, struggling to teach during the madness of Homecoming week.

Pep assemblies and football hype are only the beginning. Each day has a different costume theme—students appear in robes and slippers, beachwear. Cross-dressing is almost *de rigueur*. Kids, and even teachers, offering themselves up at the "elf auction" to raise money for charity, submit to being garbed in outrageous and humiliating creations. One three-sport athlete and A-student has been dressed as a girl. If anyone speaks to him, he has to whip a mirror out of his lacy purse, primp, and cry in falsetto, "Oh, I am *so* beautiful!"

The winner of the "lazy student" drawing lounges in a recliner mounted on a creaky cart wheeled late into class. Rooms buzz with plotting and bragging to do with the midnight raids of the "junior-senior wars"—attacks and retributions and near-disasters in which trees and bushes are splendidly festooned with toilet paper, girls are plastic-wrapped to trees, and cars full of kids lead cops on wild rides through the dark streets.

Such cognitive dissonance! All this youth and exuberance is painfully ironic when set against images of Dad in his separate emptiness waiting for someone who loves him. And Mama drugged and strapped to a chair in her lonely room wanting to die.

Today, penciled on a student's desk, I discover a little stick figure in a jaunty hat smoking a cigarette as he saunters down a mountain. Scrawled below it, an almost certainly unintentional quote from a James Wright poem reads, *I have wasted my life*. It's hard to resist adding the words that have coursed across my school computer screen ever since Dad gave me his last advice:

Appreciate your time.

☙

JOURNAL | *Decision*

October 12, 2000

NEEDED OR NOT, I've never gotten counseling or therapy. Better to be the helper. But torn between my parents and a demanding job, I'm screwed up and fragile. Trying to buck up and carry it all exacerbates the facial twitch that has plagued me off and on. Massage, acupuncture, moxibuxtion, a muscle relaxant—nothing works for long. Only a pill will help me let go, and that means a psychiatrist. As his office phone rings, a line from Eliot's *Ash Wednesday* comes into my head:

> *Teach us to care and not to care.*
> *Teach us to sit still.*

The psychiatrist doesn't call it depression. Wanting to keep it simple, he prescribes Neurontin, a brand-name miracle that provides great sleep and relaxation in situations that would have sent me over the top. My face doesn't twitch, but I feel vague and less articulate.

After two weeks, it all falls apart. Neurontin allows, or causes, sudden spasms on the left side of my face that last for ten to twenty seconds. When I get up the courage to explain to new classes what is already obvious, they are mostly kind. But this can't go on.

It's back to the doctor for a tranquilizer. And now lorazepam allows me to function and sleep—and dulls my reactions to the world.

I'm the one who wanted to drug Mom and Dad. Though my sisters had serious reservations, once the doctor recommended it, they went along. Why should our parents suffer, I argued, especially when they have limited capacity to understand what's happening to them? My own tranquilizer and the Paxil given to them are simply pain-avoidance. Theirs and ours.

Paxil's side effects raise different questions. Does my parents' frequent talk of suicide and death reflect their hopeless situation? Or is it spurred by the drug itself? Their fatigue and weight gain are certainly linked to it. In a recent email, Jan describes Mama in a condition that has to be drug-related:

I visited Mom and Dad yesterday. Mom was napping so they weren't to-gether. It was really hard to rouse her. Even sitting in the wheelchair she didn't open her eyes very often. She was listening in good spirits and wanted me to stay. Periodically she said, "I love you so much," but her eyes remained closed most of the time.

Last June, due to his lethargy and lack of appetite, Dad's dosage of Paxil was reduced. Almost immediately, he became desperate. In what may have been withdrawal, or simply waking to reality, he raged against his fate and attempted a breakout. He was tortured by dreams that placed him back in the war again. Not surprisingly, this was also when he gave me his wisest counsel: "Appreciate your time." In August, when his drug dose was increased, he became vague and mellow again.

As unclear as this situation may be, it's one thing for someone with normal mental clarity to decide to forgo drugs, to tough it out. It's quite another for a caretaker to choose that suffering for someone with dementia. Despite unknowns about side effects, I think we're doing the right thing. Of course, drugging them—and myself—also dulls my own anguish.

એ૭

JOURNAL | *Circle*

October 15, 2000

CALLING AHEAD, I ASK THE STAFF to guide Dad to Mama's room so we can take them to the lakes. As Joe and I wheel Mama out, we stop again to look at the birds in their glass case. Tiny bright birds, orange and black or blue-headed pairs nesting up in the corners, sing within their strange prison society. As before, Mama focuses on certain ones, making her little bird sounds. She does not ask to set them free.

She keeps calling for Dad, her link to the world, who is following behind.

"Oh!" she exclaims in delight as we wheel her outside.

At the park, sunshine gilds the trees and warms our skin. Runners and dog walkers circle the sparkling lake. Mama repeatedly begs to get into the water. We'd need a skyhook to do that now.

"It's too cold, Mama. Too cold."

"Are you sure?"

"It's the middle of October."

My little performance—patient, upbeat, loving—is easy enough to handle once in three weeks.

Returning to her hated space, the "Oh!" Mama expels is the same as the "Oh!" she released when we wheeled her out into the sunshine and flowers of the court-yard. But Dad is confused. He doesn't remember being in this place before, so Joe explains, "Your room is right down that hall."

"I guess I don't know much about where I live—"

"Lois's room is on the other side of the building," Joe adds.

"Oh, are we separated?"

Today, in what felt like an act of penance, I reread one of Dad's letters from France. War and its stressors and temptations never weakened the intensity of his love. Because they hadn't had a double-ring ceremony, after almost two years of separation, Mama sent him a wedding ring. In a letter full of need for her, he wrote:

April 30, 1945—France

...Just when I was feeling lowest, you came through as you always do when I need you most. Four letters and the envelope containing the ring. Words can't tell how much of a lift they gave me. Of course, I don't have to tell you how the ring and the note with it affected me. Still just as soft as ever, even after a term of twenty months in the army. Well, I told you I wouldn't change, didn't I....

I am feeling much better tonight and somehow feeling very close to you—must be the ring, which is a little tight. Won't come off easily. Love, Ralph

ের

Ralph and Lois toast each other and their love.

A Song at Twilight

Just a song at twilight, when the lamps are low;
And the flick'ring shadows softly come and go.
Tho' the heart be weary, sad the day and long,
Still to us at twilight comes love's old song,
Comes love's old sweet song.
—J. CLIFTON BINGHAM, *Love's Old Sweet Song*

November 4, 2000

FOR THEIR SIXTIETH ANNIVERSARY, Jan asks Dad if he wants to give sixty roses to Mama, one for each year of their marriage. As he says yes, his voice breaks.

In the sunroom of the dementia unit, Dad slouches in a chair by the wall. Mama sits alone at a table, staring into space. Swollen ankles bulge her white support stockings. Though the staff knew about our celebration, Mama's hair lies flat against her head. The attendant says she has had a permanent, but there is no sign of it. Someone has, however, manicured and polished her nails, dressed her in her good purple sheath, and clipped on some earrings.

"Mama?" I touch her shoulder. She clings to me and begins to cry.

"Nancy!" Dad exclaims brightly.

He stumps after us as I wheel Mama's chair out into the hall. Jan and Ginger arrive then with Mama's old friend Lucy, who shared so many late-night Christmas Eves with our family.

"It's Lucy," I say, but Mama shows no sign of recognition. Lucy looks small and sad as she tries to talk with her.

Mama's pale skin, thin and mottled, is drawn as smooth as polished marble. A little rouge and lipstick help her seem more lifelike. Ginger fluffs up a few frail curls. Dad wears slacks and a handsome shirt but has not shaved. His nose sprouts tufts. Despite our efforts, his stubborn hair sticks up like a rooster's crest.

In the chapel, Mama cannot see Dad's sixty red roses till we bring them close to her face. "Yes, they're pretty," she agrees, but does not seem to grasp each rose represents one year of their long life together.

"Can you believe it's been sixty years?" Dad asks sweetly, patting her hand and pointing to their framed wedding picture set before her. Mama's face remains impassive.

When Will and Pearl arrive, Ginger takes these good and faithful family friends to greet Dad, who is touched by their presence. Mama stares dully at them. Nor does she seem to understand the meaning of the congratulatory cards read to her. Dad hugs her close, and his eyes fill with tears as Jan's friend Sue sings *Our Love Is Here to Stay*.

Then Jan hands around the words to old love songs, and Sue's fine strong voice leads the group in singing *Always*, *When I Fall in Love*, and *Time After Time*.

Though we cannot hear her voice, Mama sings along! She is connected. Her lips form words she knows by heart.

"Oh, thank you!" she exclaims after each song. "That was wonderful!"

Holding Mama's hand, Dad declares, "I love you just as much today as when I first married you."

We wheel Mama into the conservatory, a room of big windows, plants, and wrought-iron tables. Jan's bright pink-frosted carrot cake is set out beside her heart-shaped shortbread cookies and two bottles of champagne. We try to be celebratory as we toast our parents' wonderful life together, but Mama chokes on her first sip. Ginger gives her water, but she chokes again. When she cannot take a bite, I put a piece of cookie into her mouth.

"Do you want to hold the rest of it?"

"I'd just drop it," she groans, then refuses the cake entirely, even the coffee. This from a woman whose typical response to food was "Oh, num-num!"

"I want to go to bed," she murmurs. With her hand firmly held in his, her desperate voice calls, "Ralph?"

It occurs to me then we have forgotten to sing *Yesterday*. Not the Beatles' song, *their* song. I heard it first as a child on the front porch of Dad's family home. That summer night, June bugs bounced against the dark screens. And, hand in hand, my parents rocked on the old rasping glider. Light from the window shone on Dad's face as he sang that song to Mama. It was simple, heartfelt, and perfectly attuned to their love.

Many years later, imperfectly on this bittersweet afternoon, we sing it again for them. The words clear in his mind, Dad's voice is thick with feeling:

> *What a day was yesterday*
> *For yesterday gave me you.*
> *All my schemes and golden dreams*
> *At last it seems have come true.*

> *Until I found you, the skies were always gray,*
> *Then like the sunshine you drove the clouds away.*
> *You'll never guess my happiness*
> *When you said "yes," yesterday.*

Afterward, our parents once again in their separate rooms, we sisters meet in the conservatory to decompress. Soon the chaplain and a retired nurse volunteer sit down at our table and talk pleasantly about our little anniversary party.

"We know and like your parents, and we want to prepare you for what is coming," the chaplain says. "You will have to make some important decisions. Soon. And, if you're willing, we can help you make the *right* decisions."

With some shock, I realize they are talking about end-of-life decisions. My mind spins away in denial. Surely it is too soon for that! Then an ancient woman maneuvers her wheelchair in close to our table. She smiles, mumbles unintelligibly—a mute and perhaps uncomprehending witness to our talk of death.

The chaplain lends us *The Vanishing Line*, a film in which a physician advocates letting death come naturally. He explains people are not hungry when their organs are shutting down. If they do not want to eat, it is cruel to force-feed them.

The nurse shows us a medal she wears outside her clothes whenever she travels: DO NOT RESUSCITATE, DO NOT INTUBATE. "I'd have it tattooed on my chest if that weren't so painful!" she laughs. Many years of nursing and a near-death experience of heaven have convinced her of the fruitlessness of medical procedures that prolong dying rather than save lives.

While she talks, a recent dream returns to me. Mama is lying in our old claw-foot tub. As I help her take a bubble bath, she sinks back into the water, drenching the hair I will have to fix again. She is vague, almost unconscious, and would have relaxed down under the water had I not pulled her back.

∾

Lullaby

Love isn't what we remember; it's what we are.
—RICHARD CORLISS

November 2000

AS WORLD WAR II ENDED, I was three years old, living in my grandmother's house and secure in my mother's love. But the arms that so tenderly held me longed for my father still in France. Mama's low voice sang Tennyson's lullaby to soothe me—and herself.

Sweet and low, sweet and low,
Wind of the western sea,
Low, low, breathe and blow,
Wind of the western sea.
Over the rolling waters go,
Come from the dying moon, and blow,
Blow him again to me;
While my little one, while my pretty one, sleeps.

Sleep and rest, sleep and rest,
Father will come to thee soon;
Rest, rest, on mother's breast,
Father will come to thee soon.
Father will come to his babe in the nest,
Silver sails all out of the west
Under the silver moon.
Sleep, my little one, sleep, my pretty one, sleep.

So many years later, when Alzheimer's had confined my parents to the Tower, I told Mama my memory of that time and, as her face melted in an intermingling of love and sorrow, sang that lullaby for her.

"How could I *forget* that?" she whispered.

Only four years ago, Jan and Ginger took our parents to a live performance of *I Love a Piano*, a song-and-dance program of Irving Berlin's music. On the way home, Mama was glowing but distracted. When asked a question, she said, "I'm sorry, I didn't hear you. I was *back there*."

What is memory? A ghost of feeling haunting the mind. The silver snail trail of the soul's wandering. Electrochemical connections. Synaptic pathways etched in mutable flesh. "Remember, remember," a dying friend once told Mama. But Mama cannot remember. And when she forgets my childhood, my mind's anchor drops into depths of an uncharted sea. The end of its rope dangles, frayed strands adrift in the tide. Sages of the East tell us to let go of attachments and float free. But do we float free if we simply forget?

છ

ON NOVEMBER 12, Joe and I plan to take my parents for a ride, but at the door of Mama's room, we discover a full medical emergency. Mama moans, and her every breath whistles, as intent medics give her an EKG. She started abdominal breathing during lunch, the nurse says. Tests are necessary to diagnose pneumonia or congestive heart failure.

"Is my mother dying?"

The answer comes in acronyms.

"Would you tell me that in English?"

She does, adding perhaps to calm me, "Some of her moaning is theatrics."

Doubting that, I ask her to give Mama a sedative, but she has done that.

Mom and Dad want no heroic measures to revive them when their hearts stop. But such orders do not cover this situation. Oxygen, antibiotics, and heart stimulants are keeping Mama alive. Out in the hall, helpless, I am comforted by Joe's calm hand on my shoulder. He is being present with me. When the medics finish, we are allowed into the room. Mama lies in the raised bed, breathing hard. Oxygen tubes run into her nose. She seems to know us.

"Mama, I'm sorry you're not feeling well—"

"Not *feeling* well! I'm dying!"

Her subsequent speech is partly muffled, partly incoherent, but what she wants is clear—and unattainable: *I want my husband. Why am I in this place?*

And then Mama says, "I want to go *back there*."

"You need to be here so they can take care of you. Until you're better." A lie as brittle as the sixty roses from the anniversary party shriveled in a vase on the dresser.

Back there! Does that mean her old life, active and involved, doing things for people? Or just the other side of the building with Dad? Each well-meaning move has robbed her. In the Tower, she longed for White Bear. In the dementia unit, she wanted to go "back up high" to the Tower. This last move to the isolation of a total-care room has destroyed her.

"Then I want to die," she'd hissed.

Helpless, as Mama remains agitated, I grope for a story.

"When I was a little girl, you used to sing to me. Remember? You sang *Sweet and Low*, that old lullaby, and I've always loved it."

She relaxes into my singing: *Sleep and rest, sleep and rest, Father will come to thee soon*— But he is in the other wing in a fog that protects him, most of the time, from knowing her dying.

Looking for something to distract her, I wind up a music box Jan gave her with little penguin skaters circling to *The Skaters' Waltz*. It plays a few bars and breaks down. I hold Mama's hands, lay my head lightly against her chest, rub her shoulders until she seems asleep.

Sleep, my little one, sleep.

☙

A LOCKED DOOR SEPARATES MY MOTHER'S BED from the single room where Dad waits alone. Throughout the two years since we moved our parents to the dementia unit, I dreaded the warning sign at the far north end of the hall: THIS DOOR IS ALARMED. What horror waited beyond? Now, standing on the other side of that door, I know this is a place of death. Afraid that a touch of the code buttons will set off the alarm, we ask an aide for help. It screams out at us anyway as we hurry through. Dad is sleeping in his chair with his coat on when we arrive and touch his arm. "Do you want to go for a ride?"

"Anything," he sighs. "Is Mama coming?"

"She isn't feeling well—"

He is concerned but does not ask to see her. Should we give Mama what she is calling for or protect Dad from what the nurse said would upset him? We just go on with our outing. Though the day is gray and cold, Joe drives our usual route around our chain of lakes—Calhoun, Harriet, and Lake of the Isles.

At each lake, as always, Dad asks, "What lake is this?" And again and again, "Did you say Mama isn't feeling well?"

"She isn't feeling well."

Stopping in the Harriet parking lot for the coffee and cookies we've brought along, we watch joggers and dogs. Dad is sweet, appreciative, and interested in it all. When an inline skater whooshes past, Joe says, "Ralph, I'll bet those rollerbladers remind you of your long-blade skating."

"Oh, those were the days! Mama and I glided around the Hippodrome rink—like we were one person."

Later, as we walk down the hall to his room, Dad notices the little box on the wall bearing its EMPLOYEES ONLY sign. He laughs and repeats his old corny joke: "Do they make them that small?" He chokes up a little as we hug good-bye.

On the way back to Mama's room, we take elevators to avoid the screaming door. Relaxed and fairly coherent, Mama touches the oxygen tube. "What's this?"

"Oxygen to help you breathe better."

"Where's Ralph?"

"He'll come to see you tomorrow. You need to rest now."

She accepts this, then looks me full in the face. "You're beautiful." My cheek contorts in a spasm that won't release.

"You're beautiful, too," Joe tells her.

"Hah!" she exclaims scornfully. It is a real interaction, a bit of her old self.

"I love you, Mama."

Her eyes meet mine, and she whispers almost fiercely, "I love you, too."

After a few minutes, her eyes close, and we feel we can go.

☙

DURING OUR CHILDHOOD, Mama would read Ludwig Bemelmans' *Madeline* aloud to us until we all knew it by heart. Often, she put us to bed with its final lines. As she stood silhouetted in the bright doorway of our darkened room, her voice gradually fell to a whisper:

> *"Good night, little girls!*
> *Thank the Lord you are well.*
> *And now go to sleep!"*
> *said Miss Clavel.*
> *And she turned out the light—*
>   *and closed the door—*
>   *and that's all there is—*
>   *there isn't any more.*

Then, the door would close to a crack of light and Mama would be gone.

෨

Thanksgiving

I believe what I did was right and that belief sustains me
except for a slight desire to be dead but that will pass.
—FLETCHER CHRISTIAN, *Mutiny on the Bounty*

November 2000

MAMA'S DYING CROUCHES SOMEWHERE in the dark beyond my busy fluorescent-lit days at school. She'd come close to death from congestive heart failure, but they'd "saved" her with diuretics, heart stimulants, and anti-anxiety medication.

She was suffering, and the medics eased that, in the short term. But nothing they can do will ease the suffering caused by the way she is—and *where* she is. Alone. Her life is over, but goes on. What is the right thing to do?

A voice in my head counsels, "follow your heart," and my heart knows the Zen sage Katagiri offers the best advice: *Nothing to grasp. Nothing to throw away. Just be present.* These words translate into no heroic measures to save her, no dramatic measures to end her life. Help her to be comfortable. And be present with her passing.

From this distance, the specter of Mama, long past doing anything meaningful, haunts my days. "Tell me, what is it you plan to do / with your one wild and precious life?" asks poet Mary Oliver. That question hangs on my classroom wall, as well as in my mind. In this Thanksgiving season, my answer is, "find gratitude." In the midst of loss, to reaffirm my gratitude for family, and Joe, and a mind that still functions. And gratitude, even for the job that so tests me—the kids and colleagues, the chance to contribute.

With no gratitude for the time left in my parents' lives, their slow agony of decline, I search for acceptance. And for all that is *wild and precious* in my life.

၅

JAN'S NOVEMBER 13 EMAIL presents a dismal picture of Mama's deterioration and Dad's uncomprehending despair:

> *Because Mom wanted supper in her room, we decided to take Daddy to Ginger's for supper and called to let him know. When we drove up we could see him already waiting in the hall chair by his room with his hat on. In her room, Mom was sitting up in the wheelchair and very alert. She didn't seem to be distressed, but her breathing was a little shallow and wheezy. We had a nice visit, went to supper and had an okay time. Dad asked several times about Mom, then just withdrew. As we were leaving the house, he walked a few steps and stopped— overcome. Back at his room he asked, "Did Mama die?"*
>
> *We spent the next half hour assuring him that Mom had not died and he would see her in the morning. He said, "If I live that long." He was convinced that he had heard someone say she had died. He kept coming back to it. He said it was a huge blow and his life would be over if it was true. He remained distraught even when we assured him. We offered to take him over to see Mama, but he said to let her sleep. "I know everyone has to die," he said, "but I'm older and should die first." When we left he was better, but still distressed. We let the staff know that he would probably ask again about Mama.*

၅

JAN TAKES DAD TO VISIT MAMA on the day before Thanksgiving. And it is a scene no one could be thankful for. Lifted by machine from her bed, Mama drools and keeps her eyes closed. She does not respond to Dad's voice.

"Look, she's asleep, even though her daughters are here," he says. "And my old magic isn't working now that I'm old."

After a time with no response, Jan says, "Bye, Mama—"

"Bye?" Mama cries out in dismay.

They stay and hold her hand, but her eyes do not open.

The nurse told Jan that Mama calls less for Dad now. That fact, along with her closed eyes and the drooling, suggests she is heavily drugged or shutting down or both. We do not object. We want only to ease her suffering.

When Jan and Ginger next visit, Mama lies in bed calling out for Dad. Her eyes are crusty, her skin seems drawn away from her features, but she knows her daughters.

"Where *am* I?" she asks.

"In your room, in the nursing home. Surrounded by people who love you."

Uncomforted, she murmurs, "Soon—"

ℰℒ

A RINGING PHONE WAKES ME AT 3:00 on Saturday morning to the thought that Mama has died. And to a vain attempt to convince myself that I have done my grieving. But the phantom ring of the phone in the darkness is the sound of my own longing to be with her, to tell her joys or sorrows, to laugh like fools, to listen to her enthusiasm for projects, recipes, family stories—anything. Mama has been slipping away for years, and now even the body that held her remarkable mind—held it and let it go—is dying.

And yet my journals record every detail of her dissolution, as if this effort could put her back together again. Not with all the king's horses and all the king's men.

ℰℒ

JOURNAL | *Unglued*

December 8, 2000

WHEN JOE AND I GREET HER, Mama responds with agitation but no apparent pleasure. Still trying to preserve some part of our traditions, we've brought Dad to her room to decorate a tiny Christmas tree. Sad and fragile, Dad holds Mama's hand and talks sweetly to her. In only a month, he's dropped the weight he gained in the nursing home. His size-40 slacks seem in danger of falling off. And he's lost another tooth.

All of this Christmas work is just for myself. Maybe Daddy, too. He was pleased when Jan strung lights around the window in his room and lit their little ceramic tree on his dresser. Listening or not to the Christmas CD we brought, Mama doesn't open her eyes while we work. One string of lights is enough. I plug in the cord to test it, then looking for *some* reaction, bring the bright bulbs close to Mama's face. Startled, she doesn't laugh.

"Mama, open your eyes for a minute. See this little wreath you made."

Her eyes stay closed, and there is no "I love it!" when Joe lights the tree.

The little red sled ornament Mom and Dad put together when they lived in San Diego has come unglued and lies scattered on the bottom of the box.

ᗱ

"THE STAFF IS ARRANGING FOR HOSPICE CARE," Jan told me. That means special comfort care for Mama and support help for Dad, and for us. "Ginger and I checked 'yes' to reject all the remaining treatment options, except antibiotics. I *had* pneumonia. And I know what it's like when you can't breathe."

They learned Mama is incontinent, diapered. The doctor said he might try eliminating diuretics to see what will happen. He must *know*.

There is no good day for our mother to die! We all want the ordeal to be over, but almost nothing in this world is harder than to let things be what they are.

ᗱ

JOURNAL | *Choices*

December 9, 2000

THIS MORNING, I WAKE ON THE EDGE OF A DREAM—trying to write a haiku that went something like this:

> *my ink as it dries*
> *drowns in the helpless torrent*
> *of my wordless tears*

Joe and I decide it's too cold to comfortably cut a Christmas tree out in the country. It's just as well—with piles of papers to correct and mid-quarter fail notices due on Monday. Then Jan calls. Hadn't I read her email? The hospice people have set up a meeting the whole family must attend. Today.

Joe is working out a problem with his publisher. He should stay home. But he worries that driving through city traffic at ten below zero under the influence of tranquilizers might be dangerous for me. He sets aside his work and lets me relax into his care.

In the conference room, the caseworker and a nurse explain the hospice program that Medical Assistance provides. They give us *Hard Choices for Loving People*, a good booklet about end-of-life care decisions. Jan signs lots of papers. Of various options, we choose comfort care only. Once Mama can no longer eat, she won't be fed. She will get anxiety and pain-relief drugs, if necessary. Backrubs, music therapy, visits from volunteers. Hospice—this most compassionate service—lifts some weight from us.

After the meeting, Jan says, "Ginger and I had planned to bring Santa Lucia to Mom and Dad this morning. But we're going to wait till tomorrow. Mama might think Alia is the angel of death, but Daddy will like it."

Jan's grief-filled email awaits me at home:

> *I had trouble getting to sleep. I was trying to hold the good thoughts about Mom, but I was haunted by the vision of her alone in that bed. Christmas is such a sweet time for our family and Mama made it that way. I certainly have tried to do many of the things she did to make Christmas special. It was making me so sad when I was with her in her room to think she will miss it. Not only miss the good*

times, but be miserable in the living hell she appears to be in. I hope she will be more peaceful and comfortable (and as a result easier on our minds and hearts) now with the hospice care.

Hard Choices for Loving People says if you grasp at life as if it's a coin clutched in your fist, you become tense and afraid of losing it. The alternative is to open your hand, palm up, and hold your life as a gift. If it leaves, it is no longer yours.

ço

JOURNAL | *Shadow*

December 21, 2000

ON THE PHONE, Jan describes a meeting with four colleagues, all of whom are losing or had recently lost parents. And how, later that day, she'd cried as choirboys sang carols in the lobby. Then she says, "When Ginger visited today, Mama was not responsive."

After more talk, I return to correcting papers but cannot focus. And finally realize why. Jan had told me our mother is actually dying. And even though her life dangles from a flimsy scaffold stretched over the valley of the shadow of death, I just went on working.

∾

Christmas Without Mama

December 2000

OUR CHRISTMAS IS A MERE ORNAMENT, shiny on the outside and empty within. We go through the motions, pretending, doing all the things Mama did—wrapping gifts, making delicate almond cookies, spritz, and pecan butter-balls, setting candles in the windows, decking the tree with old family ornaments and her crazy baubles made from Styrofoam, sequins, pipe cleaners, glitter, and glue. Our festival of the sun's return in darkest winter scintillates with artificial light. But the lights do not produce a glow, feasting does not fulfill, well-wishing leaves things as they are. Despite gleaming packaging, darkness sucks at the heart of it all. We celebrate birth—trying to ignore the death's head leering from the shadows.

On Christmas Eve morning, amid the preparations at Jan's, Ginger calls. She has been to see Mama and advises Jan not to go.

"Shouldn't I go, either?"

"Yes, Nano, you *should*. You might not see her alive again."

Once two tranquilizers have wrapped my nerve endings, Joe and I go to see Mama—laden with Jan's cookie plates for the staff.

Drugged and on oxygen, Mama is agitated, unresponsive. Her mouth hangs open; her belly is distended. Joe stands behind my chair, his hands gentle on my shoulders. I stroke Mama's arm to soothe her and thank her for all the years of love and care.

It is like talking to the dead.

ᕦᕤ

IN JAN'S LIVING ROOM, just before Christmas Eve dinner, Dad suddenly jumps up and looks around.

"Where's Mama?"

"She's sick and can't be here."

"Oh," he groans. "I can't eat."

A few minutes later, he sits down at the table.

After dinner, Dad and I hold hands on the couch. Now and then, he asks about Mama but with diminishing intensity.

"I'm in a room full of people and hardly know any of them," he muses.

"That's Marguerite's daughter, Karen, and those are her children, Don and Christine—" He seems to want me to stop.

"This short-term memory loss is—" he says, giving up an attempt to characterize it.

I am surprised he knows what to call it.

"Whose house is this?" he asks several times. "I don't have a house. Where do I live?"

Then he remembers Christmas 1944. "I was in a bar in the northwest of France, but I can't remember the town— I was alone, but don't know why I was there, maybe AWOL."

"You were not AWOL. I know, because you told me your war stories, on tape."

This Christmas without Mama may be stirring grim memories of the time he witnessed a procession of ambulances. Soldiers of the 66th Combat Infantry Division had been singing carols on the deck of the S. S. Leopoldville when a German U-boat sank that ship. Then, too, Dad was separated from Mama.

> About twelve of us Transportation Corps guys went up behind General Patton's army. Right during the Battle of the Bulge. Patton had lost a whole bunch of jeeps to the Germans. And he came back and took all *our* jeeps. Twelve of them. We *needed* them! Jeez! We had to do all kinds of traveling around, seeing that things were going straight. So they asked for volunteers to go back to Cherbourg to get more jeeps. That was right before Christmas of '44. And I volunteered because I didn't want to spend Christmas Eve doing nothing.
>
> We rode across France, from one end to the other. Cherbourg is on the coast, right opposite England—"Share-boo," they pronounced it. We rode in a weapons carrier. That's like a small pickup with a top on it. Terrible ride. Cold.

We got into Cherbourg late in the afternoon, and the only place we could find to sleep was in the grandstand of a cycle track. There was a lot of snow on the ground, but we had our raincoats and overcoats and one blanket each, and we slept outside in the snow on the grandstand seats.

Well, then we went into town and we spent Christmas Eve day in a soldiers' canteen having coffee and donuts and stuff like that.

All day long there were ambulances coming up from the harbor and going by on the way to the hospital. A troop ship had been hit out in the Channel. Eight hundred guys got killed. Some of them were rescued, I suppose. But, oh, that was a depressing time. Oh, Jeez, a regular parade of ambulances going up to the hospital, coming back and going up again. I could have walked under a snake with a high hat on, being away from home on Christmas Eve and seeing that—

Here on the couch, he rests his head on my chest. We try to let the glow of Christmas comfort us. In silence and sweet sorrow, I hold my father close.

After the guests leave, our friend Ed arrives. He'd lost his father just a few days before and needs to discuss with Jan the medical choices he made. Dad sits there, hearing or not hearing it all. Finally, I give him his night pill and go upstairs. For what seems like hours, Ed's intense voice rises up the stairs with stories about his father's life and death.

Long into the night—as he has always done—Dad gazes at the Christmas tree. Very late, he asks Jan, "Is there a place where I can lay my weary head?"

The next morning, Dad is still sleeping with a cat curled up against him. As he wakes, he seems confused and a little frightened.

"It's good to see a familiar face. Where *am* I?"

"At Jan's."

"How did I get here?"

"Joe and I brought you."

"In my sleep?"

"No, it's Christmas morning. Merry Christmas!"

Dad does not remember his Christmas without Mama. My being with him was only for that time. Lovely and melancholy and soulful in this darkest season, that time was a gift for *me*.

❧

Journal | *Now*

December 28, 2000

JAN AND GINGER TAKE DAD to visit Mama on Christmas Day. "Is *that* Mama?" he gasps in horror and won't go near her.

Mama lies bloated, almost comatose on the bed.

"She's *not* the woman she used to be! Does she know *you*? She doesn't speak to me."

Shocked by his reaction, Ginger decides they should take him out of there. But, as they are leaving, Mama calls out, "Rau, Raau!" And becomes so agitated the nurse gives her more morphine.

Twice, out in the hall, Dad almost collapses in grief. And in his room, he slumps onto the bed, disoriented.

"What's next?" he asks. "Is *this* where I live?"

After a bit, he recovers enough to thank his daughters for a good Christmas.

Three months ago, when the nursing home staff moved Mama to a separate ward, we were horrified. Our parents *had* to be together. We considered moving them into Jan's guest room. If we had, and Mama's health had deteriorated at this same rate, Jan's house would now be an intensive-care ward with round-the-clock aides. Could Dad, or any of us, have lived with the sight of her and borne the sounds of her slow dying?

❧

AT HOME, THE AGONY OF CHRISTMAS BEHIND US, I wake with a peaceful feeling about Mama. It seems when we die we re-enter the godhead, bringing with us what we have learned of the world. Mama learned love and floating free of the body's weight of sorrow. If only this were not a dream—

❧

JOURNAL | *Mercy*

December 29, 2000

DAD IS SOBBING IN THE BACKGROUND when Jan calls. They'd taken him to say good-bye to Mama, a necessary cruelty. We drive to the nursing home, where Mama lies, oxygen tubes in her nose, mouth hanging open. She gargles horribly with each breath, but, heavily sedated, seems free of pain. Periodically, a nurse comes in to turn her a little. One puts a tube down her throat through which a machine sucks cloudy fluid into a jar. It doesn't stop the gargling. Because they haven't eaten all day, Jan and Ginger go out for food. Holding Mama's hand, rubbing her arm, I thank her for all her years of care and wisdom, enthusiasm, energy. Her love of life. And love of *me*. I tell her she can let go. Though she seems to lightly press my hand, she is beyond reach.

Then Mama opens her one good eye and looks at me.

That eye is the crack between worlds. It holds a spark, a light of consciousness as detached and dispassionate as the eye of God. Is Mama already in another realm, taking a last look at a grieving mortal so tangled up in life? Or is this nothing more than a neural reaction to a voice? Why do I think of the impenetrable eye of the shark that once stared back at me through aquarium glass?

After Jan and Ginger return, the minister from our parents' old church who has dutifully visited them in the nursing home rushes over from St. Paul. His presence is somehow comforting as he anoints Mama's forehead with oil and prays and sings hymns unself-consciously. When Mama falls asleep, Joe takes me to feed Jan's cats, and Ginger leaves to feed her kids. But Jan stays. She doesn't want Mama to die alone.

At Jan's, I light a candle and pray, "If there is any mercy in the universe, let her die now." A little later, Jan returns. A kind nurse had come on duty, turned Mama on her side, and drained out the fluid. As the gargling stopped, the nurse said gently, "You can go. I'll take care of your mother."

The called-for mercy showed up. It was human. Always, it is human.

&

JOURNAL | *Last Kiss*

December 30, 2000

JAN AND I TALK LATE, and in the morning she joins Ginger to sit with Mama. Telling myself that all good-byes have been said and there's no need to watch Mama's last breath, I clean up the kitchen. A half hour later, Jan calls. Mama is gone.

As my sisters wait in the silence of Mama's room, Ginger wants to hear the little penguin music box play *The Skaters' Waltz* once more. But the mechanism remains locked tight—until she sets it down. Then it plays the entire song, the two little penguin skaters spinning and flopping crazily around their mirror rink until—halfway through a second time—it stops for good.

"Both Jan and I got the feeling Mama was free and skating away from us. Saying good-bye," Ginger said later. "We just shook our heads in amazement and looked at each other. I get chills just thinking about it."

When Joe and I arrive, Mama's face is pale, her mouth agape. I kiss her smooth forehead, not yet cold, and think of Juliet—her lost Romeo just slipped beyond reach. After one last kiss, she utters her saddest words: *Thy lips are warm!*

Comparing ourselves to the Four Horsemen of the Apocalypse, we walk slowly, four abreast, down the long corridors to Dad's door.

"It must be serious if you're all here," he says, pleased to see us.

As he comprehends our news, he breaks down.

Unsummoned, a woman minister appears, and we crowd into Dad's room to recite the Twenty-third Psalm together. Gasping as if trapped, Dad repeatedly rises to his feet. His eyes flit about, his hands move ineffectually.

"He could go, too, you know," the minister whispers in my ear. Her words strike like a blow.

We take Dad over to Jan's house. Every now and then he asks, "Did I hear right? Did Mama die?" Or "Where's Mama?"

On the couch, holding on to him, I answer those same questions again and again, until we are both depleted.

In the morning, Dad seems cheerful, until he asks about Mama. Then new grief washes over him. After a while, my sisters' friends begin arriving with flowers and soup and salad. They greet Dad sweetly, and he flirts a bit with them, holding on to their hands. During every lull, he sinks into himself.

"Now this is a whole different life for me," he says after a while. "I was supposed to go first. What is left for me now? You're supposed to have some function in this world, but I'm just being taken care of."

❦

JOURNAL | *Emergency*

January 1, 2001

A S ALWAYS, JOE AND I SPEND New Year's Eve in St. Paul with our dear friends Sharon and Steve. We all try to find some comfort in our traditions.

In the morning, when we arrive at Jan's, she tells me, "I didn't take Dad back to the nursing home after Christmas. He shouldn't have to be alone there. And last night, Ginger and I and Ned took turns going to Romaine's New Year's party so someone would be with Dad. The situation was not lost to him. He asked, 'Do I need a babysitter?' And this morning he looked out the window and said, 'So this is my new life.'"

A bit later, Dad tells us, "Mama pulled a fast one on me."

Joe stays with him while we sisters make arrangements at the Cremation Society. For the first time, we talk about what to do with Mama's ashes. Jan and Ginger want to scatter them in various bodies of water Mama loved. I don't want to simply throw them all away.

Uncertain as to its eventual use, we buy a large green cloisonné urn. Then Joe and I go home with Mama's ashes—and thus miss Dad's emergency. Jan's email describes what happened:

> *Dad seems finally to really have it in his head that Mom has died. Many times he said, "Mama really pulled a fast one on me." Fast?*
>
> *I was in the kitchen when Dad fell. I came out to see him crumpled on the floor by the fireplace. Was he dead? How could it be? Ned and David helped him up. He said he was all right, though his hip hurt. Could he stand? With trouble.*
>
> *"I was just going to close the fireplace door and slipped on the hearthrug," he said. (My rug that I hadn't secured properly. It was my fault.) What if his hip was broken? We called 911 and nice guys came. Dad joked with them.*
>
> *Later he said, "If I'd done a better job I could have joined Mama."*
>
> *Ginger rode with him in the ambulance. I followed in my car. We waited with him as he was x-rayed and checked out. Nothing was broken. But he couldn't walk very easily and he would be stiff in the morning and need assistance. He probably couldn't ride in my car: if he got in, could we get him out?*
>
> *The paramedics put him in a maroon body bag so he wouldn't get chilled on the ride to the nursing home. The bag looked a lot like the bag the Cremation Society people had put Mama in when they took her away. It was spooky. I wondered if*

we were going to lose him. But Dad was making jokes about getting worse bruises playing hockey—and finishing the game. It's hard for him to be an old guy.

Losing Mom has made Dad even more precious. He loves the attention but other than us, what does he have? He knows that, I think. I am beating myself up about the slippery rug. But I am strangely comforted that there were three caring, concerned nurses at the nursing home when we arrived. We can't sit and hold his hand full time. As we left him tonight, Ginger said she would see him tomorrow and he said, "Don't put me before your family." He said earlier that he knew he was a burden and we would be free otherwise. I told him "freedom's just another word for nothing left to lose." I just made that up !>)

So another day went by and the planning isn't done. Because of the holiday, the obituary deadline was 2 rather than 7 so the notice will be in on Wednesday/Thursday. We don't have to have the service on Thursday as the notice isn't in, but I do want to do it. Your thoughts? I hope the delay isn't for a reason, like we will have a double service.

೮౨

JOURNAL | *Dad*

January 2, 2001

"Dad seemed okay this morning," Jan said. He got up and went to the bathroom with a walker. Whether or not Dad can stand Mama's funeral, we have to take him there. He won't be as lucky as Joe's Aunt Stella's husband, who looked into her casket and asked who she was! My principal freed me to concentrate all week on Mama's eulogy, but Jan's email described what happened when she and Ginger went to see Daddy:

> *We were busy with preparations for Mom's service. Ginger and I had dinner out and decided that even though it was late we should go see Dad. I also wanted to look for a photograph to add to the picture boards for the funeral.*
>
> *"Ginger! Janny!" he said when we arrived. He was so pleasant. He wanted to sit out in the hall and talk. When the nurse came to give him his meds and take his blood pressure, he joked with her.*
>
> *I was busy in his room looking for the picture until he asked Ginger, "What is she doing in there?"*
>
> *Then I realized that I had come to see him, but here I was tending to business. I went to sit with him.*
>
> *"You sure are nice to the nurses," I said.*
>
> *"Well, I figure if you need to be taken care of you should at least be pleasant to the people taking care of you."*
>
> *"I'll remember that," I said.*
>
> *We talked a little about Mama. Then he said, "I don't really have anything to live for anymore. What is left for me?"*
>
> *I thought, but didn't say, what about us? He is so sweet and gentle. I don't want to lose him. As we said good night, he stayed where he was sitting. When we reached the end of the hall, I turned to see his hand wave a little bye-bye. At the front door of the nursing home, Dolores, that wonderful nurse, caught up with us:*
>
> *"I'm so sorry about your mom. And I'm worried about him."*
>
> *"He told us he doesn't have a reason to live now," I said, and she replied, "He's right, you know."*

❦

Journal | *Release*

January 3, 2001

WHEN THE PHONE RANG in the darkness this morning, I thought, *Oh no—* Jan was sobbing, could hardly speak. Only a few moments earlier, the head nurse had called her:

Ralph Pearson got up this morning, went to the bathroom and, on the way back to his bed, he fell. We helped him into his bed—and then, he died.

In the aftershock, we realize we have the rest of our lives to grieve but must decide right now what to do about Mama's funeral scheduled for tomorrow. Cancel it? Too late for that. Have a funeral for Mama and then another for Dad in a few days? The mind can be calculating when the heart is breaking. I refine Dad's roughed-out eulogy and combine it with Mama's—cut and paste. My sisters begin to plan a double funeral.

When Joe and I arrive, we find Dad in his bed. His mouth hangs open like Mama's. And his pale forehead is cool to my lips. I lay my hands on his shoulders— still warm after all these hours—and thank him for his unfaltering love and respect for our mother, his steadfastness and fidelity to our family, his good example, his sweetness, stories, and corny humor. As we leave, I gather up a blue quilt from the dresser. It holds his good clean smell.

ANCIENTS BELIEVED THAT AS ONE YEAR ENDS and another begins, a crack opens between the worlds. At this time, the dead walk the earth and must be honored, placated, and fed—or they cannot return to their rest. Our world cracked at the turning of this year and, released from their trials, our parents fell into the unknown. Only by dying young could we have avoided this loss.

Somehow we must learn to be present with their absence—and at the same time to feed their ghosts with the sweetness of our love.

The Greatest of These

*Love is everything. All the rest is standing on the edge
and staring into the abyss.*

—BERTRAND RUSSELL

January 4, 2001

AFTER A DEATH, WE ARE STUNNED by a stark fact: a person is actually gone
from this world. The loved one whose suffering was breaking our hearts, calling on us to solve the problem, is simply no more. The problem is solved, and yet
unsolved. It is over, but not over. Though released, we remain forever entangled.

We were ready for Mama's death; for years we had mourned her as she slipped
away. But even as we wondered whether Dad had a white shirt and a suit that
fit and how we could help him endure Mama's funeral, he found his longed-for
off-switch. Dad died four days after Mama, exactly one hundred days after we
separated them.

We rewrite the obituary. Ginger adds more images of Dad to the slide show.
Late into the night, Jan and I place new pictures in the photo display and include
a little red wooden valentine Dad had made for Mama: *Lois will you please be my
valentine? Love Ralph.*

Funerals are socially sanctioned channels into which we pour our grief. They
distract us with ceremony and condolence, and help us become accustomed to
our loss. With lit trees, wreaths, and banks of poinsettias, our old church is still
decorated for Christmas. Memorial bouquets and flowering plants line the chancel
behind enlarged photographs of Mama smiling near the sea and Dad toasting us
all with a cup of Christmas punch.

We thought few would attend, but the church fills with relatives, friends, co-workers from Jan's office and my school, former neighbors, The Baloney Club. Even our old family friend Ellis, frail in his late eighties, comes escorted by his daughter. He is the husband of Charlotte, Mama's long-ago swimming buddy who died last year.

"As some of you may not have known until you came in this morning," the minister begins, "this is not only the funeral of Lois Pearson but also of her beloved husband, Ralph Pearson, who died on January third—" Gasps rise from the congregation. "And so this day we commend both of them to Almighty God. They are in God's eternal presence, forever enjoying a carefree eternity."

The first hymn is Dad's favorite. Its sweet, familiar words and old Swedish melody are comforting.

> *Children of the heav'nly Father*
> *Safely in his bosom gather;*
> *Nestling bird or star in heaven*
> *Such a refuge ne'er was given.*

Then from a modern rendition, the good minister reads Biblical passages we've chosen. In Ecclesiastes 3, we hear there is *a right time for everything, a time to hug and a time not to hug, a time to tear and a time to repair*. In I Corinthians 13, the love upon which my parents based their marriage is characterized as *not irritable or touchy*. Only in the Twenty-third Psalm, which had helped Dad through all his trials, does the splendor of the language at times flicker through.

After the sermon, Joe reads my eulogy—because I couldn't. Then follow the Lord's Prayer, *For All the Saints*, and the benediction. Finally, as the organist plays *The Skaters' Waltz*, row by row we leave the nave. The music nurtures a fantasy that on the morning Dad died, Mama glided by on long blades, looking just as she did on the night he first saw her. And as she passed, she pulled him free of his old body, as if a milkweed seed released from its husk to float on the wind. Young and strong, he glided into her arms.

Far too much Hollywood sugars such an ending, but their life was such a romance. And the heart aches to accept images the mind cannot hold.

ℰℐ

The Old Smoothies at St. Paul's Aldrich Arena—1972

EPILOGUE

Amaryllis

ALL TANGLES RESOLVED, all signs of pain and sorrow obliterated, Mama rests in her cloisonné urn inside a velvet bag in my study; Dad is enshrined at Jan's amid pictures of his sports triumphs and his family, and the little wooden valentine he made for Mama.

Wanting just one handful, I scoop up my father's ashes—clean and grayish-white with little shards of bone—and let them go into the bag that Jan holds. Then, as she clasps my hand in hers, we rub his dust into our palms. Taking into my hands the ashes of my father makes one thing clear: all that he has been and done—corny jokes, faith, sweet devotion, athletic triumphs, wisdom hard-won—all of the works of his life have been reduced to dust, unless we remember.

Later, at home, Joe and I mix a handful of Mama's ashes with Dad's. Plunging my hands into my mother's ashes brings us full circle from the first moment she pulled me, newborn, toward her breast, eyes filled with tears of love. Of hello. Now good-bye. Meeting and parting is life.

This intimacy with ashes is the intimacy of the family's one flesh. The child is shaped from entwined DNA of parents whose scents and resonances are imprinted as deeply as the beating of the heart, the breath. Gentle arms rock to sleep, hands guide the suckling mouth to breast, bathe and oil the delicate skin, wipe the plump bottom, dry tears from the flushed cheek, tenderly test the temperature of the fevered forehead. And, even then, parents' eager faces encourage first steps of separation.

With my parents' ashes in my hands, that separation is complete.

❧

AT HOME SOME TIME LATER, I wake in gratitude for a good night's sleep, for our parents' release, for our family's sharing of burden and grief, for Joe's immeasurable help, and that of all who assisted us. And in gratitude, too, for whatever time remains in my own life. But, as the day wears on, emptiness swallows me. My parents are gone, and neither the decisions we made nor anything that happened, for good or ill, can be changed. Trying not to hear the football game blaring from the next room, the mindless roaring of snowmobiles next door, I concentrate on water trickling over pebbles in my tiny fountain and watch the snow sift down outside.

Then my dear friend Kate arrives.

"Oh, Nancy, I'm so sorry," she says tenderly and holds out a gift—an amaryllis.

Unplanted in its dark box, the bulb has sprouted. Such life energy bursting forth! While we drink tea, I pot it and tell Kate about my parents' lives.

In the following weeks, the stalk grows tall. Its green muscular stem reaching out of the dark is the exact emblem of healing. Grief is dry and dead as the skin of a dormant bulb, but life forces itself through, cracks open its tomb, and rises. Crinkled as new wings of butterflies, blood-red petals unfurl. Stamens tremble in opening throats. And life begins to flow back to me.

Pollinated without ministry of bees in that winter of my parents' deaths, the seeds of Kate's amaryllis ripen even as petals shrivel into dark crepe paper shrouds. When its long stem bows low, black disks spill over the table. Planted, they sprout slender leaves that promise new bloom.

On Father's Day, Jan, Ginger and her kids, and Joe and I gather in a place we love. We mix Dad's ashes into Mama's and with our own hands release them into nature. At rest beyond will or resistance, their ashes wash in the relentless, ceaseless ebb and flow, to be drawn again into life's sentient tangles.

❧

FIVE YEARS LATER, big feathery flakes drift down in the dark, clinging to each twig, muting harsh outlines, melting in glowing caves around each tiny white light strung on spruce boughs in our window boxes. It may have been that radiance that brought Dad to mind. Sixty years before, just days after he returned from war, he had smiled at my prissy reluctance to leave the shoveled path.

"I don't want my little girl to be a sissy," he'd said, and flopped into a snowdrift to make an angel for me.

And now, called out into the luminous night, I let myself fall backward into the soft snow. My legs plow angel robes; spread arms beat angel wings. And for a timeless moment, the sweetness is real.

In the morning, the angel—the empty tracing of an impulse, a memory—is gone. New fallen snow, white as the fine ash of bone, has erased it as all things must be erased. Life, a gift freely given, must turn to ashes. But while there is consciousness, I will appreciate the time I have.

Events sometimes juxtapose in ways that defy probability. Five years after its parthenogenesis, one offspring of Kate's amaryllis brings forth a bud, borne of its longing, that opens, ghostly pale, on my mother's February birthday. An amaryllis come full term. Precious *because* it is passing away.

⁝

THE AUTHOR, AGE THREE

NOTES

Introduction, A Crack in the Armor, and *What the Heart Demands*
> Whyte, David. *The Heart Aroused: Poetry and the Preservation of the Soul in Corporate America.* New York: Random House, Inc., Currency/Doubleday, 1994.

This Too Will Pass, Love Made Flesh, No Choice in the Matter, Purple Hearts,
and *Thanksgiving*
> Katagiri, Dainin. *Returning to Silence: Zen Practice in Daily Life.* Boston: Shambhala Dragon Editions, 1988.

The Life We Had
> Garner, Dwight. 'Kiss' Summit: No Tongue Action. *Salon,* April 10, 1997.

Journal: Moments—December 20, 1994
> Poetry in the Schools is a program of COMPAS of St. Paul, Minnesota. Established in 1974, COMPAS is a resource for arts residencies, workshops, and performances statewide.

The Hanging Angel
> Kushner, Howard I. *Self-Destruction in the Promised Land: A Psychocultural Biology of American Suicide.* Piscataway, New Jersey: Rutgers University Press, 1989.
> Menninger, Karl A. Spoken comment. Menninger Clinic.
> Shakespeare, William. *Macbeth.* In *The Complete Works of Shakespeare.* Edited by Hardin Craig. Chicago: Scott, Foresman & Co., 1951.

Garage Sale at the End of the World
> Zorba the Greek (film). Screenplay and direction by Michael Cacoyannis, 1964. Based on *Zorba the Greek,* by Nikos Kazantzakis. London: John Lehmann Ltd., 1952.

The Baloney Club Brunch
> Wikipedia, s.v. "St. Lucy's Day," http://en.wikipedia.org/wiki/Saint_Lucy's_Day (accessed February 5, 2010).

In the Tower
> Douglas, Alfred. *The Tarot: The Origins, Meaning and Uses of the Cards.* New York: Taplinger Publishing Co, Inc., 1972.

Journal: Being—March 15, 1998
> Millay, Edna St. Vincent. "Lament." *Second April.* New York: Mitchell Kennerley, 1921.

Such Stuff as Dreams Are Made On
> Kowalski, Gary. "Such Stuff As Dreams Are Made On." First Unitarian Universalist Society of Burlington. http://uusociety.org (accessed November 14, 2004).
> Shakespeare, William. *The Tempest.* In *The Complete Works of Shakespeare.* Edited by Hardin Craig. Chicago: Scott, Foresman & Co., 1951.

Journal: Hope—May 14, 1998
> Porter, Katherine Anne. "The Jilting of Granny Weatherall." *Flowering Judas and Other Short Stories.* New York: Harcourt, Brace and Company, 1935.

Nevermore
> Eliot, T. S. *The Waste Land.* New York: Boni and Liveright, 1922.

A Rooted Sorrow
> BBC News. "Memory Loss Link to Early Stress." *BBC News,* October 11, 2005, http://news.bbc.co.uk/2/hi/health/4327992.stm (accessed February 5, 2010).

Cheney, Karen. Living Longer: Balance. *AARP, The Magazine*, September/October 2006.

McEwen, Bruce. *The End of Stress as We Know It*. Washington, D.C.: The National Academies Press, 2002.

Shakespeare, William. *Macbeth*. In *The Complete Works of Shakespeare*. Edited by Hardin Craig. Chicago: Scott, Foresman & Co., 1951.

Happy Birthday To Me, All Right

Shenk, David. *The Forgetting. Alzheimer's: Portrait of an Epidemic*. New York: Doubleday, 2001.

Journal: Halloween—October 24, 1998

Dylan, Bob. "What Good Am I?," in *Oh mercy*. New York: Columbia, 1989.

Journal: Alone—October 29, 1998

FitzGerald, Edward J. *Rubáiyát of Omar Khayyám*. New York: The Book League of America. Country Life Press, Quatrain xcix.

Journal: Escape—November 16, 1998

Smith, Dinitia. "Kurt Vonnegut, Novelist Who Caught the Imagination of His Age, Is Dead at 84." *The New York Times*, April 12, 2007.

Journal: Chronic—November 17, 1998

Kane, Robert L. and Joan C. West. *It Shouldn't Be This Way: The Failure of Long-Term-Care*. Nashville: Vanderbilt University Press, 2005.

The Old Smoothies

Waldteufel, Emil. "*The Skaters' Waltz*" ("Les Patineurs"), Opus 183.

Journal: Christmas Eve—December 24, 1998

Eliot, T. S. "The Lovesong of J. Alfred Prufrock." *Prufrock and Other Observations*. London: The Egoist Ltd., 1917.

Hegg, Tom. *A Cup of Christmas Tea*. Waldman House Press, 1992.

Journal: Birthday—February 7, 1999

Minnesota Poetry Outloud, a touring troupe of various poets and musicians, was founded in the mid-1970s by poet John Calvin Rezmerski.

DaVinci's Inquest, a Canadian dramatic TV series of ninety-one episodes, aired on CBC, 1998–2005.

Unsinkable and *One for Grandma*

Hanh, Thich Nhat. *The Long Road Turns to Joy: A Guide to Walking Meditation*. Berkeley, California: Parallax Press, 1996.

A Crack in the Armor

Crossley-Holland, Kevin. *The Norse Myths*. New York: Pantheon Books/Random House, 1980.

Remen, Rachel Naomi. *Kitchen Table Wisdom: Stories That Heal*. New York: Riverhead Books, 1997.

A Christmas to Remember

Blane, Ralph (lyrics). *Have Yourself A Merry Little Christmas*. Music by Hugh Martin, 1943.

Wilder, Thornton. *The Bridge of San Luis Rey*. New York: Albert and Charles Boni, 1927.

It's Good to Get Out

Paddock, Joe. "So Wet." *A Sort of Honey*. Northfield, Minnesota: Red Dragonfly Press, 2007.

A Long, Long Way
> Judge, Jack and Harry Williams (lyrics and music). *It's a Long Way to Tipperary*. 1912.

What the Heart Demands
> Lozoff, Bo. *It's a Meaningful Life: It Just Takes Practice*. New York: The Viking Press/ Penguin Press, 2000.
> "Cider with Rosie," *ExxonMobil Masterpiece Theater*. December 5, 1999; adaptation of *Cider with Rosie*, by Laurie Lee. London: The Hogarth Press, 1959.

A Perfect Place
> Aurelius, Marcus. *Meditations*. Translated with an introd. by Maxwell Staniforth. Baltimore: Penguin Books, 1964.
> Baker, Beth. Small World. *AARP Bulletin*, Vol. 46, No. 9. October 2005.
> Berman, Barry. "New Markets Tax Credits and Private Donations Finance First Green House Homes in Massachusetts." Press release, *ncb capital impact eNewsletter*. July 28, 2008. Additional resource: Green House Project (thegreenhouseproject.com).
> Dembner, Alice. "'Green Houses' for golden years: Innovative units comes to Mass." *The Boston Globe*, September 30, 2006.
> Hamilton, William L. "The New Nursing Home, Emphasis on Home." *The New York Times*. April 23, 2005.
> Milton, John. *Paradise Lost*. Edited and with introduction and notes by James Holly Hanford. New York: The Ronald Press Company, 1936. Lines 242–270.
> Mooney, Rose. "Spirits High at Irish Nursing Home that Provides a Pub." SeniorJournal. com. November 17, 2005. Based on Eastley, Tony & Kerri Ritchie. "A Nursing Home with a Twist." www.abc.net.au. November 15, 2005.
> Sartre, John-Paul. "No Exit." *No Exit and Three Other Plays*. New York: Vintage, 1989.
> Shapiro, Joseph. "Reformers Seek to Reinvent Nursing Homes." *Morning Edition*. National Public Radio. June 22, 2005.
> "The Boy in the Bubble," David Phillip Vetter (1971–1984), suffered from a rare genetic disease, SCID (Severe Combined Immune Deficiency syndrome), which confined him for life to isolation in a sterile environment.
> Thomas, William H. *What Are Old People For? How Elders Will Save the World*. Acton, Massachusetts: VanderWyk & Burnham, 2004.
> Tzu, Lao. No. 48, *The Way of Life, Lao Tzu: A New Translation of the Tao Te Ching*. Translated by R. B. Blakney. New York: A Mentor Book, The New American Library, 1955.

Journal: Efficiency—September 17, 2000
> Heller, Joseph. *Catch-22*. New York: Simon & Schuster, 1961.

The Crack Between Worlds
> Shakespeare, William. "Sonnet CXVI," in *The Complete Works of Shakespeare*. Edited by Hardin Craig. Chicago: Scott, Foresman & Co., 1951.

Journal: Dissonance—September 27, 2000
> Wright, James. "Lying in a Hammock at William Duffy's Farm in Pine Island, Minnesota." *The Branch Will Not Break*. Middletown, Connecticut: Wesleyan University Press, 1959.

Journal: Decision—October 12, 2000
> Eliot, T.S. "Ash Wednesday." *Collected Poems 1909–1962*. London: Faber & Faber Ltd., 1963.

A Song at Twilight

Bingham, J. Clifton (lyrics). *Love's Old Sweet Song*. Melody by James L. Molloy. 1884.

Ayer, Nat D. (lyrics). *Yesterday*. Recorded by Eddie Miller's Dance Orchestra, 1927.

Monsen, Maren. *The Vanishing Line* (film.) New York: First Run/Icarus Films. 1998.

Lullaby

Bemelmans, Ludwig. *Madeline*. New York: Simon and Schuster, 1939.

Corliss, Richard. "Do I Love You? (I Forget)." Film review of *Eternal Sunshine of the Spotless Mind*. *Time*, April 19, 2004.

Roderick, Ray and Michael Berkeley. *Irving Berlin's I Love a Piano*.

Tennyson, Alfred. "Sweet and Low." *The Princess A Medley*. 3rd Ed. London: E. Moxen, 1850.

Thanksgiving

Jennings, Talbot; Jules Furthman and Carey Wilson, screenwriters. *Mutiny on the Bounty* (film). 1935.

Oliver, Mary. "The Summer Day." *New and Selected Poems*. Boston: Beacon Press, 1992.

Journal: Choices—December 9, 2000

Dunn, Hank. *Hard Choices For Loving People: CPR, Artificial Feeding, Comfort Measures Only and the Elderly Patient*. Fairfax Nursing Center, Inc. Herndon, Virginia: A&A Publishers, Inc., 1994.

The Greatest of These

McGilligan, Patrick. *Jack's Life: A Biography of Jack Nicholson*. W.W. Norton & Co., 1996. Nicholson attributes quote to Bertrand Russell.

Sandell-Berg, Caroline V. (Swedish text). "Children of the Heav'nly Father." Translated by Ernst W. Olson.

&

ACKNOWLEDGMENTS

I AM DEEPLY INDEBTED to my husband, Joe Paddock, for his immeasurable support and counsel throughout not only the writing and editing of this book but the events described within it. And to my sisters, Janet Pearson and Virginia Pearson, for their steadfast love and help as we lived this story.

Many friends have read all or part of this manuscript and helped me to improve it. I am grateful to Connie Szarke for her careful consideration of content and language, to Margot Fortunato Galt for her memoir-writing workshop and encouragement, and to readers of all or part of the manuscript: Carole Wendt, Roseann Lloyd, Stephen Wilbers, Pam Joern, Beth Waterhouse, Don Maronde, Jean Replinger, Pam McClanahan, Ken Meter, Tom and Barb Balcom, Orlo Otteson, Virginia Pearson, and Janet Pearson.

Thanks also to Charles Woodard, Florence Dacey, Jill Breckenridge, Kate Weyrens, Judith Mattsson, Nicole Kubesh, and Edith and John Rylander for their interest in and encouragement of my work; and to the Southwest Minnesota Arts & Humanities Council of Marshall, Minnesota, which, with grant funds from the McKnight Foundation, helped support some of my writing time.

Sincere thanks to John Gaterud and Abbey Gaterud of Blueroad Press for believing in my book and helping me refine it. And for their expertise in creating its beautiful design.

∽

THE AUTHOR

NANCY PADDOCK lives and gardens in Litchfield, Minnesota, with her husband, Joe. Her poems have appeared in many journals and anthologies, including *To Sing Along the Way: Minnesota Women Poets From Pre-Territorial Days to the Present*; *The Writer Dreaming in the Artist's House*; *As Far As I Can See: Contemporary Writing of the Middle Plains*; *Beloved on the Earth: 150 Poems of Grief and Gratitude*; *From the Other World: Poems in Memory of James Wright*; *Farming Words*; and *County Lines*.

Her book *Trust the Wild Heart*, a finalist for the 2006 Minnesota Book Award in poetry, was published by Red Dragonfly Press, which will also release *Cooking With Pavarotti* in 2011.

Born in St. Paul in 1942, Nancy has been a writer-in-residence for COMPAS Writers and Artists in the Schools, the Southwest Minnesota Arts & Humanities Council, Minnesota Public Radio station KRSW, and other organizations. She worked for the National Endowment for the Humanities/Farmers Union-sponsored American Farm Project, which engaged young farmers in humanities-based discussions about land and environment, and for the Minnesota-based Land Stewardship Project, an organization dedicated to sustainable and environmentally sound agriculture. In connection with that work, she wrote two environmental plays and, with Joe Paddock and Carol Bly, co-authored *Soil and Survival: Land Stewardship and the Future of American Agriculture* (Sierra Club, 1986).

ᴄ⁄ᴐ

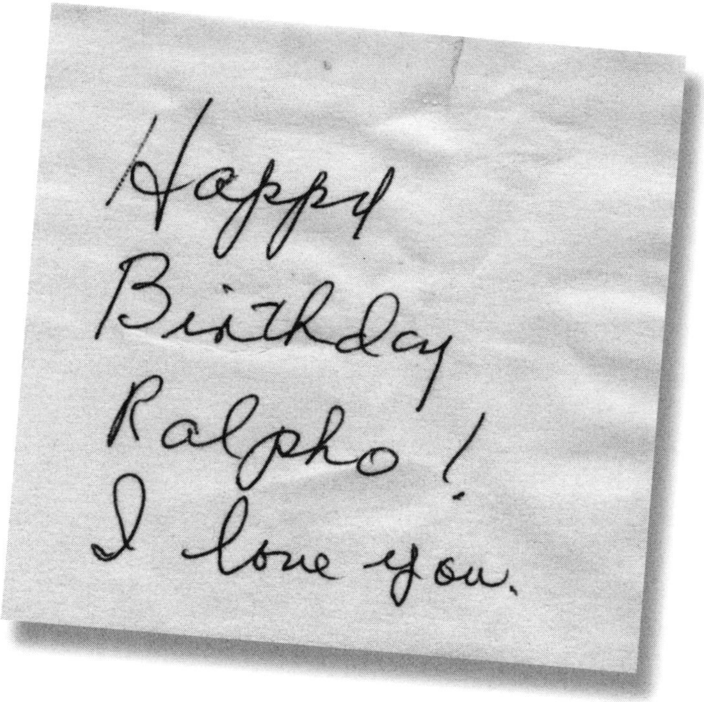
Happy
Birthday
Ralpho!
I love you.